MARTIN ZWEIG'S WINNING ON WALL STREET

MARTIN ZWEIG'S

WINNING ON WALL STREET

Martin E. Zweig

With the editorial assistance of
Morrie Goldfischer

WARNER BOOKS

A Warner Communications Company

Ⓦ A Warner Communications Company

Printed in the United States of America
First Printing: April 1986
10 9 8 7 6 5 4 3

Book design: H. Roberts

Library of Congress Cataloging-in-Publication Data

Zweig, Martin.
    Martin Zweig's Winning on Wall Street.

    1. Stocks—United States.   2. Speculation.
3. Investments—United States.   I. Title   II. Title:
Winning on Wall Street.
HG6049.Z87   1986   332.63'22   85-43167
ISBN 0-446-51234-6

To my wife Mollie for her constant encouragement of my career and her patience and support during the writing of this book.

Acknowledgments

I'd like to thank those whose contributions made this book possible: Joan Graff and Lisa Liss who typed and retyped the drafts; Joe DiMenna, Carol Whitehead, and Tim Clark of Zweig Securities, Ned Davis of Ned Davis Research and Ken Tower of Delafield, Harvey, Tabell for their research help; Debbie Drake (and Ned once again) of Ned Davis Research for their generous aid in doing the graphics; Jim Frost, Larry Kirshbaum and everyone else at Warner Books; Nat Sobel, my agent; Lou Rukeyser of *Wall $treet Week* and Alan Abelson of *Barron's* who each, many years ago, gave me the opportunity to be heard or read when my career was embryonic; Jonathan Weiss, who taught me to trust my own stock market judgment; my mom and late father for obvious reasons; my late Uncle Mort who first encouraged me to learn about the stock market; and most of all my friend and collaborator Morrie Goldfischer who first urged me to write this book and then diligently edited the manuscript and gave it cohesive direction, all the while abiding my idiosyncrasies and time constraints.

Contents

CHAPTER 1

How This Book Is Different from All Other Books on the Stock Market and What It Can Do for You

*I*f you are looking for a simple, reliable, and *workable* system for playing—and beating—the stock market, this book was written for you. I will show you how to avoid the most common investment errors, preserve your capital, and make a good deal of money as well. All you need is a willingness to spend half an hour or so a week keeping up with the market indicators that I will describe, and a commitment to maintain a discipline.

Let's face it. No one is smarter than the market all the time. If market forecasting were easy, everyone would be rich. Even Bernard Baruch, the legendary Wall Street financier, went broke early in his career. I don't have a crystal ball—and wouldn't want one. I've found that investors who rely on crystal balls frequently wind up with crushed glass. I'm satisfied if I can predict a market trend, get in tune with it, and stay with that trend as long as it lasts.

Since becoming an investment advisor, I have read most of the books on the stock market—not that I buy them; publishers send them to me hoping I'll promote them in my market letter. Sad to say, most of them are not very helpful.

Some books dangle the *get-rich-quick* bait. *How I made $1,000,000 overnight without trying.* These are just plain hype. What they're selling is the end of the rainbow. Greed is a very powerful emotion, and a lot of people buy these books hoping that, by following an offbeat formula, they will immediately find that elusive pot of gold. Of course that's impossible. The world just doesn't work that way.

1

Other books may not make extravagant promises but offer systems—simple or complicated—for playing the market or picking stocks. A system is not necessarily a bad tool, but many of these are ineffective or worse. It is said that no girl was ever ruined by a book, but I suspect some would-be market plungers would come pretty close to ruining themselves if they tried to implement these schemes.

Then there are the virtual encyclopedias on investments, books that span the spectrum from options to precious metals, from Ginnie Maes to Freddie Macs, from commodities to collectibles. They describe every vehicle comprehensively, but I don't think such overwhelming detail equips you very well for the nitty-gritty of investment decisions.

I should also mention books like those by Adam Smith and Andrew Tobias. They entertain with great anecdotes, humor, and bits of wisdom. And that's fine; they serve a purpose and the general reader will get useful advice from these books. But they don't offer a system for making money in the market.

However, don't despair. There is valid academic work that proves conclusively that *a few methods do exist for "beating the market."* I have incorporated these tools into my stock selection techniques and have junked those methods that are popular but, unfortunately, futile. With this book, you *can* find the proverbial "edge" in playing the market.

I am proud of my winning Wall Street track record. Among all of the stock market advisors rated by the independent *Hulbert Financial Digest*, I was the *number one* stock picker two years straight and my *Zweig Forecast* was only one of four to show a profit, *including all commissions*, each and every year since mid-1980, when the *Hulbert* ratings began.

The job of selecting stocks should never be taken lightly. It's tough to be a consistent winner. Although Wall Street spends millions each year analyzing stocks, the best available research indicates (1) that analysts cannot consistently predict earnings—which makes such strategies as buying growth stocks at any price multiple rather risky (as many institutions have found in recent years); (2) that mutual funds and other institutions as a group have failed to beat the broad market averages over the years regardless of their methods; (3) that such technical tools as charting and relative strength don't predict any better than pure chance; and (4) that expensive and lengthy research reports from brokerage houses generally fail to pinpoint stocks that outperform the broad market.

My proven methods for market forecasting and stock selection, painstakingly developed through trial and error over the years, are suitable for both conservative investors and those who wish to trade more actively. My principles have been extensively tested and are all verifiable and thoroughly documented in this book. They work!

I can't possibly include all the variables I track on market activity because it would get hopelessly complicated. So I have simplified my approach to make it understandable and workable for the nonprofessional reader. In this regard, I have tried to follow Albert Einstein's dictum: "Don't make things simple. Make them simpler."

THE FUNDAMENTAL INDICATORS

First I would like to tell you about my basic approach to investment decisions. Most people think of me as a technician, but actually, I use anything that works. If they worked, I'd track the planets or sunspots, or even use a Ouija board. Instead, I rely heavily on a group of fundamental indicators.

The major direction of the market is dominated by monetary considerations, primarily Federal Reserve policy and the movement of interest rates. To monitor these and other vital trends, I have devised several simple indicators, described fully later in the book, that I have found very reliable.

My guidelines include purely technical indicators. I refer to this factor as the tape action, or momentum, in the market. Here I combine various price and volume indicators to measure the actual behavior of an individual stock or the overall market. To appreciate the role of momentum, think about a rocket ship being launched to the moon. If it takes off with a lot of thrust, it has a chance of making it out of the earth's atmosphere. If it doesn't, it will turn around and flop back. Broadly speaking, the market behaves in a similar fashion. *To me, the "tape" is the final arbiter of any investment decision. I have a cardinal rule: "Never fight the tape."*

If you buy aggressively into a bear market or into individual stocks that are performing badly, it is akin to trying to catch a falling safe. Investors are sometimes so eager for its valuable contents that they will ignore the laws of physics and attempt to snatch the safe from the air as if it were a pop fly. You can get hurt doing this: witness the records of the bottom pickers on the Street. Not only is this game dangerous, it is pointless as well. It is easier, safer, and, in almost all cases, just as rewarding to wait for the safe to hit the pavement and take a little bounce before grabbing the contents.

I also follow closely the degree of optimism and pessimism in the marketplace and will share with you my key sentiment indicators, which provide an early-warning system to detect market trends. I believe you'll be surprised at how wrong so-called expert opinion can be.

Last but not least, I monitor what I call the fundamentals—the actual value of a particular stock. That includes analyzing earnings, dividends, and balance sheets. Fundamental analysis doesn't do much for forecasting the broad market direction but is very important for individual stocks. I use fundamentals for probably 80 percent of my input on stock selection but for not more than 5 percent of the weight in predicting the market as a whole.

Big money is made in the stock market by being on the right side of the major moves. I don't believe in swimming against the tide. It's rare for me to recommend stock purchases when my market-timing models are bearish, or a short sale when the reverse is true. I would like to be fully invested when the market goes up and fully in cash when it goes down. But the market couldn't care less about what I like. The idea is to get in harmony with the market. It's suicidal to fight trends. They have a higher probability of continuing than not.

Actually, about two-thirds of the time markets are either neutral, or rising or declining moderately. Under these conditions, the trend of the market isn't so crucial and you might trade profitably by selecting the right individual stocks, although the returns would not be nearly as great as those in a strong bull market.

PICKING WINNING STOCKS

In addition to describing my various indicators and how you can use them, I will discuss my criteria for choosing individual stocks. Here I look at two main areas. One covers the earnings and the relationship of the price to the earnings (the P/E ratio), the earnings trend, and a few balance sheet items. I don't get that much involved in the product being produced. If a company can show nice consistent earnings for four or five years, I don't care if it makes broomsticks or computer parts.

The second factor I examine is the action of the stock itself, to see whether it is performing well. If the stock is going to climb, I'd rather let somebody else buy it at the bottom. I want to see if the stock acts well relative to the market before I buy it. I find that buying on strength gives you an edge. You must pay a premium, but you increase the probability of being right.

People somehow think you must buy at the bottom and sell at the top to be successful in the market. That's nonsense. *The idea is to buy when the probability is greatest that the market is going to advance.* If a bear market were to bottom at 800 on the Dow, and eventually go to 1400, you don't have to buy at 800. You can buy at 900 if the probability were, say, 90 percent that it would go higher.

And you don't have to sell at the peak. You might sell after the top or maybe a little before. Let's say you get out at 1300 when the probability is very good that the market will decline. There's nothing wrong with buying at 900 and selling at 1300 and giving the other guy the last hundred points either side. What you are concerned with is the probability of success or, alternatively, the probability of losing money. You want to avoid loss. So it's fine to buy above the bottom and to sell below the top.

According to my rulebook, the only consistent way to make money in the market is to cut losses and run with profits. You can be right on individual stocks as little as 30 percent of the time and still do well if you can get out when the getting is good.

Regrettably, many investors haven't learned this lesson. Ego prevents them from admitting a mistake. Perhaps there's something macho about it. A slap in the face, as represented by a 15 percent price decline, is greeted with stubborn persistence to hang around for a severe pummeling. *I'm a trend follower, not a trend fighter.* I'm smart enough to realize that a slap is easier to recover from than a beating that, in this case, leaves you unable to pursue future gains.

I have found that, in this business, you usually have to make mistakes in order to come up with something that really works. In fact, the whole idea of using momentum as a stock market indicator (which you'll read about in chapter 5) came to me as a result of mistakes that made me miss a major market move. Several years ago a client of mine gave me an abstract painting incorporating this quotation from Benjamin Franklin: "The things which hurt, instruct." I keep that painting and its message in a prominent place in my office.

As a risk-control strategy, I use a system of stops (sell orders at predetermined levels) that I will describe in depth later in the book. This gives me the discipline to avoid fighting crippling battles. Basically what I do is place a stop, generally 10 to 20 percent below the current price, whenever I buy a stock. The exact level depends on my own analysis of the stock's trading pattern. If a stock violates this stop, I'm out with no second-guessing and no regrets. I admit my mistake, but also view it as an opportunity to find something better. If the stock goes up, I'll tell you how to raise the stop to lock in profits. That way you can let your profits ride...but with the protection of the trailing stop.

To illustrate this market strategy, I will give real-life examples of the stocks I have recommended in the past, both winners and losers. I'll relate when stops took me out of stocks that eventually became disasters and, unfortunately, when I was stopped out at the low point and wistfully watched the stock climb higher. If it's a volatile stock, a random downward move might take you out. That's happened before. But so what? There's always another stock. In the long run, the probabilities favor using stops.

A FLEXIBLE INVESTMENT PHILOSOPHY

And now a word about my investment philosophy. I consider myself both conservative and aggressive. By nature I'm conservative. I'm very risk averse. I want to protect myself and the people who follow my advice. But there are times when you have to be aggressive. *The problem with most people who play the market is that they are not flexible.*

The conservative person tends to stick with such instruments as utility stocks and Treasury bills. He never makes a lot of money, but he doesn't get hurt. The aggressive investor buys wild stocks or drills for oil or speculates with high leverage in real estate. During boom times he makes fortunes, only to lose it all in the bad times.

I don't think either approach is sound by itself. If you're an aggressive trader, that's okay, but there's still a time to be conservative. If you're conservative, that's fine, too, but there's a time to be aggressive. That moment may not come very often, but when it does, pounce on it and take advantage of it. The rest of the time you can cut back and be your conservative self.

People sometimes ask me what traits an investor should have if he wants to succeed in the market. I tell them *discipline* is the most important—the discipline to follow your method or system and not give in to all the temptations that might weaken your resolve. The broker calls you with a hot tip. Forget it. Someone else says, "Why don't you buy some call options on Interplanetary Bionics? You'll make a fortune." Forget it. Stay with your discipline.

The second trait necessary for beating the market is *flexibility*. Let me give you an example. I remember back in February 1980, when I thought the market was going to get the stuffing beat out of it. Sure enough, it started to unravel and came down very hard. That was around the time the Hunt brothers cornered the silver market and everything began to collapse around them. Some brokerage houses were on the verge of going under because of bad loans to the Hunts, and we were close to a financial panic. I was very bearish.

Then, one day in March, without advance warning, the Federal Reserve came to the rescue with the bailout provision for Bache & Co., one of the brokerage firms involved, and stemmed the tide. What they did was send a message to Wall Street that no brokerage firm was going to sink because of the debacle. The market, which was off 27 points at 3:30 P.M., spurted and closed down only two points on the day. That was one hell of a rally in the last half hour. The next day the market went through the roof.

I was sitting there looking at conditions and being as bearish as I could be—but the market had reversed. Things began to change as the Fed reduced interest rates and eased credit controls. Even though I had preconceived ideas that we were heading toward some type of 1929 calamity, I responded to changing conditions. Each day I got less bearish and more bullish. By May I was a screaming bull and 100 percent invested in the market. A pretty decent bull market ensued for the next year or so.

Summing up, to succeed in the market you must have discipline, flexibility—and patience. You have to wait for the tape to give its message before you buy or sell. That means you must forget about trying to catch the exact tops or bottoms, which no one can consistently do anyhow. But success in the market doesn't require catching those tops and bottoms. Success means making profits and avoiding losses. By using the indicators in this book and waiting for a trend to develop, you can make money, stay in tune with the tape and interest rates, and, best of all, sleep better at night.

C H A P T E R   2

How and Why I Got into Market Analysis and Stock Selection

*T*he fall of 1948 was a special time in my life. I had just started first grade in East Cleveland, Ohio, and I thought school was great. The whole town was nuts over the baseball team. The Cleveland Indians were about to win their first world series in twenty-eight years (they haven't won one since), and their march toward the championship became our special project in room 10. I was the kid who knew most about the team, thanks to my dad, who used to take me to games even if it meant playing hookey some afternoons.

I knew every player's uniform number and even had a vague idea about what batting averages meant. So I was in my element when we cut out little paper Indians, drew numbers on their backs, and hung them in the classroom. I had begun to love numbers. Perhaps this was a tip-off that I would later gravitate to the stock market and apply my numbers approach to it.

Later that fall came the presidential election in which Thomas Dewey was supposed to trounce Harry Truman. A church next door to my house was used as a polling place. Its parking lot, which I had always regarded as my private playground, was decorated with American flags. Cars and people were everywhere, making it necessary to call off my daily game between the Indians and the Boston Red Sox in which I played for both teams. Somehow, the Indians invariably won, although some of the games were exceedingly close.

I was disappointed the day after the election when I found an empty parking lot, no American flags, and no fun. There was also little joy in my house that evening. Usually my father would look up from the *Cleveland Press* sports page to tell me the latest news about the Indians from the hot stove league. This time his face was buried in the stock market pages. His expression was as sour as it had been the day I broke the living room window with a baseball.

My father mumbled something about Truman and what a disaster he was for the stock market. I had no inkling what he meant. To me the stock market was a fuzzy thousand numbers in the newspaper, none of which I understood at six years of age. In fact, I thought it had something to do with socks or stockings. But I surely knew my dad was unhappy.

I eventually learned why my father was so distraught that day, aside from the fact that he had voted for Dewey. Wall Street thought Dewey, the Republican, was a sure winner and was shocked when Truman, the Democrat, scored an upset. The market reaction was devastating. The Dow Industrials plunged 3.8 percent the day after the election, roughly the equivalent of a sixty-point drop today. On the New York Stock Exchange, thirty-six stocks had declined for every one that advanced. In all the years since then, the daily advance/decline ratio has never been worse.

My father died when I was nine years old. A year later my mother remarried and we moved from Cleveland, where I was born, to Miami, Florida. My interest in the stock market began in earnest when I was thirteen. For my birthday, my uncle Mort, my father's brother, gave me a gift of six shares of General Motors stock. I thought that was terrific. Each day I would search the stock listings to see how General Motors had fared. I didn't know why prices fluctuated, but I enjoyed tracking my own stock. I also looked forward to receiving the small dividend payments every three months. The checks whetted my interest even further, and I began to follow a few other stocks of the day.

Later on, in a high school American history class, we learned about the famous industrialists (some called them robber barons). By chance I chose to write a report on a book about J. P. Morgan. I was fascinated by his life story, and I believe it was at that point I decided that I wanted to become a millionaire—and that I would do it via the stock market. Nothing in J. P. Morgan's life proved to be any guide to me, then or now—he's not one of my heroes. It was just a case of an enterprising man making it big in the market, which served to inspire me.

I began to pay more attention to the performance of various stocks. I remember an occasion during my junior year in high school when, in a discussion about the market, the teacher asked, "Does anyone know the name of the stock that sells at the highest price?" Well, no one else in the class knew beans about the stock market, but I raised my hand and said, "I believe it's Christiana Securities." I was right—and the teacher almost fainted. (I think the stock was around $1500 at the time.) I even managed to say I thought Superior Oil might be the next-highest stock. Again I was correct and the teacher was incredulous. So far my stock market knowledge was only secondhand.

I graduated from Coral Gables Senior High School in 1960 and was accepted at my first and only college choice—the University of Pennsylvania's Wharton School of Finance. I had selected Wharton because I wanted to study business and, of course, the stock market. Also, it was the best undergraduate business school in the country. It still is. (To be fair, Harvard and Chicago don't have undergraduate business schools.)

In the fall of 1960 I began my four years at the Wharton School, still eager to learn about the stock market. But our first-term class schedule, which was set automatically, didn't include any stock market study. That was for upperclassmen. The course closest to my interest was economics, taught by Professor Murray Brown, and I vividly remember his opening remarks. He said most of us had probably come to Wharton to learn how to make money and his course would not be much help in that regard. Well, he was only partly right. If you master the lessons of economics and the laws of supply and demand, it's bound to be beneficial in business or the stock market.

My first few weeks with Professor Brown were touch-and-go, from his side as well as mine. Things came to a head when we were discussing the coming presidential election between Richard Nixon and John Kennedy. Professor Brown went around the class asking each of us, "Are you a Nixon supporter or a Kennedy supporter?" I resented this inquiry, believing that my political convictions were my own private business. When he came to me with the same question, I replied, "Neither. I'm an athletic supporter."

The class cracked up and Professor Brown was appalled. He responded with a snappy comeback: "You mean you're a jock?" Well, I had been a jock of sorts in high school. I was on the basketball team and had played just about every other sport as well. But I really didn't mean to be a wise guy. I was just trying to puncture what I thought was a hot-air balloon. Unfortunately, he had a terrible impression of me from the incident.

I may have been irreverent but I was serious about learning all I could about economics and business. I just wasn't comfortable with the Ivy League atmosphere. Perhaps I was still in a state of cultural shock coming from Miami to Philaldephia, although nowadays I go into culture shock going *to* Miami. But that's another story.

So there I was in my first year at Wharton, hoping to learn about the stock market and instead suffering through the laws of supply and demand and struggling with debits and credits in accounting classes—the latter subject a bore but one I figured correctly would help me later in my market activities.

It was early that freshman year when I met Maurice Falk, a classmate. He was always dropping the name of a stock that had been in the news or had come out with a good earnings report. Maurice and I, along with a few other friends, including Tony Rosenberg, my poker buddy, and Lou Eisenpresser considered setting up some kind of investment partnership at that time. We were going to call it Dynamic Growth Associates. With that name, I suppose we could have gone far, but somehow we never did pool our money. I think it significant that at our young ages we were even *considering* something so ambitious.

The drawback in getting started was in working more or less by committee. I've learned over the years that "committee" decisions in the market tend to be mediocre. I've never heard of a great investor who operated by committee. So it perhaps just as well that we never operated.

At least the investment idea whetted my appetite to know more about the stock market than I did. In the summer of 1961, when my freshman year ended, I went back to Coral Gables to look for a summer job at a brokerage house. I went from one to the other and tried to impress them that I was a young Wharton student, eager to learn, and would work cheap. Alas, there were no jobs.

I was willing to settle for a "chalk boy" position. In those days, electronic equipment was just beginning to take over in brokerage firms. Usually prices and quotations came across on the old ticker tape. The tape was blown up on a screen and you could watch the prices go by. But the only way to recall those prices during the day was to have a so-called chalk boy write down periodic quotes of the leading stocks on a large blackboard. Usually, the fifty or so most important stocks would constantly be posted in chalk. There was one house left with the old chalkboard, but I guess I didn't qualify for the chalk boy position, even at a lowly buck an hour.

Rather than seek a low-paying, dead-end job in another field, I decided it would be in my long-term best interest to spend my full time studying the market activity at a brokerage house. That's exactly what I did. I went to the local branch of the old Hayden Stone and practically moved in for the next couple of months.

Each day I would read *The Wall Street Journal* and all of the investment information Hayden Stone put out. I also spent a lot more time going through reports by Standard & Poor's, Moody's, and other statistical services. I pored over earnings reports and, having had some accounting background, was able to adjust earnings for a few items here and there. Soon I began to understand the role of earnings in valuing stocks. Also becoming clearer was the relationship between the price and earnings, the P/E ratio.

MY FIRST INVESTMENT

Late that summer I finally decided to test my knowledge by putting some money where my heart was. I had a couple of thousand dollars in savings and was ready for the big plunge. My first purchase, not surprisingly, was General Motors. I bought fourteen shares to round out my position to an even twenty. The stock was selling in the low forties at the time, and I would eventually double my money in it, excluding the dividends, which were fairly hefty. Years later I discovered this was a typical first-time investment. The novice feels more secure buying the blue chips, and there were few stocks higher on the blue chip scale than GM. Besides, I was comfortable with it, having followed the stock for a long time. Turned out to be a darn good invest-ment, too.

Of course I wanted a diversified portfolio, so I busied myself trying to select more stocks. My second choice turned out to be an immediate disaster and taught me a lesson. Never listen to a broker. Well, at least almost never. The broker recommended American Cyanamid, a large chemical company. I had analyzed the earnings and done the statistical work, and the investment seemed to make sense. I purchased twenty shares. And, wham, my first day in it the stock dropped four points, a 10 percent plunge. I couldn't believe it because the market had been very quiet that summer and price movements of even half a point were a lot. What the heck had happened?

It turned out, as I recall, that the company was hit by some kind of government antitrust suit. What mattered, though, is that there was unexpected bad news in the stock and suddenly I was down 10 percent before I had barely gotten my feet wet. I did hang on to the stock, and I wound up making money on it. But it was a pretty lousy way to start out. Over the next couple of weeks I also bought some odd-lots of Gulf Oil and Dan River Mills. Thus I began my portfolio.

Although I had been buying odd-lots in the summer of 1961, I really didn't want to see the market take off at the time. In a few years, when I turned twenty-one, I was going to inherit several thousand dollars from my father's estate, and I was hoping I could invest that money when stocks were cheaper. As it turned out, I didn't have to worry about it. From the spring of 1961 on, the market began to churn on extremely light volume. If you think the tape is slow today when seventy million shares are traded, imagine how lethargic it was on those summer days when trading failed to reach even two million shares.

The market had had a huge run-up from the fall of 1960 into the spring of 1961, when the momentum waned. Prices then stayed in a very narrow range for the rest of the year and into the first quarter of 1962. In the early spring of 1962, the market began to cave in.

I was then in my sophomore year at Penn. Just about when school finished for the spring, the market collapsed in what became known as the 1962 crash. The debacle was blamed on President Kennedy's strong words against the steel industry, but that was just the catalyst, triggering a break in a very weak market. Actually, I found the dramatic slump in the market exciting to watch, especially since I had very little invested and very little to lose. But I noticed the pain around me.

In the summer of 1962 I spent a few weeks in New York visiting school friends. I vividly recall a night in early June at a friend's home. His father was there with his accountant, and they were furiously going through stock transactions and other records. There was anguish on his father's face, and I knew something was seriously wrong.

My friend filled me in on a few of the details. Apparently his father had been heavily margined in the stock market and had been hurt during the break, especially in his big Polaroid holdings, one of the day's chief glamour stocks. Now he was scrambling to raise money from his other assets to meet the margin calls. Polaroid had climbed smartly for years, but the 1962 break hacked the price considerably. At least that story ended happily. My friend's father survived the crisis and the market rebounded, with Polaroid one of the leading stocks in the ensuing bull market.

The point of the story, however, has nothing to due with Polaroid. Indelibly etched in my mind was the agonized image of my friend's father that spring night of 1962. Watching the wound inflicted by stock market reverses gave me concern. It increased my respect for the impact of any future stock market break. I had had something of a hang-up about 1929 anyhow and couldn't help worrying about what would happen if I were in the market and another 1929 occurred. I had just witnessed a miniature version of it. That incident lit a red light in my mind to alert me never to get caught in a stock market collapse. At that time I still knew absolutely nothing about the warning signs of such a break, but I was determined to find out.

I finished my four years at Wharton, majoring in finance my last two years and specifically concentrating on investments and the stock market. I took every stock market course offered, but I knew my education was far from complete. About the only thing they really taught us was how to evaluate individual stocks, using as a text *Security Analysis* by Benjamin Graham, David L. Dodd, and Sidney Cottle, a bible of fundamental analysis. The whole idea with Graham, Dodd, and Cottle is to buy stocks with good value that are selling at reasonable multiples and paying satisfactory dividends, and to make allowances for risks. That's okay as far as it goes, but, to my mind, it left a lot of important things unsaid.

Nothing was taught about movements of the market as a whole, about technical factors such as the market's own price action, crowd psychology, or the impact of the Federal Reserve and monetary and economic variables. In other words, when I left Wharton I had at best just one tool to work with, and that clearly wasn't enough.

I started in the M.B.A. program at New York University in the fall of 1964. I selected that school because it was located next door to the American Stock Exchange and because they had numerous stock market courses listed in their catalog. Unfortunately, during that first term I had to repeat the same fundamental courses I had just completed at Wharton. That rankled me because I felt I wasn't learning anything new. I had also just gotten engaged to my future wife, Mollie, and she was in Miami going to college. Tired of being away from home, I decided to return to Miami.

Resuming my education, I enrolled at the University of Miami, taking courses at night. I opted to work during the day because I needed the money. Unlike my previous job-hunting experience, I was immediately offered jobs by three brokerage houses. I mean I was *offered* the jobs—I didn't ask for them. I had already gotten a modest reputation as a trader in the market, not necessarily a good one, just an active one. Active enough to earn the nickname Trader Horn from my friends.

I had carried an account for a couple of years with Bache & Co. in Surfside, Florida. The branch manager there, Edwin Crooks, offered me a job as a broker. I accepted it against competing offers from two other firms because I liked and respected Crooks. I stayed there only about seven months, just long enough to get my license and then relinquish it, because I wanted to return to school. But my time at Bache was not wasted, thanks to Crooks.

Crooks was an old-timer who, early in his career, was the youngest member of the New York Stock Exchange at the time of the 1929 crash. He loved to talk about the old days, and I was his best listener. Of the many stock market stories Crooks told me, I found most fascinating his descriptions of what it was like working for Jesse Livermore, one of the most fabulous traders of all time. Later I read a great deal about Livermore, and if there is anyone who is even close to being my hero in market lore, it is Livermore. His emphasis on letting your profits run and cutting your losses has always stood me in good stead.

Leaving Bache at the time Mollie and I were married in 1965, I went to the University of Miami as a full-time graduate student. I picked up my master's degree in one year, again taking every stock market course available. All these courses were taught by Professor Wade Young, who was heavily oriented to the technical side of the market. Technical analysis, as we'll see later in the book, in its purest form is a study of only those variables that you can see on the ticker tape, namely price and volume.

At first I did not agree with Professor Young's methods, even though I had studied technical analysis on my own. But years later I recalled some of his advice such as "Buy on strength and sell on weakness," and I began to appreciate the value of that approach more and more. But in those days, like most novices, I thought the trick was to buy on weakness and sell on strength. That's exactly how most people get themselves into trouble in the market.

While finishing my M.B.A. work during the summer of 1966, I taught a course in corporate finance at Miami and enjoyed the experience tremendously. For several years I had dreamed of getting up in front of a class and lecturing on finance or stocks, and finally I had my chance. I knew I didn't want to spend my life as a cloistered college professor but found the work most rewarding. However, the more I taught, the more I realized how much I had to learn.

The next step was my decision to go for a Ph.D. in finance. Miami did not have such a program, so in the fall of 1966 I took off for Lansing, Michigan, where I enrolled in the doctoral program at Michigan State University. Determined more than ever to improve my formal education in the whys and wherefores of the stock market, I naturally majored in finance and special-ized in the stock market. I spent three years at MSU, finishing in 1969.

At Michigan State I learned a lot about economics and more about the fundamental analysis of common stocks. I was also exposed to the academic theories of the market, which boiled down to the idea that the market moves in a so-called random walk in which past pricing patterns do not necessarily predict what will happen in the future. Moreover, the academic community generally favored the concept of an efficient market, one in which no amount of economic, fundamental, or technical data could hope to forecast stock prices any better than you or I could by buying a large, diversified portfolio, putting it away, and forgetting about it.

I rebelled at these ideas. In fact, one of my professors, Alden Olsen, didn't agree either. Professor Olsen apparently had been rather successful in managing money for himself and others and generally proceeded on the basis of value and contrary opinion. That is, he bought stocks that were out of favor and that were undervalued.

But most of what I learned in my three years at Michigan State I picked up on my own, particularly as a result of research for my Ph.D. dissertation on the puts-and-calls option market, my main interest at the time. (Basically, when you buy a put, you acquire the right to sell a hundred shares of a company's stock at a stated price within a specified period of time. Conversely, a call is an option to buy a hundred shares of a company's stock over a stated time period.)

These were the days long before there was a Chicago Board Options Exchange or any other listed exchange on which to trade options. Back then, puts and calls were traded by dealers who specialized in them. The market was small and not very liquid. I was hoping to find a way to make big money in options but, after studying the results of fifty-four different trading strategies, I concluded in my dissertation that the returns on a risk-adjusted basis didn't warrant playing the options market, largely because of the huge transaction costs. Those findings do not necessarily apply to today's options market because transaction costs are lower and liquidity has improved. Nevertheless, I'm still not enthusiastic about trading options.

I was disappointed that all my work on options had failed to uncover a way to beat the market. But I did discover something that proved to be more valuable in the long run. In accumulating data for my dissertation, I unearthed some figures from the Securities and Exchange Commission going back to World War II and found that when options investors got too optimistic—buying lots of calls and shunning puts—the stock market was generally heading for trouble. The reverse was also true. When the options players were very bearish on the market—favoring puts and selling or avoiding calls—the market usually was near a bottom.

It also became apparent to me that when options players were extremely active, it was a negative sign, and when they shunned the market and options volume dropped off, it was frequently a good time to buy stock. In other words, it was the old game of contrary opinion—don't follow the "crowd." My studies also indicated that most speculators were not very successful. Because they invariably lost money on balance, it followed that they weren't right very often, regardless of whether, as a group, they were bullish or bearish.

It was shortly after finishing my dissertation that I invented the puts/calls ratio, which is now a widely used technical benchmark, especially because there are so many new options markets against which to apply this ratio. This discovery was important to me not so much because of that particular indicator, but because I began to integrate various numbers that measure market sentiment and to use the result as a forecasting guide. I did the same for monetary and technical indicators. This helped build a bag of useful tools that I've been using in my advisory letter and in my money management business for years.

I finished my Ph.D. work in the summer of 1969 and, eager to be in New York near Wall Street, accepted a position as assistant professor at the City University of New York. In the back of my mind was the hope that somehow I could become involved in the Street on a consulting basis. In my first year of teaching I got that chance. I was engaged as a consultant by the Chicago Board Options Exchange, which didn't even have that name at the time. They were trying to get SEC clearance to set up their exchange, and it took them four more years before they got going. I also parlayed my options knowledge into a brief stint teaching the options business to beginning brokers at E.F. Hutton.

Although my work was varied and interesting, I wanted something more stimulating and rewarding. My old college friend Ron Rothstein opened a new door for me. He had become a partner in a brokerage firm and invited me to join them as a consultant. I grasped this opportunity even though the company was small and relatively unknown. After working on several projects, we decided that I would write a stock market letter geared to institutional investors.

THE ZWEIG FORECAST IS LAUNCHED

The launching pad for the market letter and my subsequent career was built on a few articles I had written for *Barron's* over the prior year. The first was in spring 1970, as the market had just suffered its most violent crash since the 1930s. It was virtually at the bottom in May when *The Wall Street Journal* carried a report from a second-rate brokerage firm recommending the sale of American Telephone & Telegraph stock. It was rare that Wall Street firms put out sell recommendations and it was virtually unheard of for the bluest of all blue chips.

I read the so-called reasoning behind the sell recommendation and immediately concluded that (1) it would scare the hell out of all the widows and orphans who were in the stock, (2) it was based on faulty logic, and (3) it was so much gobbledygook. Although I had no particular interest in AT&T, the report made my blood boil and I decided to do something about it. I sat down and wrote a rebuttal, but it was much too long for *The Wall Street Journal*. So I sent it to *Barron's*, which, like the *Journal*, is published by Dow Jones.

Luckily for me, Alan Abelson, then managing editor of *Barron's*, liked what I wrote and had his secretary, Shirley Lazo, call me immediately to tell me they would run it. Only much later did I realize my good fortune, because *Barron's* receives hundreds of submissions and only a few are published.

In June of 1970 my first article, called "Tea and Sympathy," ran in *Barron's*, refuting the brokerage firm's bearish recommendation on Telephone. I proved to be right. Both the stock market and Telephone were virtually at their bottoms. Moreover, the brokerage firm responsible for the misguided recommendation went out of business a few months later.

Naturally, I felt very good about being published in *Barron's*, especially since I had been correct. But writing about Telephone wasn't my specialty; I really wanted to write about stock market indicators. Having had one article published gave me an opening to write additional pieces.

A couple of months later I sent Alan Abelson another article, this one dealing with options activity, utilizing the data I had uncovered for my Ph.D. dissertation. I invented an indicator called the option activity ratio, which gave bullish signals for the market when volume in options was low and bearish signals when volume was high. The article, published in late November of 1970, predicted a very bullish outlook. What timing! The day *Barron's* hit the newstand, the market exploded, and it continued to rally sharply for the next several months.

It was gratifying to be right again, and it made me even more eager to write another article. The next one was on the puts/calls ratio, to which I referred previously. This came out in the spring of 1971, when that indicator had just turned bearish. For the next seven months the market went down, and again I had hit the nail on the head. The two articles on technical indicators brought mail to me from investors who wondered if I was writing, or planned to write, a stock market letter. I saw this as an ideal opening because I was ready and eager to get started in this direction.

Soon after, I began to write a market letter for the brokerage house, gearing it to institutions. I favored the institutional approach because I thought it would permit me to provide more sophisticated information, which is what I really wanted to do. In the fall of 1971 I wrote the first issue. As I was writing the second, the brokerage firm went under. One of the partners allegedly had embezzled a couple of million dollars, and the firm collapsed.

So there I was with my new stock market letter and no brokerage firm. What to do? I had received about 120 pieces of mail from *Barron's* readers who were interested in my work. On the chance that they might want to buy a letter from me, I wrote to each individual. Over the next few months I managed to pick up about 40 subscribers to my new letter, which I decided to call *The Zweig Forecast*. And that's how I started, almost through the back door.

In the spring of 1972 I published still another technical indicator in *Barron's*, this one on short-selling activity. Again I predicted a down market and again the market obliged by easing lower over several months. That didn't hurt my new business. I began to advertise *The Zweig Forecast* in *Barron's* in the spring of 1972, and it quickly built into a real business. Soon income from my letter and my money management activities surpassed my college-teaching earnings. However, I really enjoyed teaching and accepted a position as associate professor at Iona College in New Rochelle, New York, where I taught for seven more years, finally taking a leave of absence only because I couldn't devote enough time to my teaching chores.

When time permits, I'd like to teach again at the college level. What I enjoy most about teaching is the stimulation. I prod the students into asking questions and am not embarrassed if I don't know the answers. I never try to finesse my way through. If I don't really know, I tell them so. Often they will force me to think through an issue. In the thinking process I frequently get new ideas, some of which have led to theories I have used in market forecasting.

Ever since I can remember, I have had an almost overwhelming desire to learn all I could about the stock market and to play it successfully. Perhaps my urge was not too different from that attributed to the mountain climber who must assault the mountain just because it's there. Now, I don't relate particularly well to mountains, but from an early age I wanted to surmount the summit of the stock market, so to speak. It was a challenge I couldn't resist.

It hasn't been all peaches and cream. The stock market at times has driven me up the wall. Then again, it has also earned me a fair sum of money and given me many emotional highs. But, no matter how rough the stock market road, it has never, never bored me. I always find the market fascinating and filled with surprises. Perhaps that's because no one on this planet will ever know all there is to know about the market—and no one can expect to be right all of the time or even most of the time.

You can, however, be right more often than you are wrong. If you are right 60 percent of the time, ride your profits, and rein in your losses, you'll find that when you're right you're very right, and when you're wrong you're only moderately wrong. In the long run, a 60 percent success rate translates into huge gains, a 50 percent rate into solid gains, and even a 40 percent rate can beat the market.

In playing the market, remember you must deal with probabilities, employ sensible strategies to limit risk, and get aggressive only when conditions warrant. I've spent my adult life trying to fathom the stock market and, in the following chapters, will try to give you the best information I've acquired.

CHAPTER 3

The Market Averages— What They Mean

The world's best-known stock market index is the Dow Jones Industrial Average. It has been maintained since 1897, when it consisted of 12 large industrial corporations. In 1916 the list was expanded to 20 stocks, and it grew to its present size of 30 industrials in 1928. Many of the biggest manufacturing firms in major U.S. industries are included. They are:

Allied–Signal	General Electric	Owens-Illinois
Aluminum Co.	General Motors	Philip Morris
Amer Can	Goodyear	Procter & Gamble
Amer Express	Inco	Sears Roebuck
AT&T	IBM	Texaco
Bethlehem Steel	Inter Harvester	Union Carbide
Chevron	Inter Paper	United Tech
DuPont	McDonald's	US Steel
Eastman Kodak	Merck	Westinghouse
Exxon	Minn. M&M	Woolworth

Originally, when the Industrial Average included 12 stocks, it was calculated by adding the prices of the 12 issues and dividing by 12. The same rule would apply today for 30 stocks if the average were brand-new (except that the appropriate divisor would be 30). However, over the years stocks frequently split. Moreover, Dow Jones has on occasion substituted one industrial firm for another. The most recent changes came in October 1985, when Philip Morris superseded General Foods, and McDonald's replaced American Brands.

Such switches and splits require a change in the divisor to keep the average continuous. If there were just two stocks, with A at $20 and B at $40, one could calculate the average by adding the prices ($60) and dividing by the divisor (2). The answer, of course, is $30. However, suppose B split 2-for-1 and the price went to $20 (no "real" change). If you added the prices of both stocks and divided by 2, your ministock average would fall from $30 to $20. Obviously, that's not realistic, since there was no real change in value (B may sell for one-half its former price, but it has twice as many shares, so stockholders are equally well off).

A downward adjustment to the divisor is required to maintain the old average at the appropriate $30 level. Now the sum of the two current prices (after the split) is $20 for A plus $20 for B, or $40. By dividing the $40 total by 1.333, you would get $30, the true average. Thus, the new divisor would be only 1.333, even though there are two stocks in the average. Over the years the 30 Dow Industrials have undergone so many splits and changes that the divisor is down to 1.090. In other words, you could add up the prices of the 30 Industrials, divide by 1.090, and wind up with the actual Dow Jones Industrial Average.

Most investors will not need to use the divisors, but it is important to understand what is meant by a Dow Jones Industrial Average of 1000, or 1200, or whatever.

There are two other Dow Jones averages, the Transportation Average and the Utility Average, plus a 65-stock average that combines all three. You'll often see them mentioned in the financial newspapers, but since they cover narrow industry groups, I don't see much point in discussing them in detail in this book. Occasionally, the Utility Average, because it represents a group of stocks that are very sensitive to interest rates, can be an effective leading indicator for the rest of the stock market. There is such a tendency, but it is not overwhelming.

AVERAGES AND MARKET ACTIVITY

Let's see how the most significant averages reflect market activity. The top half of graph A (pp. 28–29) shows the monthly plot of the Dow Jones Industrial Average back to 1962. Each vertical dash on the graph represents the range between the

Dow's high and low for the month. You ought to take a minute or two to look at the graph and familiarize yourself with the market's history over this span. You can readily see that there were bear markets in 1962, 1966, 1969–70, 1973–74, 1976–78, early 1980, and in 1981–82. The 1973–74 bear market, when the Dow fell from 1052 to 578, was the worst since the Depression in the 1930s. The 1969–70 bear market was the second worst.

There was a long bull market between 1962 and early 1966, when the Dow nearly doubled. Other bull markets occurred in 1967–68, 1970–73, late 1974–76, 1980–81, and 1982–83. You'll also find periods of intermediate-type advances and declines, including the sell-off of 1983 and 1984, which I would classify as an intermediate-type decline.

The lower half of graph A shows the Standard & Poor's 500 Stock Index. This average concerns institutional investors the most since performance of their own results is usually compared to this benchmark. As its name implies, the S&P consists of 500 stocks, most of which are blue chips. The S&P is weighted by market capitalization. This means that if a stock has 100,000,000 shares outstanding and sells for $20 per share, its market capitalization is 100,000,000 × $20, or $2,000,000,000. The greater the capitalization, the greater the weight given in the S&P Index. Currently, IBM easily is the most heavily weighted stock, accounting for approximately 6% of the index value. Other heavily weighted stocks include Exxon, General Motors, General Electric, and American Telephone. Since the S&P 500 is dominated by very large companies, stocks of the smaller firms have correspondingly less weight.

As graph A shows, the Dow Industrials and the S&P Index generally move in the same direction. However, the magnitude of the gains and declines can differ. For example, in April 1981 the Dow peaked at about 1024, slightly under its high of 1052 in early 1973. Meanwhile, the S&P peaked earlier at over 140 in November 1980, considerably above its top of 120 in 1973. While the Dow actually declined almost 3% between the peaks, the S&P climbed nearly 17%.

This can happen when one is dealing with a fully weighted sample of 500 stocks vis-à-vis a much smaller sample of 30 stocks weighted solely for price and not market capitalization. It may seem frustrating at times, but there is no perfect gauge of the

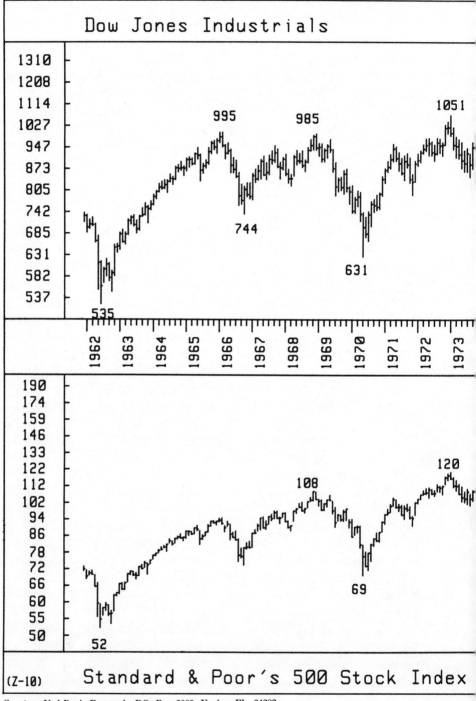

Dow Jones Industrials

1310
1208
1114
1027
947
873
805
742
685
631
582
537

995
985
1051
744
631
535

1962 1963 1964 1965 1966 1967 1968 1969 1970 1971 1972 1973

190
174
159
146
133
122
112
102
94
86
78
72
66
60
55
50

108
120
69
52

(Z-10)   Standard & Poor's 500 Stock Index

Courtesy Ned Davis Research, P.O. Box 2089, Venice, Fl., 34282

Monthly Data 12/31/61 - 10/31/85 (Log Scale)

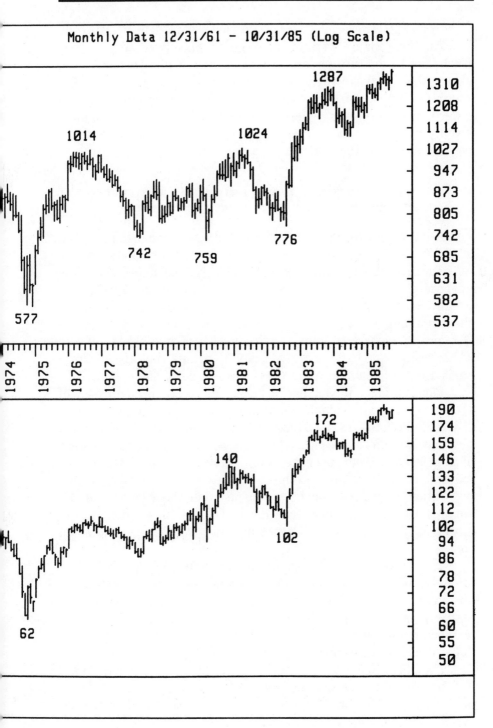

stock market. There are merely alternative ways to measure it.

Another major market average is the New York Stock Exchange Composite Index. It is constructed like the S&P 500, except that it gives weight to every common stock on the NYSE, roughly 1700 stocks. That is, it uses market capitalization to determine the weights, where once again IBM would be the most heavily weighted stock. The movements of the New York Composite Index and the S&P 500 are very similar.

THE UNWEIGHTED PRICE INDEX

Another way to measure the market's performance is to look at the broad spectrum of stocks not weighted for capitalization. Such an average is called an unweighted price index. For this purpose, I constructed my own measure, called the Zweig Unweighted Price Index, or ZUPI for short, whose base is 100 at the beginning of 1965. I get the raw input for my ZUPI from Quotron, a basic computer service for stock quotations. If the ZUPI rises, say 1%, on a given day, it means that the average stock rose 1% that day regardless of the size of the company.

For example, if you had a two-stock average comprised of IBM and some very small company, on a weighted basis such as the S&P 500 the performance of the small stock would make virtually no difference and IBM would account for 90-odd percent of the weight. Your average would almost reflect IBM's price movement. But in an unweighted index of two stocks, IBM's percentage change would be given just half the weight and the small stock's price change the other half. When this is done for all stocks on the exchange, IBM has no more weight than the small company.

The unweighted average is quite useful for the individual investor, who has the flexibility to buy stock in any company, large or small. But the S&P 500 is probably a better measure for institutional investors, who buy millions of dollars' worth of IBM or Exxon but who would have difficulty acquiring very large dollar amounts of extremely small companies.

The performance of the ZUPI can occasionally differ markedly from that of the Dow or the S&P 500. That's because the ZUPI is heavily biased toward the performance of the smaller stocks, often called secondary stocks, while the major averages are dominated by the blue chips. There are times when blue chips do fairly well, such as from the spring of 1972 to early 1973, while the secondary stocks decline. At other times, such as in 1977, the secondaries can rise while the blue chips come under pressure and fall. But in a major bear market such as 1973–74, most stocks weaken and all the averages drop significantly. It's a reflection of the old saw, "When the paddy wagons come they take the good girls with the bad." Similarly, during major bull markets, both the weighted and unweighted averages will tend to advance.

In the studies that follow, I have tried to test various indicators and models against both the ZUPI and the S&P 500 Index. Occasionally, tests will be made against the Dow Industrials or the Value Line Composite Index. The Value Line is seen on the lower half of graph B (pp. 32–33) just under the ZUPI. This index is constructed by Arnold Bernhard & Co., publishers of the Value Line service. This is an unweighted index of approximately 1700 stocks (about the same size as the NYSE Composite) the bulk of which are on the New York Stock Exchange. It is constructed exactly the same as the ZUPI except that the ZUPI recognizes all common stocks on the NYSE and none from the AMEX and OTC markets. The Value Line ignores a few hundred stocks on the NYSE but includes some from the AMEX and OTC. As seen in the graph, the two unweighted indexes perform almost identically, although they may deviate by small fractions in the short run.

In the spring of 1982, the Kansas City Board of Trade began the first trading ever of stock index futures and based the activity on the Value Line Composite Index. The futures can trade at prices above or below the actual value of the index. But discounts and premiums aside, you can buy or sell the market as a whole as measured by the Value Line unweighted index. Also in 1982, stock index futures began trading in Chicago on the S&P 500 Index. Later that year a third market in stock index futures began in New York with trading on the New York Composite Index.

The activity in the S&P 500 Index is by far the largest, and the combined dollar volume in the three stock index futures now exceeds the dollar volume of all stocks traded on the NYSE. On a recent typical day the dollar volume of all shares traded on S&P

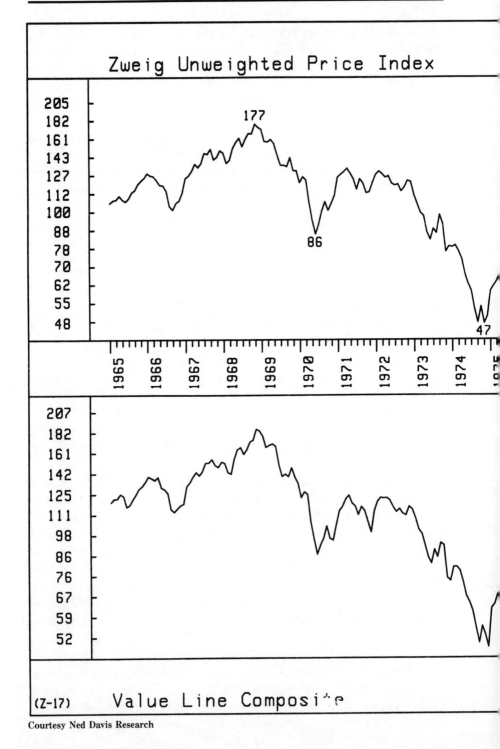

Zweig Unweighted Price Index

Value Line Composite

(Z-17)

Courtesy Ned Davis Research

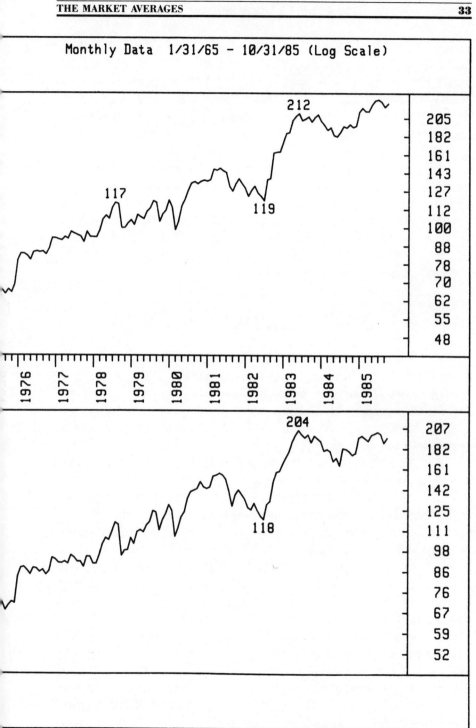

Monthly Data   1/31/65 - 10/31/85 (Log Scale)

futures was $6.8 billion, Value Line futures traded $600 million, and New York Composite futures traded $1 billion, bringing index futures to $8.4 billion, nearly $3 billion greater than the NYSE volume. Clearly, stock index futures have grown tremendously since their origins a few years ago and are becoming increasingly important to the investment community and to speculators.

I cannot cover stock index futures in greater detail here because this is a whole subject in itself. However, in later chapters, when you see tests run of an indicator or of a model, bear in mind that you could approximate the results of those tests by trading stock index futures. That way you can avoid most of the transaction costs associated with trading stocks and get the diversification of the market average involved.

INFLATION ADJUSTMENTS

Graph C (pp. 36–37) shows the Dow Jones Industrial Average plotted monthly since 1921. It's similar to the Dow in graph A except that it goes back much further. Also note that the price scale is in percentages. Thus, a rise in the Dow from 100 to 200 is a gain of 100% and would run the same vertical distance on the graph as a move from 500 to 1000, which is also a gain of 100%. The problem with using nominal prices (prices as they appeared at the time) to construct the market average is that over time they are distorted by the effects of inflation or extreme deflation. On a short-term basis this usually doesn't matter too much, say over a period of a few days or a few weeks. Or, if the inflation rate is "normal," say in the 2%-to-4% range, even over a period of one to two years, the effects are not that significant. But if inflation gets up to 10% or so, as it did not long ago, or if you have extreme deflation as seen in the early 1930s, it causes a tremendous distortion in the nominal price averages.

For example, assume that you invested money in the Dow Industrials when the Dow Average stood at 1000. Suppose that over the next five years the cumulative ravages of inflation doubled the consumer price index, a compounded inflation rate of about 15% a year. Consequently, you would need $2000 to purchase what $1000 would have bought five years earlier. Now, suppose that while inflation doubled, the Dow remained at 1000. To conclude that your investment was even at the end of that period is nonsense. Your net worth had actually declined by 50%. The greater the inflation rate, the greater the adjustment necessary in the stock price averages.

Graph D (pp. 38–39) shows the Dow Jones Industrials plotted monthly from 1921, adjusted for the effects of inflation and deflation. It is properly called "Deflated Dow Jones Industrials." This shows how the Dow performed in "real" dollars, the actual buying power of the dollars that you might have invested in the market. Thus, using the example above, had the Dow in nominal terms remained unchanged over a five-year span while the inflation rate doubled, a graph of the deflated Dow would show a gradual decline from 1000 down to 500 during that period, losing one-half in real terms from its beginning point.

To brush up on the performance of the market averages during most of this century, study graph D of the deflated Dow. On a long-term basis there was a tremendous bull market from 1921 to the peak in 1929. This was probably the greatest bull market in our history. Interestingly, prices were quite stable during the decade of the 1920s, with no significant inflation.

WHAT REALLY HAPPENED IN 1929

The market peaked around Labor Day of 1929 and began to sink lower through September. In October the decline picked up steam, and prices literally collapsed on October 23 and October 28 of that year. Indeed, the decline on October 28 was the largest one-day drop in the history of the stock exchange. On that day alone, the Dow plunged from 298.97 to 260.64, a sickening crash of 12.8%! (The October 23 decline had been a whopping 6.3%.) Nowadays, with the Dow in the 1500s, a percentage drop like that of October 28, 1929, would lop an amazing 200 points off the Dow...and create a splash on the network evening news!

Most people think the market simply crashed on October 29, 1929, and know little about what happened before or after. True, stocks did collapse that day, with the Dow closing at 230.07, down a hefty 11.7%, but the drop was somewhat less severe than the prior day's loss. Volume hit an all-time-record 16.4 million

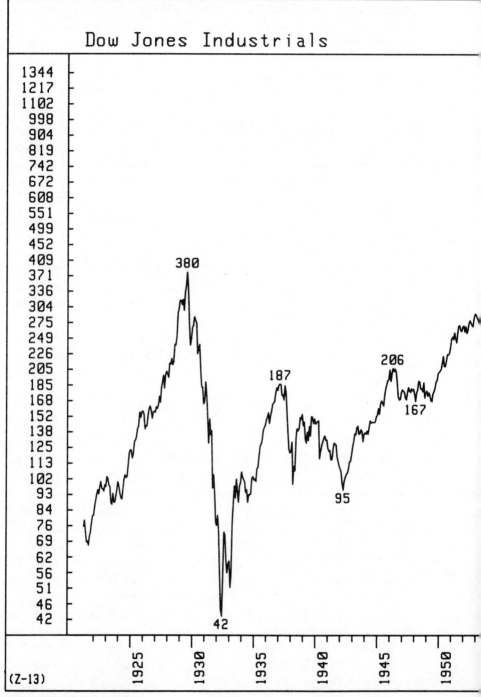

Dow Jones Industrials

(Z-13)

Courtesy Ned Davis Research

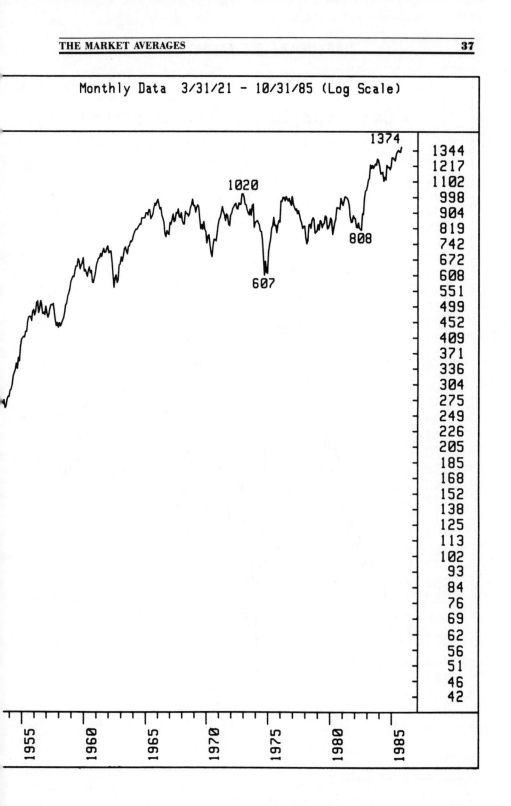

Monthly Data   3/31/21 - 10/31/85 (Log Scale)

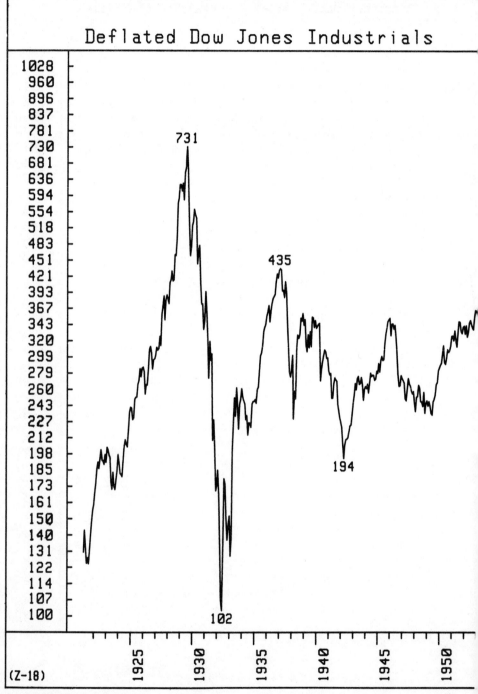

Deflated Dow Jones Industrials

(Z-18)

Courtesy Ned Davis Research

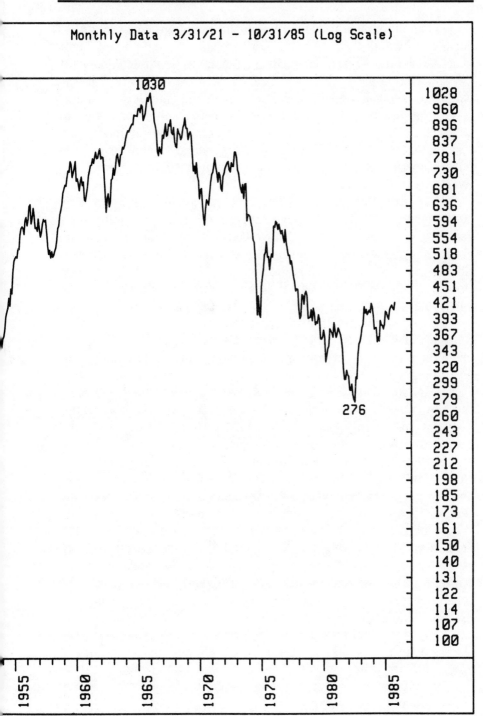

Monthly Data 3/31/21 - 10/31/85 (Log Scale)

shares, an amount not seen again on the exchange for another 3½ decades! Actually, on October 29, stocks put on one of their greatest rallies ever during the last hour of trading. The next day, on October 30, the Dow soared 12.3% to 258.47. But the rally was short-lived, and by mid-November the Dow closed at about 199, down by nearly one-half from its September 3 high of above 381. That so-called 1929 crash encompassed far more than just October 29 and represented the greatest decline ever in a fairly short period. But the major damage really occurred between 1930 and 1932.

From mid-November of 1929 the Dow rallied smartly to a top of 294 in April 1930. That move represented a bull market with a gain of some 48%. A similar move today would take the Dow up about 700 points in five months. After that, though, the Depression began, and it was all downhill. By July of 1932 the Dow closed at 41, down an incredible 86% from the spring highs of 1930, and off an amazing 89% from the 1929 peak.

After the devastation of the early thirties, stocks reversed course and a mighty bull market persisted until 1937. The Depression picked up steam once again and prices fell anew, not bottoming on a real basis until April 1942, a few months after Pearl Harbor. Then the great bull market commenced, carrying the Dow up to a peak of almost 1000 in 1966. Even in real terms, the Dow Industrials gained more than fivefold between 1942 and the top in 1966.

Here is the point I want to emphasize. In nominal terms, the Dow struck 995 in 1966, about the time the Vietnam War was heating up. With that war came the beginning of heavy inflation that distorted most economic factors, including stock averages. When the bear market bottomed in August of 1982, at 777 on the Dow, it represented about a 22% nominal decline over a sixteen-year span. However, during that interval the inflation rate roughly tripled. Indeed, between January 1966 and August 1982, the consumer price index rose from 95.4 to 308.6, a huge gain of 223.5%. That's an annualized inflation rate of 7.3% for more than sixteen years. Using the 1966 price level, when the Dow Industrials were trading at 777 in August 1982, it was the equivalent of only 240. In other words, the Dow had lost roughly three-quarters of its value over a sixteen-year period, and that, in my book, is a real bear market.

Graph D clearly shows this long-term bear trend from 1966 to 1982. Of course, there were interim bull markets within this extensive down cycle. These bull markets occurred in 1967–68, 1970–73, 1974–76, and, to a lesser degree, in 1980. But in all cases the bull market highs came at real prices below the previous bull market peaks, and the subsequent bear market lows came at lower real levels than the previous bear market bottoms. The succession of lower highs and lower lows was part of the ongoing long-term bear market.

This cycle was broken after the 1982 bottom. In the huge bull advance that followed to 1983, the "real" Dow Jones bettered its 1980–81 peak, the first time in about two decades that it surpassed a prior high. The sell-off that followed into 1984 likewise bottomed at real prices considerably above those at the 1982 lows. Then the 1985 rally blasted "real" prices to above the 1983 high.

The 7.3% compounded inflation rate from 1966 to 1982 was, in fact, a culprit in helping to create that long-term bear market. Stocks generally do not do well in periods of extreme inflation— it's the second worse environment for stocks. The worst, of course, is extreme deflation, such as that seen in the early thirties and then again in 1937–38. The stock market likes stable prices such as those in the decade of the 1920s and in the first half of the 1960s. The higher inflation rate of the late sixties and the seventies caused individual investors to abandon the stock market and move money into collectibles, gold, and real estate.

From the early 1960s on, the individual investor became a net liquidator of stock and continued selling relentlessly until 1983, when the public, for the first time in two decades, turned to the buy side. However, the public temporarily reversed that trend, on balance going back to selling in 1984. During much of that period, real estate prices boomed, especially the prices of homes, fueled by intense speculation. Gold also made an enormous move, running from $35 an ounce to a peak of about $875 in early 1980 before collapsing. Prices of all sorts of collectibles, including art, antiques, coins, and stamps, went sky-high during this span, as people perceived them as hedges against inflation.

The worst thing about inflation, as far as the stock market is concerned, is that the cure is more damaging than the disease. When inflation gets too intense, the Federal Reserve starts acting to reduce the growth in the money supply, thereby increasing interest rates. This slows economic activity and hurts corporate profits. The result is often a bear market.

When Paul Volcker became chairman of the Federal Reserve Board in 1979, he called inflation the number one enemy and took restrictive monetary steps to do battle. By 1981 his war was won and the inflation rate was nose-diving. By 1982 stocks had stopped going down on a major-trend basis. With the disinflationary period at hand, stocks began to rise in what is probably the beginning of a very-long-term bull market, perhaps similar to that of the 1920s or the period from 1942 through 1966.

If the inflation rate behaves over the next decade or so as it did in the early 1980s, stocks will become more attractive, while real estate, collectibles, and precious metals will have less allure. The public, which has shunned the stock market for a generation, will return, driving stock prices higher. Of course, it won't be a one-way street on the upside. There will be interim bear markets during this long-term major bull market that I foresee, just as there were interim bull markets from 1966 to 1982 during that major long-term downtrend.

In subsequent chapters I will show you how to time your investments so that you can get in and out of the market at optimal moments. But do keep in mind the lesson of these last few pages. If inflation were to heat up, it would tend to work against stock prices and also distort the nominal price averages that are reported. So, in a period of rapid inflation or deflation, be sure to make the proper adjustments to the stock averages to avoid being stuck with a rubber yardstick.

CHAPTER 4

Monetary Indicators—
"Don't Fight the Fed"

*I*n *the stock market, as with horse racing, money makes the mare go. Monetary conditions exert an enormous influence on stock prices. Indeed, the monetary climate—primarily the trend in interest rates and Federal Reserve policy—is the dominant factor in determining the stock market's major direction. Once established, the trend typically lasts from one to three years.*

Combining to produce a monetary "climate" are loan demand in the economy, liquidity in the banking system, inflation or deflation, and, of course, policy decisions by the Federal Reserve Board. These are the major factors that create a trend in interest rates. Generally, a rising trend in rates is bearish for stocks; a falling trend is bullish. Let's see why.

First, falling interest rates reduce the competition on stocks from other investments, especially short-term instruments such as Treasury bills, certificates of deposit, or money market funds. For example, when an investor sees yields on CDs drop from, say, 12% to 8%, he becomes a lot less enthusiastic about "rolling over" his CDs and reinvesting them. The newer and lower yields just aren't as good. Stocks begin to look more attractive. Obviously, the reverse is true when interest rates rise.

Second, when interest rates fall, it costs corporations less to borrow. That reduces a major expense, especially for companies that are heavy borrowers such as airlines, public utilities, or savings and loans. As expenses fall, profits rise. Wall Street loves the idea that future earnings will go up. So, as interest rates drop, investors tend to bid prices higher, partly on the expectation of better earnings. The opposite effect occurs when interest rates rise.

So much for theory. Now let's see how it works out in practice. I'll take you through three different monetary indicators, each very simple to construct and easy to understand. Although I keep tabs on a much wider range of economic data for my forecasting, I have found that these three indicators are so effective and so much less complicated than my entire system, that they fall into the category of "less is better."

PRIME RATE INDICATOR

The prime rate is that interest rate that banks charge their best customers, principally the top-quality major corporations. Most rates on bank loans are based off the prime rate, with the charge increasing relative to the prime rate as the riskiness of the loan rises. In other words, the less credit-worthy the borrower, the more above the prime rate he will pay. Movements in the prime rate are plotted in graph E (pp. 46–47) against the Dow Jones Industrials.

The beauty of using the prime rate as a stock market indicator is that it does not change every day as do other interest rates. Over the twenty years through 1984, the prime rate changed an average of 11.6 times a year, or roughly just once a month. Also, it's difficult not to notice a prime-rate change since such moves always make headlines in the financial pages and usually are noted on the evening news as well. So, for the busy investor, following the prime rate is certainly easy enough.

The prime rate has another virtue: it lags behind other interest rates. The prime rate usually falls only after a drop in federal funds rates or in the yields on certificates of deposit or commercial paper. But that's exactly what an investor wants to keep his eye on, because changes in interest rates generally *lead* changes in the stock market. An interest rate that moves a little behind other interest rates can often mark just that point when stocks finally begin to respond to the changes in rates.

__Rules:__ First, I made a somewhat arbitrary decision that 8% or above is a relatively high interest rate and below 8% is relatively low. Therefore, small declines in rates *below* 8% are enough to give a bullish signal for stocks, but somewhat larger declines in rates are necessary for a bullish signal if they come from *above* the 8% level. Conversely, minor increases in rates at levels above the "high" 8% zone are enough to give bearish signals for stocks. But at levels below 8%, somewhat larger increases in rates are needed to give bearish signals. While the 8% demarcation is open to debate, clearly both the level and the direction of rates are important, although all of my studies show that the *trend* of interest rates is more significant than the level itself. In any case, there is logic to these rules, and, most of all, simplicity.

Buy Signals: 1. Any initial cut in the prime rate if the prime's peak was less than 8%. *Example:* The prime has risen several times from, say, 5% to 7% over a period of months. Finally, it is cut one day to 6½%. That day immediately marks a buy signal for stocks based on this indicator.

2. If the prime's peak is 8% or higher, a buy signal comes on either the second of two cuts or on a full 1% cut in the rate. *Example:* The prime has risen several times from 6% to 10%. Then it is cut to 9½%. That's not enough for a signal. Later it is cut again, to 9%. That's the second cut, and that's when the buy signal flashes. If the first cut had been a full percentage point to 9%, the buy signal would have come at that time. Changes in the prime rate usually come in ¼% or ½% increments. A full-point change at one time is much rarer (about one in twenty cases) and also more significant.

Sell Signals: 1. Any initial hike in the prime rate if the prime's low is 8% or greater. *Example:* The prime has fallen several times from 12% down to 10%. Then, it's boosted to 10½%. That day marks a sell signal.

2. If the prime's low is less than 8%, a sell signal comes on the second of two hikes or on a full 1% jump in the rate. *Example:* The prime has fallen several times from 10% to 6%. Then it is lifted to 6½%. That's not enough for a signal. Later it is raised again, to 7%. That's the second increase, and that flashes the sell signal. If the first rise had been a full percentage point to 7%, the sell signal would have come at that time.

Table 1 shows the performance of the Prime Rate Indicator when tested against my Zweig Unweighted Price Index, a market average that gives equal weight to all Big Board stocks. Its movements are very similar to the Value Line Index, against

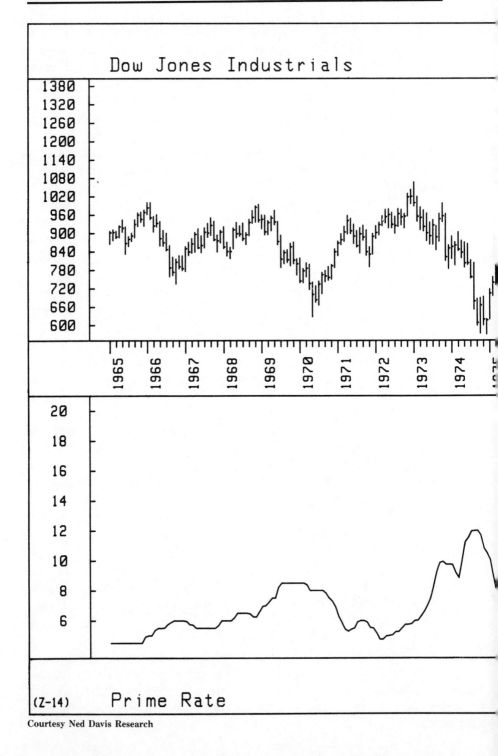

(Z-14)   Prime Rate

Courtesy Ned Davis Research

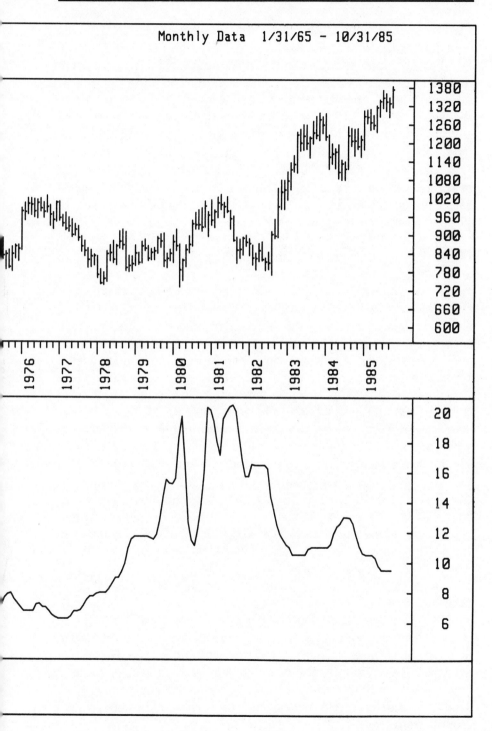

Monthly Data   1/31/65 - 10/31/85

which one can now trade stock index futures (the ZUPI was explained fully in chapter 3).

For example, the first buy signal came in March 1954 when the ZUPI stood at 33.73. Some nineteen months later the indicator gave a sell signal in October 1955, as seen on the right side of the table. The ZUPI at that time had climbed to 48.29. The percentage gain on the buy signal was 43.2% and is shown in the "% Change" column under "Buy Signals."

After the 1955 sell signal the Prime Rate Indicator stayed bearish until January 1958, when it gave the second buy signal listed in the table. At that point the ZUPI had drifted back to 47.66. That was 1.3% lower than the level at the 1955 sell signal and is noted in the first entry on the far-right column under "% Change" for "Sell Signals." The rest of the table should be easy to follow.

In all, nineteen buy signals have been given by the indicator, although the last one is still "on" as of this writing. Of the eighteen prior buys, sixteen of them produced profits, an 89% success rate. Indeed, the only losses were insignificant fractional ones in 1981 and 1982, when the prime rate whipped back within a week or two.

Some of the gains are startling, such as the one coming on the July 1982 buy signal; it produced a hefty 61.2% profit in just over a year. That signal essentially caught the entire 1982–83 bull advance. In all, the indicator was in its bullish position (or mode) a cumulative total of 16.1 years. Had you invested $10,000 in a basket of typical stocks (or mutual funds) that moved in line with the Zweig Unweighted Price Index, it would have grown to $266,544. That's an annualized rate of 22.6%. By contrast, had you bought stocks or funds similar to the ZUPI and held constantly for thirty years—the approach called "buy-and-hold"—$10,000 would have increased to only $57,696. These calculations, and all others in the book, except where noted, ignore dividends and taxes.

Now, suppose that you had bought the "market" (ZUPI) on the buy signals, sold stock on the sell signals, and then invested in short-term money market instruments (such as CDs) at an average rate of 7% until the next buy signal. That strategy would have grown a $10,000 stake into $711,348 over a 30.6-year period. That's a healthy 14.9% a year, far in excess of buy-and-hold's 5.9% a year.

TABLE 1

PRIME RATE INDICATOR
VS. ZWEIG UNWEIGHTED PRICE INDEX: 1954 to 1984

BUY SIGNALS			SELL SIGNALS		
Date	ZUPI	% Change	Date	ZUPI	% Change
3/17/54	33.73	+43.2	10/14/55	48.29	− 1.3
1/22/58	47.66	+57.2	5/18/59	74.93	− 1.6
8/23/60	73.74	+70.1	3/10/66	125.43	− 3.3
1/26/67	121.28	+20.8	4/19/68	146.45	+12.2
9/25/68	164.98	+ 7.7	12/2/68	177.68	−42.7
9/21/70	101.86	+21.9	7/6/71	124.17	− 6.1
10/20/71	116.59	+ 3.8	6/26/72	121.02	−34.6
1/29/74	79.17	+ 2.2	3/22/74	80.95	−33.5
10/21/74	53.83	+31.0	7/28/75	70.53	− 5.6
11/5/75	66.59	+20.1	6/7/76	79.95	+ 6.1
8/2/76	84.79	+ 8.0	5/31/77	91.57	+21.2
12/7/79	110.96	+ 5.5	2/19/80	117.09	−11.4
5/1/80	103.73	+27.3	8/26/80	132.08	+ .6
12/22/80	132.87	+11.7	4/24/81	148.46	+ .9
6/16/81	149.84	− .5	6/22/81	149.02	−14.7
9/21/81	127.04	+ 1.3	2/1/82	128.68	− 5.9
3/8/82	121.07	− .1	3/16/82	120.96	+ 2.8
7/26/82	124.39	+61.2	8/10/83	200.53	− 3.0
10/15/84	194.61	—			

$10,000 becomes: $266,544 $2,164

Annualized Return = +22.6%   −10.0%

Buy-and-hold return = +5.9% per year

Percentage of signals

correct: 89%   67%

The sell signals also produced solid results, although, as is generally true with monetary indicators, the record is not as good as it is on buy signals. Nonetheless, a dozen of the eighteen sell signals "worked"; that is, prices fell. That's a healthy success average of 67%. (See Table 1, bottom line.) Moreover, you would have avoided the bulk of both the 1969–70 and 1973–74 bear markets, the two worst since the Depression. To be sure, the fact that 1962 monetary conditions were okay did not prevent the 1962 crash (a lot of other factors, especially the overly extended price/earnings ratios, were terrible then). But the more recent 1980 and 1981 downturns were nailed.

Had you been hapless enough to have ignored the warnings of rising interest rates and insisted on owning stocks during the "sell modes" (the spans from sell signals to the next buy signal), a $10,000 investment would have shrunk to only $2,164. That's an annualized loss rate of 10.0%.

Table 2 shows a similar test of the Prime Rate Indicator against the Standard & Poor's 500 Index. Recall from chapter 3 that the S&P is not as volatile as the ZUPI and virtually never will provide returns on any indicator as good as those on the ZUPI. The S&P test shows gains on the buy signals of 17.2% per annum vs. buy-and-hold of only 6.2%. The buys enabled $10,000 to grow into $128,377. Had you then, in the sell modes, gone into money market instruments at average yields of 7%, the $10,000 investment would have appreciated to $342,610, a nice 12.2% annualized gain, or about double that of buy-and-hold.

On the buy signals, the S&P went up fifteen times in eighteen tries, a success rate of 83%. On the sell signals, the S&P 500 Index fell ten times, stayed even once, and rose seven times. That's good for a 59% batting average. A $10,000 stake by a "wrong-way" investor would have slipped to $4,854 during the sell modes, a loss of 4.9% per annum.

FED INDICATOR

It's been said that the Federal Reserve writes the script for the stock market. The evidence supports that theory. The Fed, as it is commonly called, has the job of adjusting the growth of the nation's money supply, monitoring the trend of credit or

TABLE 2

PRIME RATE INDICATOR
VS. STANDARD & POOR'S 500 INDEX: 1954 to 1984

	BUY SIGNALS			SELL SIGNALS	
Date	S&P	% Change	Date	S&P	% Change
3/17/54	26.62	+54.8	10/14/55	41.22	0
1/22/58	41.20	+41.1	5/18/59	58.15	− .7
8/23/60	57.75	+54.0	3/10/66	88.96	− 3.5
1/26/67	85.81	+11.7	4/19/68	95.85	+ 6.8
9/25/68	102.36	+ 5.6	12/2/68	108.12	−24.2
9/21/70	81.91	+21.8	7/6/71	99.76	− 4.1
10/20/71	95.65	+12.4	6/26/72	107.48	−10.7
1/29/74	96.01	+ 1.3	3/22/74	97.27	−24.4
10/21/74	73.50	+20.7	7/28/75	88.69	+ .5
11/5/75	89.15	+10.6	6/7/76	98.63	+ 4.6
8/2/76	103.19	− 6.9	5/31/77	96.12	+11.9
12/7/79	107.52	+ 6.6	2/19/80	114.60	− 8.0
5/1/80	105.46	+18.4	8/26/80	124.84	+ 8.8
12/22/80	135.78	− .5	4/24/81	135.14	− 2.2
6/16/81	132.15	− .2	6/22/81	131.95	−11.1
9/21/81	117.24	+ .5	2/1/82	117.78	− 8.9
3/8/82	107.34	+ 1.8	3/16/82	109.28	+ 1.0
7/26/82	110.36	+46.4	8/10/83	161.54	+ 2.6
10/15/84	165.77	—			

$10,000 becomes: $128,377 $4,854
Annualized Return = +17.2%   −4.9%
Buy-and-hold return = +6.2% per year
Percentage of signals
          correct: 83%   59%

borrowings, and influencing the level of interest rates. It does not necessarily tackle all of these tasks at any one time, but whatever goal the Fed has in mind, it is certain to have a major impact on interest rates and ultimately on stock prices.

Among the weapons in the Fed's arsenal are two potent and overt vehicles, the *discount rate* and *reserve requirements*. The discount rate is the interest rate the Fed charges banks that wish to borrow from the Fed's "discount window." Such borrowings are made when banks strive to obtain required reserves. The level of reserve requirements can either liberalize or restrict the ability of banks to make loans.

The Fed has the power both to determine the discount rate and to set reserve requirements. When it does so, the news is always prominently displayed in the financial section of major newspapers and usually makes the national news on television. Ten years ago I developed a model for monetary changes in these guideposts (plus the less effective impact of stock margin requirements) and dubbed it the Fed Indicator. I recently simplified the rules and came up with a better mousetrap.

It's very easy to keep abreast of the data you will require in order to maintain the Fed Indicator. All you need know is the direction of change in either of the two tools. Between them they've only been changed an average of three times a year in the past, so this is truly a "lazy man's indicator."

Rules: To calculate the Fed Indicator, you must grade the discount rate and the reserve requirements separately. Then their scores are combined. In the following examples, I'll stick with just the discount rate, but the rules would work exactly the same for reserve requirements. (At this writing, the Fed hasn't touched reserve requirements since the fall of 1981.)

Negative Points: An increase in either the discount rate or reserve requirements is bearish (recall: rising interest rates are usually negative for stock prices). A hike in either one receives minus one point for that component of the Fed Indicator. It would also wipe out any positive points that might have been there at the time. The negative point remains for six months, after which it becomes "stale" and is discarded.

Example: Suppose the discount rate were raised on January 1. It would give that element a − 1 rating. If no more changes were made by the Fed, the discount rate score would revert to zero on July 1. Alternatively, if a second discount rate hike came on, say, March 1, the score would drop to −2 points. On July 1 the rating would go to −1 as the first move faded. Then on September 1, the second negative point would drop and the score would be zero again. A change in the discount rate does not affect the score on reserve requirements, nor vice versa. Here is how the scoring would look in tabular form:

Jan. 1	Rate rises	−1
July 1	(No further changes)	0

Alternatively:

Jan. 1	Rate rises	−1
March 1	Rate rises again	−2
July 1	(No further changes)	−1
Sept. 1	(No further changes)	0

Positive Points: Moves by the Fed toward easing have a greater positive impact on stock prices than the negative effect created by tightening moves. So, an *initial* cut in either of the two tools not only wipes out any negative points that may have accumulated, but it also kicks in *two positive points*. An initial cut is the first one following a rise in that component. Or a cut is initial if it marks the first change in that instrument in at least two years. As an initial change grows stale, one of the two points is lost six months later and the remaining point falls out a year later.

If a second reduction were made in the discount rate, it would add one more point, for a total of three points. That point, resulting from the second cut, would become stale six months later and would drop out. Third, fourth, fifth, or even more consecutive cuts in the rate would be treated the same way.

Example: Suppose that the Fed previously had raised the discount rate one or more times . . . or that it had not changed it for at least two years. Now, assume that the discount rate were lowered on January 1. It would eliminate all negative points (if any) and add two positive points since this is an initial cut. The discount rate component would stay at +2 for six months. On July 1 it would drop to +1 as the initial move begins to grow stale. The following January 1 the rating would fall to zero as the initial cut fades away. Here is the scoring in tabular form:

Dec. 31	(Rate unchanged for 2 years)	0
Jan. 1	Rate lowered	+2
July 1	(No change since January)	+1
Jan. 1	(No further changes)	0

Now suppose that after the January 1 initial cut, the Fed slices the discount rate a second time on April 1. That would add one more point, for a score of +3. On July 1 the rating would dip to +2 as the initial cut loses a point. On October 1 the rating would ease to +1 as the secondary cut of April 1 fades away. And, of course, on the following January 1 the last point would drop and the rating would be zero. In tabular form, it looks this way:

Dec. 31	(Rate unchanged for 2 years)	0
Jan. 1	Rate lowered	+2
April 1	Rate lowered	+3
July 1	(January 1 cut fades)	+2
Oct. 1	(April 1 cut fades)	+1
Jan. 1	(Final point fades)	0

Calculating the Fed Indicator: There will be a rating for each of the components, the discount rate and reserve requirements. A move in one has no effect on the other. To calculate the Fed Indicator itself, merely add the scores of the two components. There will rarely be more than three or four points in the discount rate nor more than about two or three in reserve requirements. The Fed Indicator will normally range from −4 to −5 at the worst to about +6 or +7 at the best. However, extensive testing has found that scores below −3 don't have any greater negative effect on stocks than a −3 rating. Similarly, scores above +3 have no greater positive effect on stocks than a +3 rating. Testing has determined the following gradings on the Fed Indicator:

Extremely Bullish   = +2 or more points
Neutral   =   0 or +1 point
Moderately Bearish = −1 or −2 points
Extremely Bearish   = −3 or more points

There is no "moderately bullish" rating simply because scores of +2 points led to excellent stock market performance, and ratings of +1 point turned in ho-hum returns. There was no point total that consistently coincided with moderately good stock results.

Graph F (pp. 56–57) shows the changes in the discount rate from 1963 through 1984. Since 1914, when the Fed first regulated it, the discount rate has been hiked 69 times and lowered 71 times (through 1984). Reserve requirements, first regulated in 1936, change far less frequently. They have been raised 15 times and dropped 28 times.

From 1914 to 1936 the discount rate was the only device the Fed had. Even so, just that one indicator produced results consistent with those in periods since then. Reserve requirements were introduced in 1936, so I used the span from then through 1957 to "test" the Fed Indicator, which is how the ratings described above were formed. Once the rules were set, I applied them to the years from 1958 to the present (1984), an era in which institutional trading came to dominate the stock market. The results turned in from 1958 to 1984 did not differ significantly from the earlier days.

I first tested the Fed Indicator's performance against the Zweig Unweighted Price Index (ZUPI). As seen in table 3, when the Fed eases, stocks take off. A $10,000 investment in the broad market (ZUPI) when the Fed Indicator rated "extremely bullish" would have grown to $103,544 in a cumulative span of only 7.6 years. That's a whopping annualized return of 35.8%, miles ahead of the 5.6% a year on buy-and-hold. Indeed, the broad market has actually declined 4.6% per annum over the remaining nineteen-odd years since 1958, when the Fed was anything but "extremely bullish." The results in the "extremely bullish" zone were very similar from 1936 through 1957, with an annualized gain for the ZUPI of 33.8% vs. only 7.1% for buy-and-hold.

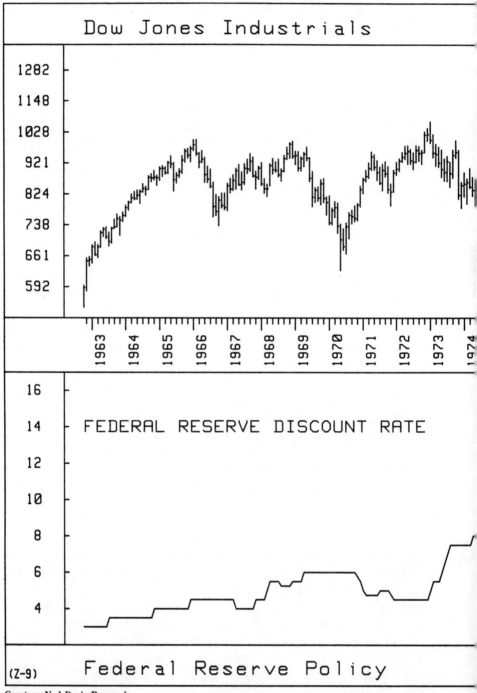

Courtesy Ned Davis Research

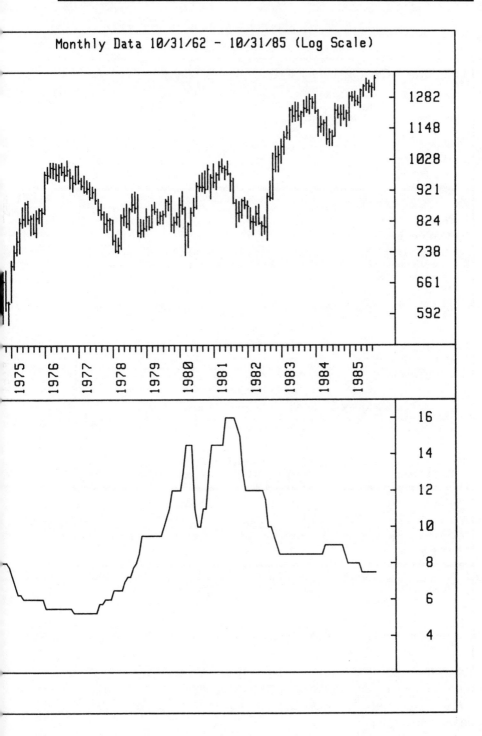

Monthly Data 10/31/62 - 10/31/85 (Log Scale)

TABLE 3

PERFORMANCE OF FED INDICATOR VS. ZWEIG UNWEIGHTED
PRICE INDEX:
January 2, 1958 to November 21, 1984

Fed Rating	Total No. of Years	% Cases Market Rose	$10,000 Investment Becomes	Return per Year	Return vs. Buy-&-Hold
Extremely Bullish	7.6	92	$103,544	+35.8%	+30.2%
Neutral	9.4	45	8,937	− 1.2%	− 6.8%
Moderately Bearish	7.4	43	6,346	− 6.0%	−11.6%
Extremely Bearish	2.5	22	7,349	−11.5%	−17.1%
Total	26.9	50	$ 43,387	+ 5.6	—

TABLE 4

PERFORMANCE OF FED INDICATOR VS. STANDARD & POOR'S
500 INDEX:
January 2, 1958 to November 21, 1984

Fed Rating	Total No. of Years	% Cases Market Rose	$10,000 Investment Becomes	Return per Year	Return vs. Buy-&-Hold
Extremely Bullish	7.6	83	$57,027	+25.6%	+20.2%
Neutral	9.4	60	11,992	+ 2.0%	− 3.4%
Moderately Bearish	7.4	43	6,770	− 5.2%	−10.6%
Extremely Bearish	2.5	22	8,837	− 4.8%	−10.2%
Total	26.9	53	$40,793	+ 5.4%	—

During "neutral" periods the ZUPI eased 1.2% a year, while
in the "moderately bearish" zones it fell 6% per annum. The
"extremely bearish" mode produced losses of 11.5% a year, or
more than 17 percentage points worse than buy-and-hold. The
market rose only twice in the nine trips it made into the most
bearish category.

Table 4 shows the returns of the Fed Indicator against the Standard & Poor's 500 Index, which is less volatile than the ZUPI. Still, the "extremely bullish" mode showed a nifty 25.6% annualized gain with the S&P rising in ten to twelve cases. That's more than 20 percentage points superior to buy-and-hold.

The "neutral" range posted a small gain of 2.0% a year. The "moderately bearish" region had a loss of 5.2% a year, and the "extremely bearish" rating actually did a tad better than that, losing 4.8% per annum (but that bottom rating against the ZUPI did much worse than the "moderately bearish" ranking, as ought to be the case.)

Table 5 shows what has happened since 1958 in the most potent Fed Indicator zone, "extremely bullish." Remember, monetary indicators generally have their greatest impact on the bullish side and only moderate impact on the bearish side.

The middle column of table 5 shows that the ZUPI declined only one time out of twelve trips into the "extremely bullish" region, and that produced only a trivial loss of 1.3% in 1981–82. Then, after a six-week hiatus, the top ranking returned in July 1982, just before the market exploded with its greatest rally in forty-nine years. By May 1983, when the "extremely bullish" rating finally gave way, the ZUPI had gained an extraordinary 64%, its tenth double-digit gain in twelve tries. Indeed, in seven of the dozen cases the gains for the ZUPI were better than 20%. No wonder I call it "extremely bullish"!

TABLE 5

PERFORMANCE OF FED INDICATOR WHEN RATED EXTREMELY BULLISH:
January 2, 1958 to November 21, 1984

Extremely Bullish Period	Return on ZUPI	Return on S&P 500
1/2/58 to 10/17/58	+40.6%	+27.6%
6/10/60 to 6/10/61	+20.5%	+14.1%
4/7/67 to 10/7/67	+16.1%	+ 9.1%
8/30/68 to 12/18/68	+12.0%	+ 8.2%

(TABLE 5 continued) Extremely Bullish Period	Return on ZUPI	Return on S&P 500
11/3/70 to 7/16/71	+22.9%	+17.7%
11/19/71 to 6/17/72	+12.7%	+18.0%
11/28/74 to 12/6/75	+26.5%	+24.4%
12/24/75 to 6/24/76	+26.2%	+16.0%
12/17/76 to 5/19/77	+ 5.2%	− 4.2%
5/22/80 to 11/14/80	+24.8%	+25.8%
9/21/81 to 6/4/82	− 1.3%	− 6.1%
7/19/82 to 5/19/83	+64.0%	+46.3%
11/21/84 to ?	—	—
Total years bullish = 7.6		
$10,000 investment =	$103,544	$57,027
Annualized return =	+35.8%	+25.6%

The right-hand column of table 5 shows the returns on the S&P 500 during each "extremely bullish" period. The S&P appreciated 8% or more in ten of the twelve spans, while the other two endured moderate losses.

The returns in the "extremely bullish" modes are so good that it would pay for a patient and risk-averse investor to stay completely out of the stock market at any time the Fed Indicator rated anything less. Since 1958 the "extremely bullish" zone was in effect for a cumulative total of just 7.6 years. Suppose one had invested in the broad market (ZUPI) only in those years and then gone into cash equivalents in the remaining 19.3 years at an average yield of 6%. Assuming no taxes or dividends, a $10,000 investment would have grown to $334,766, an annualized gain of 13.9%. That would have clobbered the buy-and-hold return of 5.6% and its final value of $43,387. Moreover, the fortunate investor would have had *no money at risk 72% of the time.* A conservative investor can't ask for much better than that, even though in some periods, such as 1962–65 and in 1978, he would have watched from the sidelines as the market moved upward. Of course, during the grim days of 1969–70 or 1973–74 he would have slept comfortably while stocks were being ravaged.

Clearly, investment strategy should never be determined merely on the basis of one indicator. But the results found here strongly argue against "fighting the Fed."

INSTALLMENT DEBT INDICATOR

Loan demand has an important effect on interest rates. When demand for loans rises excessively, it puts upward pressure on rates. When it drops dramatically, it works to lower interest rates.

There are several major sources of loan demand, including federal, state, and local government borrowings; corporate borrowings both in the short-term money markets (commercial paper and bank loans) and in the longer-term bond markets; mortgage debt; and consumer installment debt. The latter figure has maintained one of the best records at calling the shots for the stock market. Also, since it is reported only once a month, it's a very simple tool to use. So, let's try it.

I personally use a rather complicated approach in dealing with the consumer installment debt numbers. But the idea of this book is to make it easy for the "weekend investor" to make decisions. Moreover, even a very simplified model using installment debt works very well.

First, the monthly total of such debt is released by the Federal Reserve around midmonth for the month ended about six weeks earlier. In other words, the data for, say, September would come out around November 15 or so. The delay in getting the numbers is not that important since our concern here is only with the major trend, one that changes very slowly. The installment figures are reported in most major newspapers, including *The New York Times* and *The Wall Street Journal*. You can also be placed on the mailing list for the release itself by writing to the Federal Reserve Board in Washington, D.C. Ask for Federal Reserve Statistical Release G.19.

The figures are reported both on a seasonally adjusted basis and a non–seasonally adjusted basis. Use the latter... *the non–seasonally adjusted number.*

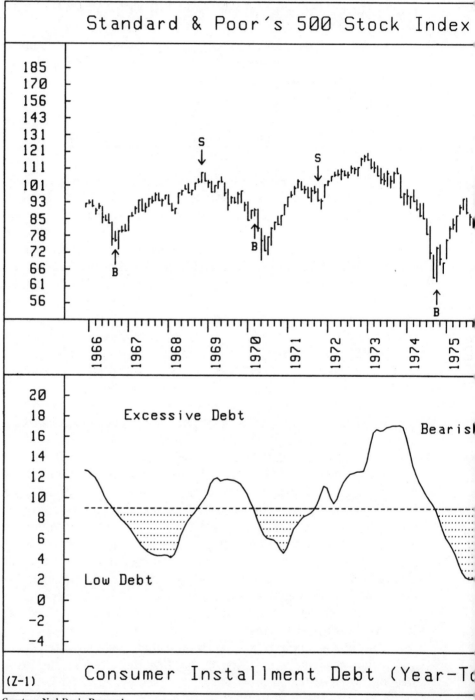

(Z-1) Consumer Installment Debt (Year-To

Courtesy Ned Davis Research

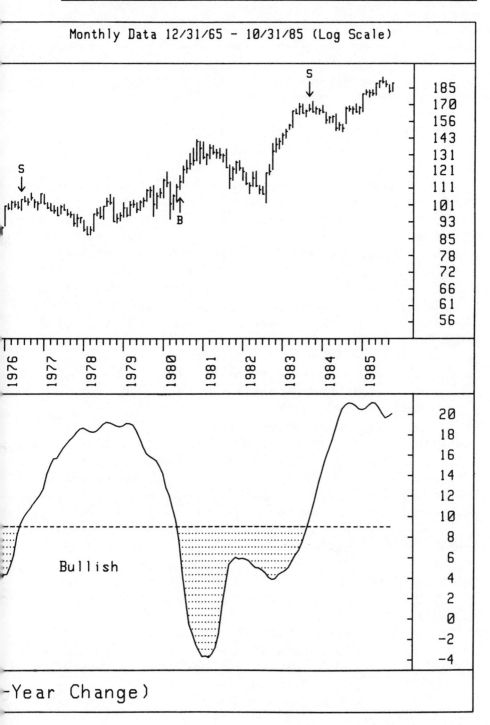

Monthly Data 12/31/65 – 10/31/85 (Log Scale)

Bullish

-Year Change)

Take that total for the month and divide by the total for the same month a year ago. Then subtract 1.000. That leaves you with the percentage change in installment debt on a year-to-year basis. When done this way, you don't need the seasonal adjustment since you are comparing January to January, February to February, etc.

Let's try an example. Take out your calculator and work along with me. Suppose on November 15, 1984, you get a release showing that non–seasonally adjusted consumer installment debt was $450.131 billion at the end of September 1984. The G.19 release will also show the non–seasonally adjusted debt for September 1983, which we'll assume was $375.246 billion. Now, divide the former by the latter and you get 1.200 (rounded upward). Subtract 1.000 and you are left with .200, which when converted from decimals equals +20.0%. In other words, in the one year ending September 1984, consumer installment debt rose by 20.0%.

The year-to-year percentage change in installment debt is *the only calculation* you have to make on this indicator. It will take you a few seconds a month.

Graph G (pp. 62–63) shows installment debt plotted on the year-to-year basis just described. Above it is the Standard & Poor's 500 Index. It is readily apparent that an expansion in installment debt tends to be bearish, as it was in late 1968, 1972, and late 1976. Conversely, when the trend of such debt plunges, it's bullish for stocks, as it was in late 1966, 1970, late 1974, and 1980.

The important question is, just how much of a year-to-year change in installment debt is needed to signify a bullish or a bearish condition for stocks? It appears that 9% is the key level. At the least, the 9% mark offers an easy method for generating good signals.

Rules: A buy signal is given when the year-to-year change in installment debt has been falling and drops to under 9%. A sell signal comes when the year-to-year change has been rising and hits 9% or more. That's it. *Example:* Table 6 shows a three-year history of consumer installment debt from 1974 to 1976. Column 1 gives the actual month of the data. Column 2 shows the approximate day you would have gotten the figures from the government. Recall, there is about a six-week lag. Column 3 provides the monthly total of installment debt (in billions of dollars). Column 4 shows the year-to-year change.

The year-to-year change was falling in 197 :, finally breaking under 9% in October when it struck 8.2%. You would have gotten that information about 6 weeks later, on December 13, the date of the buy signal. Afterward the series kept falling until mid-1975, when it bottomed at 1.6%. From there it rose again until the key 9% level was topped in June 1976 at a reading of 9.2%. That tripped a sell signal effective six weeks later, on August 13.

Table 7 shows the performance of the Installment Debt Indicator from 1951 to 1984 vs. the Zweig Unweighted Price Index. It has given only eight buy signals and eight sell signals (the sell signal of October 13, 1983, was still open when the table appeared). A $10,000 investment in the ZUPI during only the buy periods would have grown to $101,292, an annualized return of 17.0%. Buy-and-hold over that period returned only 5.4% a year. In the sell modes a $10,000 investment would have been cut nearly in half for an annualized loss of 3.0%.

TABLE 6

CALCULATING THE INSTALLMENT DEBT INDICATOR

Month of Data	Date Data Received	Consumer Installment Debt ($billions)	Year-to-Year Change in Consumer Installment Debt
1974			
January	3/18/74	$145.55	+14.9%
February	4/18/74	145.29	+14.0%
March	5/15/74	145.02	+12.6%
April	6/14/74	146.27	+12.2%
May	7/16/74	148.13	+11.5%
June	8/15/74	149.91	+10.7%
July	9/13/74	151.36	+10.1%
August	10/15/74	153.71	+ 9.9%
September	11/14/74	154.47	+ 9.4%
October	12/13/74	154.51	BUY + 8.2%

(*TABLE* 6 continued)

Month of Data	Date Data Received	Consumer Installment Debt ($billions)	Year-to-Year Change in Consumer Installment Debt
November	1/17/75	154.36	+ 6.9%
December	2/14/75	155.38	+ 6.1%
1975			
January	3/18/75	153.36	+ 5.4%
February	4/18/75	152.40	+ 4.9%
March	5/15/75	151.10	+ 4.2%
April	6/13/75	151.12	+ 3.3%
May	7/16/75	151.41	+ 2.2%
June	8/14/75	152.64	+ 1.8%
July	9/15/75	154.52	+ 2.1%
August	10/15/75	156.20	+ 1.6%
September	11/13/75	157.45	+ 1.9%
October	12/15/75	158.19	+ 2.5%
November	1/19/76	159.22	+ 3.1%
December	2/13/76	162.24	+ 4.4%
1976			
January	3/17/76	160.82	+ 4.9%
February	4/15/76	160.40	+ 5.2%
March	5/13/76	160.73	+ 6.4%
April	6/16/76	162.33	+ 7.4%
May	7/16/76	164.10	+ 8.4%
June	8/13/76	166.66	SELL + 9.2%
July	9/15/76	168.67	+ 9.2%
August	10/14/76	171.16	+ 9.6%
September	11/16/76	172.92	+ 9.8%
October	12/16/76	173.93	+10.0%
November	1/17/77	175.33	+10.1%
December	2/14/77	178.78	+10.2%

TABLE 7

INSTALLMENT DEBT INDICATOR
VS. ZWEIG UNWEIGHTED PRICE INDEX: 1951 TO 1984

BUY SIGNALS			**SELL SIGNALS**		
Date	ZUPI	% Change	Date	ZUPI	% Change
9/14/51	33.60	− 4.1	7/10/52	32.21	+11.0
6/16/54	35.75	+41.5	6/16/55	50.58	+ 8.0
4/17/57	54.64	+30.5	9/15/59	71.31	+18.5
3/17/61	84.47	−16.3	10/15/62	70.70	+53.8
11/16/66	108.75	+59.2	12/31/68	173.15	−44.1
5/14/70	96.78	+34.2	3/16/72	130.26	−63.5
12/13/74	47.49	+79.7	8/13/76	85.36	+37.6
6/16/80	117.46	+78.0	10/13/83	209.04	− 7.2
11/21/84	193.94 [a]				

$10,000 becomes: $101,292 $5,692
Annualized return = +17.0%   −3.0%
Buy-and-hold return = +5.4% per year

[a] The latest date when table was prepared (not a BUY).

Note that not all the signals were good ones. The worst was the sell in October 1962, right after a bear market bottomed. Stocks then rose for three years before hitting another bear market, during 1966. Nonetheless, the Installment Debt Indicator stayed correctly bearish during just about all of the two worst bear markets since the Depression, 1969–70 and 1973–74. It also caught most of the major bull advances of the past few decades.

Table 8 shows how the Installment Debt Indicator performed when tested against the Standard & Poor's 500 Index. The buy modes produced annualized gains of 13.6%, more than double the buy-and-hold return of 6.0%. The sell modes showed a tiny annualized gain of .3%...but that is still substantially inferior to the buy-and-hold results. One would have been much better off, and at much less risk, staying out of the market during the sell periods and keeping the money in Treasury bills or the like.

MONETARY MODEL

Thus far I've taken you through the simple calculations on three important monetary indicators—Prime Rate, the Fed, and Installment Debt. The next step is to combine them into a model. A *model* may sound like some sort of fancy mathematical word. Don't let that bother you. All *model* means in this case is that we give each of our indicators a numerical score, then combine them to get a composite reading on monetary conditions. Once we do that, we'll develop rules to make buy and sell decisions.

TABLE 8

INSTALLMENT DEBT INDICATOR
VS. STANDARD & POOR'S 500 INDEX: 1951 to 1984

BUY SIGNALS			SELL SIGNALS		
Date	S&P	% Change	Date	S&P	% Change
9/14/51	23.69	+ 4.7	7/10/52	24.81	+17.0
6/16/54	29.04	+37.6	6/16/55	39.96	+12.8
4/17/57	45.08	+25.7	9/15/59	56.68	+14.0
3/17/61	64.60	−11.3	10/15/62	57.27	+43.8
11/16/66	82.37	+26.1	12/31/68	103.86	−27.4
5/14/70	75.44	+42.5	3/16/72	107.50	−37.6
12/13/74	67.07	+55.4	8/13/76	104.25	+11.4
6/16/80	116.09	+46.3	10/13/83	169.88	− 3.2
11/21/84	164.52 [a]				

$10,000 becomes: $65,622 $10,569
Annualized return = +13.6%   +.3%
Buy-and-hold return = +6.0% per year

[a] The latest date when table was prepared (not a BUY).

The first indicator we developed is the Prime Rate Indicator. When the prime rate gives a buy signal according to our rules (see pages 44–45), give it 2 model points. When it gives a sell signal, accord it zero points. Table 9, on page 71, is a worksheet that shows the grading for the prime rate and the other indicators from the end of 1979 to the end of 1984. Each time any one of the three indicators changed, an entry was made on the worksheet.

Now, look at the Prime Rate column. As of December 31, 1979 (our starting point for the worksheet), the prime rate was on a buy signal (which had been given on December 7, 1979). Thus, it carried a score of 2. On February 19, 1980, the prime rate went bearish and the score for it fell to zero. Then on May 1, 1980, the indicator gave a buy signal and our rating went back up to 2. If you note the buy and sell signals for the prime rate that were presented in table 1, you'll see that each is recognized and given a score of either 2 or zero in the worksheet in table 9.

The next column on the worksheet grades the Fed Indicator. Recall (see pages 54–55) that I gave it four different gradings based on its past performance. Each of those gradings related to a certain number of "points" on the indicator, which I'll call "indicator points." Now, we'll convert those gradings to "model points" in order to construct our Monetary Model. The listing below shows how this is done.

FED INDICATOR GRADINGS

Indicator Points	Rating	Model Points
+2 or more points	= Extremely Bullish	= 4 Model Points
0 or +1 point	= Neutral	= 2 Model Points
−1 or −2 points	= Moderately Bearish	= 1 Model Point
−3 or fewer points	= Extremely Bearish	= 0 Model Points

Now, refer again to the worksheet in table 9. The Fed Indicator ended 1979 in its "extremely bearish" mode, so it was graded 0. It had −3 indicator points then (not shown in the table). On May 6, 1980, the Fed cut the discount rate, causing the indicator points to rise to +1, a "neutral" rating. Based on the above scoring, the worksheet shows a jump to 2 model points on May 6, 1980. Two weeks later the Fed lowered reserve requirements. That shot the indicator points up to +4, an "extremely bullish" rating. That's also worth 4 model points. On November 14, 1980, the discount rate was raised, dropping the number of indicator points to +1, a "neutral" rating. So, the worksheet shows the model points easing to 2.

Because of the conversion in scoring for the Monetary Model Worksheet, the Fed Indicator's gradings may be a bit confusing at first glance, but give it a try and you'll quickly see it's really simple. Remember this: Changes in reserve requirements and the discount rate (as explained in pages 52–54) give rise to what I call indicator points. The number of indicator points determines ratings ranging from "extremely bullish" down through "neutral" and "moderately bearish" to "extremely bearish." There is no "moderately bullish" zone simply because there was no clear pattern of moderately bullish market behavior consistent with any score on the Fed Indicator.

Finally, the indicator points must be converted to model points as shown on page 65 in order to develop our overall Monetary Model.

Gradings on the Installment Debt Indicator are much easier. When the Installment Debt Indicator gives a buy signal (see page 64), give it 2 model points. When it gives a sell signal, grade it zero model points. It's the same process as that done with the Prime Rate Indicator. Note that if the Installment Debt Indicator had a "neutral" rating, it would be given one model point. Another version of this indicator, which I keep myself, has such a range . . . but in this book I'm striving for simplicity to the fullest extent possible, so I've ignored a "neutral" rating. It wouldn't add much value anyhow.

You ought to keep a worksheet similar to that in table 9. Indeed, you can merely update the worksheet you see there. It's easy. The prime rate doesn't change that often, and the rating changes even less often. The Fed doesn't change reserve requirements or the discount rate very much either. Installment debt figures come out once a month. You have to be exceptionally lazy not to update your worksheet. It's worth it, and the task ought not to take more than a few minutes a month.

In my Monetary Model Worksheet (table 9), I have included, for illustrative purposes, various market averages (ZUPI, S&P 500, and the Dow). If, when model changes occur, you would like to post and keep track of one or more of these averages, fine. But you don't have to in order to determine the buy and sell signals.

TABLE 9

MONETARY MODEL WORKSHEET

Date	ZUPI	S&P 500	Dow	Prime Rate	Fed	Installment Debt	Monetary Model
12/31/79	112.33	107.94	839	2	0	0	2
2/19/80	117.09	114.60	876	0*	0	0	0
5/1/80	103.73	105.46	809	2*	0	0	2
5/6/80	105.52	106.25	816	2	2*	0	4
5/22/80	110.68	109.01	843	2	4*	0	6 (BUY)
6/16/80	117.46	116.09	878	2	4	2*	8
8/26/80	132.08	124.84	953	0*	4	2	6
11/14/80	138.18	137.15	986	0	2*	2	4
12/4/80	136.90	136.48	970	0	1*	2	3
12/22/80	132.87	135.78	959	2*	1	2	5
4/24/81	148.46	135.14	1020	0*	1	2	3
6/16/81	149.84	132.15	1003	2*	1	2	5
6/22/81	149.02	131.95	994	0*	1	2	3
9/9/81	128.22	118.40	854	0	2*	2	4
9/21/81	127.04	117.24	847	2*	4*	2	8
2/1/82	128.68	117.78	852	0*	4	2	6
3/8/82	121.07	107.34	795	2*	4	2	8
3/16/82	120.96	109.28	798	0*	4	2	6
6/4/82	125.50	110.09	805	0	2*	2	4
7/19/82	124.03	110.73	826	0	4*	2	6
7/26/82	124.39	110.36	825	2*	4	2	8
5/19/83	203.54	161.99	1191	2	2*	2	6
8/10/83	200.53	161.54	1176	0*	2	2	4
10/13/83	209.04	169.88	1261	0	2	0*	2 (SELL)
4/6/84	189.74	155.48	1132	0	1*	0	1
10/6/84	192.21	162.13	1178	0	2*	0	2
10/15/84	194.61	165.77	1203	2*	2	0	4
11/21/84	193.94	164.52	1202	2	4*	0	6 (BUY)

*Indicates change.

BUY AND SELL SIGNALS

The Monetary Model is merely the addition of all model points. The maximum score is 8, the minimum is zero. There is no way to get a 7 because the Fed Indicator can never hit 3, it runs only 0, 1, 2, and 4. The other two indicators get either a zero or a 2.

You can use the Monetary Model any way you wish to augment other market-timing tools. But for the long-term investor I have devised simple but consistent rules to determine buy and sell signals for the stock market. When the Monetary Model rises to 6 points, it trips a buy signal. That buy remains in effect until the model falls to 2 points, which then flashes a sell signal. The sell then remains effective until the Monetary Model increases back to 6 again, which would trigger a buy signal. To repeat, a buy signal requires 6 points; a sell signal requires 2 points. That's it.

Table 10 shows all the buy and sell signals since 1954, tracked against the Zweig Unweighted Price Index. There have been only nine buys and eight sells since 1954. The ninth buy signal came in November 1984 and was still in effect as of this writing, at which time the market was already more than 25% higher. Each of the eight prior buy signals produced profits, including five with gains of better than 50% each. Had you invested $10,000 only in the 217 months that the Monetary Model was bullish (on a buy signal), it would have grown to $222,355, an annualized gain of 18.7%. That doesn't include interest you could have earned on money market instruments (such as T-bills or certificates of deposit) during the bearish periods when the model was on a sell signal.

Assuming an average interest rate of 6% over the period (less in the early years, considerably more since the mid-1960s), you would have earned a total of 108.2% in the 151 months you were out of the stock market. When that sum is compounded onto the stock market return, the original $10,000 investment becomes $462,992 in 30.7 years. That is equal to an annualized return of 13.3%. It still does not include dividends earned while in the stock market. By contrast, buy-and-hold on the average New York stock (as per my Zweig Unweighted Price Index) would have returned only 5.9% a year, again ignoring dividends. Buy-

and-hold would have turned $10,000 into only $57,498, nowhere near the $462,992 produced by the Monetary Model.

TA B L E   1 0
====

MONETARY MODEL
VS. ZWEIG UNWEIGHTED PRICE INDEX: 1954 to 1984

BUY SIGNALS				**SELL SIGNALS**			
Date	**ZUPI**	**% Change**	**No. of Months**	**Date**	**ZUPI**	**% Change**	**No. of Months**
3/17/54	33.73	+53.4	18	9/9/55	51.75	− 12.7	26
11/15/57	45.18	+60.7	22	9/11/59	72.61	+ 1.6	11
8/23/60	73.74	+70.1	66	3/10/66	125.43	− 3.3	11
1/26/67	121.28	+20.8	15	4/19/68	146.45	+ 8.1	4
8/30/68	158.29	+ 9.4	4	12/31/68	173.15	−41.2	21
9/21/70	101.86	+18.8	21	6/26/72	121.02	−57.7	29
11/28/74	51.21	+78.8	30	5/31/77	91.57	+20.9	36
5/22/80	110.68	+88.9	41	10/31/83	209.04	− 7.2	13
11/21/84	193.94	?	?				

$10,000 becomes: $222,355   217 mo. $2,587   151 mo.
Annualized return = +18.7%   −10.2%
Buy-and-hold return = +5.9% per year

Buy-and-hold would fare somewhat better if dividends were considered. My estimate for dividends on the ZUPI (there is no precise figure) is about 3.5% a year over the period . . . somewhat less than dividends on bigger, blue chip stocks, which dominate the major stock averages. When the dividends are added to the capital gains for the buy-and-hold investor, the return increases to 9.4% a year. That would make $10,000 grow to $157,415 over the 30.7-year test period.

But, we also have to allow dividends of 3.5% during the buy periods of our Monetary Model (actually, the dividend yields would have been a bit better than that because many times our model had us buying near market lows, when yields were greater). That would have increased the total ending value on the Monetary Model to $862,511, a nice 15.6%-a-year return. In other words, if you had bought the average New York stock on the model's buy signals, allowed for dividends, and then switched to money market instruments on sell signals, you would have made about 15.6% a year for more than 30 years and would now have about 86 times your original stake.

Transaction costs (commissions) would not have been too important since the portfolio would have turned over only about once every two years. Moveover, you could have traded no-load mutual funds and avoided commissions entirely, although you would have absorbed some management fees. But at least the reinvestment of interest and dividends could have been done with only minimal cost.

I have also ignored taxes. That assumption is warranted in pension accounts, including some you may have yourself such as individual retirement accounts (IRAs) or Keogh plans. Of course, the buy-and-hold investor also has to reckon with taxes sooner or later ... whenever he decides to cash in. He also has to pay taxes along the way on dividends.

The right side of table 10 shows the results of sell signals on the model against the ZUPI. Three times, the broad market went higher on a sell signal (once, just barely); five times, it fell as predicted, including two horrendous losses in the bear markets of 1969–70 and 1972–74. Had a hapless investor stayed in the market during the sell signal periods, he would have lost about three-quarters of his money, showing a loss rate of 10.2% per annum. Had he paid attention to the Monetary Model, he could have avoided such grief.

Table 11 tracks the Monetary Model against the Standard & Poor's 500 Index. Buy periods alone would have produced annualized profits of 14.7%, while sell periods showed losses of 5.1% a year. By contrast, buy-and-hold gained 6.1% yearly. Again, all eight prior buy signals had gains, with six of them returning more than 30% each. And at presstime, the 1984 buy showed a 27% gain and the signal was still in effect. Five of eight sell signals led to market declines, and two of the three gains in sell periods were minimal. The Monetary Model is plotted in graph H (pp. 76–77) against the S&P 500 Index. The most bullish zone is the area above the upper

TABLE 11

MONETARY MODEL
VS. STANDARD & POOR'S 500 INDEX: 1954 to 1984

BUY SIGNALS				SELL SIGNALS			
Date	S&P	% Change	No. of Months	Date	S&P	% Change	No. of Months
3/17/54	26.62	+64.9	18	9/9/55	43.89	− 8.0	26
11/15/57	40.37	+42.2	22	9/11/59	57.41	+ .6	11
8/23/60	57.75	+54.0	66	3/10/66	88.96	− 3.5	11
1/26/67	85.81	+11.7	15	4/19/68	95.85	+ 3.1	4
8/30/68	98.86	+ 5.1	4	12/31/68	103.86	−21.1	21
9/21/70	81.91	+31.2	21	6/26/72	107.48	−34.9	29
11/28/74	69.97	+37.4	30	5/31/77	96.12	+13.4	36
5/22/80	109.01	+55.8	41	10/13/83	169.88	− 3.2	13
11/21/84	164.52	?	?				

$10,000 becomes: $119,066   217 mo. $5,192   151 mo.
Annualized return = +14.7%   −5.1%
Buy-and-hold return = +6.1% per year

dotted line. The most bearish zone is the area beneath the lower dotted line.

You don't have to use my buy and sell signals (6 points and 2 points respectively). You can use the rating on the Monetary Model in conjunction with other indicators to make *major* market-timing judgments or to make *partial* moves in the market. For example, rather than using the all-or-none approach of buy and sell signals, you might want to increase stock investments as the model gets better, and to decrease them as the model falls. When the model is neutral at 4 points, you might be 50% invested. If it rises to 5, you might go to 65% invested. A score of 6 might be worth 80% invested, and an 8 might entice you to go 100% long.

In the other direction, a 3 might relate to 40% invested, a 2 to 25%, 1 to 10%, and 0 to 0% invested. These are merely ballpark suggestions, not hard-and-fast rules.

It is illuminating, though, to see how you would have fared only when the Monetary Model reached its extremes of either 0

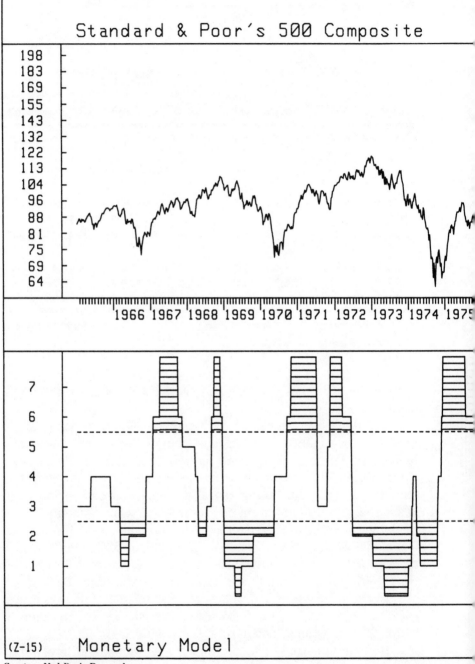

Standard & Poor's 500 Composite

1966 1967 1968 1969 1970 1971 1972 1973 1974 1975

(Z-15)   Monetary Model

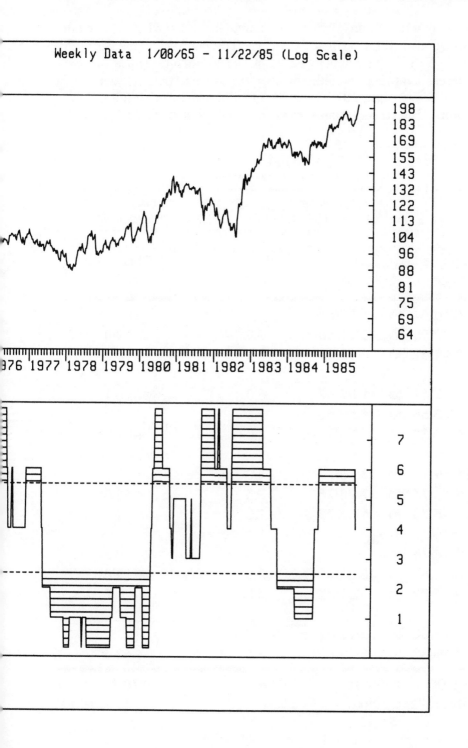

Weekly Data   1/08/65 - 11/22/85 (Log Scale)

or 8 points. Table 12 lists all fourteen cases when the model rested at 8, the best possible score. The market, as measured by the ZUPI, went higher twelve of those fourteen times, an 86% success average. Indeed, the two losses were trivial, including a 2.7% loss in late 1975 when the model temporarily fell below 8 points. But three weeks later it rebounded back to 8 and the

TABLE 12

MONETARY MODEL RATED +8 POINTS
VS. ZWEIG UNWEIGHTED PRICE INDEX: 1954 to 1984

+8 Point Span		No. of	% Change in
Start	End	Months	ZUPI
6/16/54 to	1/19/55	7.0	+28.4
1/22/58 to	10/17/58	9.0	+32.0
3/17/61 to	6/10/61	3.0	+ 4.0
4/7/67 to	10/7/67	6.0	+16.1
9/25/68 to	12/2/68	2.5	+ 7.7
11/3/70 to	7/6/71	8.0	+22.9
11/19/71 to	3/16/72	4.0	+19.7
12/13/74 to	7/28/75	7.5	+48.5
11/5/75 to	12/6/75	1.0	− 2.7
12/24/75 to	6/7/76	5.5	+20.2
6/16/80 to	8/26/80	2.5	+12.4
9/21/81 to	2/1/82	4.5	+ 1.3
3/8/82 to	3/16/82	.5	− .1
7/26/82 to	5/19/83	9.5	+63.6

$10,000 becomes:	$104,794	70.5 months
Annualized return =	+48.9%	(5.9 years)

market skyrocketed. The other loss was a meager .1% during an eight-day stretch in March 1982. Conversely, in eight of the fourteen cases the market gained 16% or more.

In all, had you invested $10,000 only during the 70.5 months when the Monetary Model was at its absolute best rating of 8 points, you would have seen the money grow to $104,794, an annualized gain of a whopping 48.9%! A truly conservative person could have then retreated to money market funds the rest of the time, having exposed himself to stock market risk for only 5.9 years of a 30.7-year period, yet far outperforming the stock market. A more typical investor might opt for the buy and sell signals described earlier, or a "partial" strategy such as that described on page 75.

Table 13 on page 80 enumerates the eight cases when the Monetary Model rested at its lowest possible score of zero. Stocks fell during six of those eight spans, for a nice 75% success average. The two times stocks rose, the gains were tiny ones of .6% and 2.5% respectively. The model was in its worst mode for a total of 19.5 months. You would have lost about 40% of your original investment in that span, an annualized rate of loss of 27.5%, fast enough to send you to the poorhouse in a hurry. *Obviously, the stock market is no place to be when monetary conditions are hostile. Yet, stocks are super attractive when the Fed is loosening and interest rates are falling. In sum, "Don't fight the Fed."*

TABLE 13

MONETARY MODEL RATED ZERO POINTS
VS. ZWEIG UNWEIGHTED PRICE INDEX: 1954 to 1984

Zero Point Span		No. of	% Change in
Start	End	Months	ZUPI
10/14/55 to	10/15/55	0	+ .6
11/18/55 to	2/5/56	2.5	+ 2.5
4/17/69 to	6/18/69	2.0	− 6.6
5/4/73 to	1/2/74	8.0	− 22.0
1/6/78 to	2/29/78	2.0	− .9
6/30/78 to	7/6/78	0	− .9
9/18/79 to	12/7/79	2.5	− 8.3
2/19/80 to	5/1/80	2.5	− 11.4

$10,000 becomes: $5,994   19.5 months
Annualized return = − 27.5%   (1.6 years)

CHAPTER 5

Momentum Indicators—
"The Trend Is Your Friend"

In the old days all stock transactions were actually printed on ticker tape that rolled out of a machine topped with a glass dome. To this day the activity on the market itself is called tape action. Of course, we now have electronic machines, and the physical ticker tape is almost obsolete. However, every transaction is still reported with the name of the stock, the price of the trade, and the volume.

Any calculation using price and volume is in the realm of technical indicators. Occasionally the sentiment-type indicators, a first cousin to tape action, are included in technical analysis, but they don't truly fit that category. We'll cover all the sentiment indicators in another chapter. Right now we're just talking about price and volume.

Of the two variables, price is more important than volume. For the moment let's concentrate on price. In the market, as we've seen in earlier chapters, you can construct a price index such as the Dow Jones Industrial Average or the S&P 500 or my unweighted index, the ZUPI. You can observe the behavior of a price index and measure tape action from it. For example, you can analyze the change in the Dow Jones average. If the average is up by X%, it's bullish; if it's down by X%, it's bearish. That would be a very simple type of indicator.

To complicate matters, some people might argue that if the

market is up by X%, it's bearish because the market is overbought and likely to decline. Conversely, one may contend that if the market is down by X%, it's bullish because the market is oversold and ready to rise. That brings us to the key question, Does strength tend to beget strength, or does strength tend to wane and lead to weakness? Let's look at it scientifically.

After years of testing various market averages, advance/decline ratios, volume figures, and other indicators, I have found that strength does indeed tend to lead to greater strength. Every single bull market that I've seen has started with a tremendous rally. The rally doesn't necessarily come the first day after the bear market ends. Occasionally you have a period of weeks or even months during which the market backs and fills and bounces around in what technicians call a basing action. If conditions are right, a rally eventually ensues.

For a raging bull market, you need falling interest rates, probably an economic recession (that helps the Fed to loosen up and rates to fall), lots of cash on the sidelines, good values in the market—namely, low price/earnings ratios—and a great deal of pessimism because, as we'll see later, pessimism means there's an abundance of cash. If all these conditions converge, the market should rally very, very strongly, and the first rally of the bull market should be the best one.

When that rally blasts off, prices should go through the roof. Remember my analogy about launching a rocket to the moon? The rocket must have sufficient thrust to get through the atmosphere and into outer space. The market works similarly. The first rally must have a tremendous surge for a major market advance. If it does, it generates more buying enthusiasm and brings in people who missed the first move. It prevents a large correction because that first rally reverses the market psychology. People who missed it are sitting there loaded with cash and eager to get aboard. So, after the smallest setback, new buyers enter and there is no sharp correction. *One of the frustrating things for people who miss the first rally in a bull market is that they wait for the big correction and it never comes. The market just keeps climbing and climbing. It feeds on itself in frenzied fashion and propels prices considerably higher for six months or so, and sometimes longer.*

ADVANCE/DECLINE INDICATOR

As our first momentum indicator, let us examine data on advances and declines on the NYSE. Advances comprise the total number of stocks that rise on a given day, and declines those that fall. We'll ignore the day's total of unchanged stocks. Here's how you calculate an advance/decline ratio: If 1000 stocks are up on the day and 500 are down, the ratio would be 2-to-1. Of course, advances predominate when the market does well, and declines predominate when the market does poorly. It is a sign of very strong momentum when advances overwhelm declines for a significant span, and vice versa.

I like to track the Advance/Decline Ratio (A/D ratio) over a ten-day period. It's very rare for advances to lead declines by a ratio of 2-to-1 over such a span. When that happens, one could rightly say the market's momentum is strong. The test then would be the market's performance after such relatively rare events.

Beginning in 1953, there have been only nine cases when the ten-day A/D ratio reached 2-to-1 or more. There were a couple of other cases, which I consider repeats since they occurred a few months after the first signal. For example, in August 1982 the ten-day ratio surpassed 2-to-1 and did it again two months later. I'm ignoring that second signal because it's superfluous. The last signal of the nine came in January 1985, and, as of this writing, it's a bit soon to track its success or failure. (By presstime for this book, the signal had worked very well.)

However, we can track the previous eight signals, as shown in table 14. The first column lists the dates of these A/D signals. The second and third columns show the percentage changes in the market as measured by the Standard & Poor's 500 Index and the Zweig Unweighted Price Index, respectively. The first A/D signal came on January 26, 1954. Three months later the S&P 500 was up 7.1% and the ZUPI had risen 5.2%. If you follow the columns down, you'll see how the other signals performed three months later.

Had you invested $10,000 in the market averages only at such signals, held for three months, and then sold, you would have had $18,770 on the S&P 500 Index and $25,267 on the ZUPI.

Bear in mind that that's in a cumulative period of only two years—eight separate three-month periods. The rate of return per quarter was 8.2% on the S&P and 12.3% on the ZUPI. The annualized returns would be more than four times the quarterly figures when compounded.

The right-hand columns in table 14 show the market's performance six months after these signals. Note that the S&P 500 and the ZUPI were up at least 10% six months later in every single case. You would have more than tripled your money in the S&P and nearly quintupled it on the ZUPI. The return per six months is 16.2% on the S&P and 22.2% on the ZUPI. Those returns are extraordinarily high in the stock market.

TABLE 14

TEN-DAY ADVANCE/DECLINE RATIO GREATER THAN 2-TO-1: 1953 to 1985

	Percentage Change in Market			
	3 Months Later		6 months Later	
Date	S&P 500	ZUPI	S&P 500	ZUPI
1/26/54	+ 7.1	+ 5.2	+16.6	+15.2
1/24/58	+ 3.4	+ 4.4	+11.8	+15.4
7/11/62	− 1.2	− 1.3	+12.3	+11.3
1/16/67	+ 7.3	+11.0	+10.0	+20.7
12/4/70	+ 9.5	+19.8	+13.2	+21.8
1/10/75	+15.4	+18.2	+30.6	+38.9
1/6/76	+10.5	+19.4	+10.7	+19.0
8/23/82	+14.5	+24.2	+26.4	+38.4
1/23/85	?	?	?	?

$10,000 becomes:
| | $18,770 | $25,267 | $33,312 | $49,761 |

Return/period =
+8.2%/qt.   +12.3%/qt.   +16.2%/half   +22.2%/half

In other words, had you patiently waited for prices to "explode" over some two-week period, and then stepped in and bought at what seemed like "high" levels at the time, you would have made abnormally large profits in the months that followed. Thus, strong momentum tends to persist. Momentum also tends to be greatest at the beginnings of bull markets. Indeed, seven of the eight listings in table 14 came near the starts of bull markets. The 1976 case was a "second leg" of an old bull market.

As indicated in the results shown in table 14, the market must push off with a lot of firepower to get off the ground. To put it succinctly, *if the tape can't ignite, conditions aren't right.*

UP VOLUME INDICATOR

A second momentum indicator uses the ratio of up volume to down volume. Up volume comprises the total volume of all stocks that rise on a given day, and down volume totals all that decline. Again, we'll ignore the volume for stocks that are unchanged on the day. The up and down volume figures are available daily in *The Wall Street Journal*, on quote machines, and in the *Barron's* weekly statistical section, as well as in the financial sections of most major newspapers.

I have found that when 90% or more of the volume (ignoring unchanged volume) is on the upside in a given day, it is a significant sign of positive momentum. In other words, when daily up volume leads down volume by a ratio of 9-to-1 or more, that tends to be an important signal for stocks. The significance of this ratio was first spotted many years ago by Lowry's Reports, Inc. However, over the years I've developed my own ways of interpreting the up/down volume.

Since 1960, there have been only ninety-two days in which the 9-to-1 ratio was on the down side—that is, where down volume exceeded up volume by more than 9-to-1. That averages just about four such very poor days per year. Conversely, there have been only fifty very positive days in which up volume topped down volume by at least 9-to-1. Thus there have been only about two 9-to-1 up days per year.

The 9-to-1 down days do have some predictive ability but are not nearly as strong an indicator as the 9-to-1 up days, so let's just concentrate on the latter. Why is a 9-to-1 up day significant?

Simply because it graphically shows the powerful thrust of the market. *Every bull market in history, and many good intermediate advances, have been launched with a buying stampede that included one or more 9-to-1 up days.**

The most spectacular one-day reading ever was 42-to-1 on August 17, 1982. Not so coincidentally, it heralded the strongest bull market in nearly five decades. Just three days later there was a 32-to-1 up day, the second greatest in the twenty-five years for which I have figures. That merely verified the enormous momentum that helped to blast off that bull market.

But even a 9-to-1 up day can fail now and then. The last to do so came on July 20, 1983. There was very little follow-through over the next few sessions, and prices began to fade, declining for about a year. In other words, while a 9-to-1 up day is an impressive positive sign, it does not guarantee a great leap forward. More thrust is required to enhance the bullish odds.

However, the 9-to-1 up day is a most encouraging sign, and having two of them within a reasonably short span is very bullish. I call it a "double 9-to-1" when two such days occur within three months of one another. As an indicator, this calculation falls into one of two types. The first and most bullish is when there are no intervening 9-to-1 down days. The second is when one or more 9-to-1 down days occur between the up days. The latter condition implies not as much thrust as does the former, but here too the record provides great comfort to the bulls.

As you will see in table 15, there have been twelve double 9-to-1 signals since 1960. In 1962 and 1975 there was a third 9-to-1 up day within several weeks of the first two. After the August 1982 double, there were two more 9-to-1 days in October (which I consider a repeat signal), an amazing display of thrust that was soon followed by another double 9-to-1, completed in early January 1983. In early August of 1984 there was an unprecedented string of three consecutive days in which up volume topped down volume by 9-to-1 or better, and about a week later there was a fourth such day.

Table 15 measures the Dow Industrials' advances after the double 9-to-1 days. At the bottom of the third column you will see that three months later, on average, the Dow's compounded

---

*Based on hard up/down volume data since 1960 and estimates of such volume in previous years.

return was up 7.6% per quarter. The next column shows that, six months after these signals, the Dow rose an average of 14.0%, and the final column shows a 20.7% gain one year later. The table reveals that the Dow was up every time but once three months after these signals, and every single time six months and twelve months later. Indeed, the smallest gain a year after such signals was 16.5% in 1963 (excluding the 1984 cases, for which a year had not yet passed when this table was prepared).

TABLE 15

DOUBLE 9-to-1 SIGNALS WITHIN THREE MONTHS VS. DOW JONES INDUSTRIAL AVERAGE: January 1, 1960 to May 3, 1985

Date	Dow	% Change 3 Mo. Later	% Change 6 Mo. Later	% Change 12 Mo. Later
11/12/62	624	+ 8.5	+15.9	+20.2
11/19/63	751	+ 6.9	+ 9.1	+16.5
10/12/66	778	+ 6.9	+ 8.6	+17.4
5/27/70	663	+14.6	+17.8	+16.5
11/19/71	830	+11.8	+17.0	+22.8
9/19/75	830	+ 1.7	+18.1	+19.9
4/22/80	790	+17.3	+20.9	+27.5
3/22/82	820	− 2.4	+13.2	+37.0
8/20/82	869	+15.1	+24.3[a]	+38.4[a]
1/6/83	1071	+ 3.9	+14.0[a]	+20.2[a]
8/2/84	1166	+ 4.4	+10.6	+ 6.9[b]
11/23/84	1220	+ 4.7	+ 2.2[a,b]	+ 2.2[a,b]

$10,000 =	$24,178	$43,071	$60,343

Compounded return

	+ 7.6%qtr.	+14.0%/half	+20.7%/year

[a] Cumulative returns adjusted for overlap 6 to 12 months later.
[b] Holding periods cut off as of 5/3/85, the last date of the study.

As usual, the results are more extreme when measured against the ZUPI, as seen in table 16. Three months after the double 9-to-1 signals, the broad market advanced 11.3%, rising every time but once. Six months later the ZUPI gained an average of 19.9%, and a year later the unweighted average was up 30.2%. In both the six-month and twelve-month cases, the market rose every single time.

Now observe the bottom line of the upper half of table 17, which compares the performance of the double 9-to-1 signals to that of an investor who merely bought the Dow Industrials and held them to the end of this study in 1985. Such an investor would have made only 2.5% a year in capital appreciation (plus something less than 4% a year in dividends, not shown on the table). Going across the top two lines of the table you'll see a summary of what had been reported in table 15, namely, the three-, six-, and twelve-month returns on the Dow following the double 9-to-1 signals. The third and fourth lines show the Dow's performance for all periods since 1960 not following the 9-to-1 signals. These results are all negative. Obviously, the Dow did a heck of a lot better in periods after these double 9-to-1 signals.

TABLE 16

DOUBLE 9-to-1 SIGNALS WITHIN THREE MONTHS
VS. ZWEIG UNWEIGHTED PRICE INDEX (ZUPI):
January 1, 1960 to May 3, 1985

Date	ZUPI	% Change 3 Mo. Later	% Change 6 Mo. Later	% Change 12 Mo. Later
11/12/62	72.10	+12.8	+19.2	+22.3
11/19/63	86.95	+ 5.2	+ 7.8	+16.2
10/12/66	100.64	+16.0	+28.1	+47.5
5/27/70	89.44	+ 8.1	+12.4	+40.9
11/19/71	109.13	+18.3	+16.3	+ 9.6
9/19/75	65.16	+ 1.0	+28.7	+32.6
4/22/80	100.76	+25.2	+35.9	+46.2

(*TABLE 16 continued*)

Date	ZUPI	% Change 3 Mo. Later	% Change 6 Mo. Later	% Change 12 Mo. Later
3/22/82	124.47	− 2.0	+12.3	+48.3
8/20/82	126.35	+27.5	+40.7[a]	+61.3[a]
1/6/83	169.91	+ 8.9	+24.6[a]	+23.8[a]
8/2/84	182.81	+ 7.8	+17.8	+17.4[b,]
11/23/84	195.96	+11.0	+ 9.6[a,b]	+ 9.6[a,b]
$10,000 =		$36,243	$75,135	$124,479
Compounded return		+11.3/qtr.	+19.9%/half	+30.2%/year

[a] Cumulative returns adjusted for overlap 6 to 12 months later.
[b] Holding periods cut off as of 5/3/85, the last date of the study.

TABLE 17

DOUBLE 9-to-1 PERIODS VS. ALL OTHER PERIODS:
January 1, 1960 to May 3, 1985

---

	3 Mo. Later	6 Mo. Later	12 Mo. Later
Vs. Dow:			
9-to-1 periods:			
$10,000 =	$24,178	$43,071	$60,343
Return =	+7.6%/qtr.	+14.0%/half	+20.7%/year
All other periods:			
$10,000 =	$7,596	$4,264	$3,043
Return =	−1.3%/qtr.	−4.4%/half	−7.7%/year
Buy-and-hold:			
$10,000 =	$18,365	$18,365	$18,365
Return =	+ .6%/qtr.	+1.2%/half	+2.5%/year

(*TABLE 17 continued*)

	3 Mo. Later	6 Mo. Later	12 Mo. Later
Vs. ZUPI:			
9-to-1 periods:			
$10,000 =	$36,243	$75,135	$124.479
Return =	+11.3%/qtr.	+19.9%/half	+30.2%/year
All other periods:			
$10,000 =	$7,813	$3,769	$2,275
Return =	− .3%/qtr.	−2.6%/half	−9.5%/year
Buy-and-hold:			
$10,000 =	$28,318	$28,318	$28,318
Return =	+1.1%/qtr.	+2.2%/half	+4.3%/year

The second half of table 17 shows similar figures for the ZUPI. The first two lines there summarize table 16, showing the three-, six-, and twelve-month returns on the ZUPI following the signals. The next two lines show the results for all other periods. In all spans not falling within one year to 9-to-1 signals, the investor who bought the broad market as measured by the ZUPI would have lost 9.5% per year, a huge difference from the 30.2% a year he would have made had he listened to the signals. The last line shows the returns on buy-and-hold on the ZUPI, which worked out to 4.3% per year.

Or, if you prefer to think of dollars instead of percentages, the investor who bought the ZUPI and held for a year after double 9-to-1 signals, would have seen a $10,000 investment appreciate to $124,479. That does not even count interest when out of the market or dividends while in stocks. By contrast, the unfortunate investor who insisted on buying only in the non–double 9-to-1 periods would have seen his $10,000 shrink to $2,275 an enormous disparity when compared with the dollars made by following the signals.

THE FOUR PERCENT MODEL INDICATOR

I've now given you two indicators that use momentum, one monitoring advances and declines and the other measuring up/down volume. These two indicators, as used here, look only for tremendous bursts of momentum that occur occasionally. They lead to terrific returns on the upside. However, these models are limited because, first, their buy signals are rare, and second, as designed, these indicators do not give sell signals. In other words, most of the time they don't tell you much because the market does not explode very often. What we need is a model that always is on either a buy or a sell signal. Of course, such a model will not give the spectacular returns over shorter periods the way the first two indicators do. But they will tell the investor the safest course on a continuous basis. *Remember, though, that no indicator or model is right all of the time.* In fact, we'll see that the model I'm about to develop is right only about half the time. But the profits derived from this model are excellent.

The Four Percent Model was developed by my close friend and colleague Ned Davis. Davis is the editor of two market letters I publish: *Futures Hotline*, which covers stock index figures, interest rate futures, foreign currencies, and precious metals; and *Business Timing Guide*, which calls the direction of both the economy and the rate of inflation. He has developed numerous computer models for these two services, all designed to follow the trend. Remember, the trend is your friend.

The Four Percent Model for the stock market works as follows. First, it uses the Value Line Composite Index, which is quoted regularly on Quotron machines and is found in your daily newspaper or in *Barron's*. You'll recall that the Value Line Index, as calculated by Arnold Bernhard & Co., is an unweighted price index of approximately seventeen hundred stocks and is very similar to my Zweig Unweighted Price Index. In fact, over long stretches the two give nearly identical results. One could just as easily apply this Four Percent Model to my ZUPI. However, the Value Line data are more readily available and easier to follow.

All you need to construct this model is the *weekly close* of the Value Line Composite. You can ignore the daily numbers if you wish. Just look in the Saturday or Sunday newspaper to find the weekly close, or in *Barron's*, which hits the newsstands on Saturdays. This trend-following model gives a buy signal when the weekly Value Line Index rallies 4% or more from any weekly close. It then gives a sell signal when the weekly close of the Value Line Composite drops by 4% or more from any weekly peak. *Note: I mean 4% of change, not four points.*

For example, if in Week One the Value Line Index closes at 200, it would require a reading of at least 208 to generate a buy signal. Let's say that happens in a week when the Value Line Index closes at 209. The buy signal continues as long as there is no 4% or greater drop in the weekly Value Line Index. Suppose the Value Line continues to rally, possibly with some small dips along the way—none of which is greater than 4%—until it reaches a closing weekly high of 240. At that point suppose the index begins to fall. It would have to drop by 4%, or to a level of 230.40 or less, to generate a sell signal. Assume that happens in a week when the Value Line closes at 229. The sell point would be 229, and the model would remain on a sell signal thereafter until there was a 4% or greater rally.

That's all there is to it. In just about a minute a week, with the aid of a calculator (or if you can remember your long division), you can calculate the Four Percent Model.

This model is designed to force you to stay with the market trend. The market can't rise for very long before you're forced into a buy signal, nor can it fall very much before you're forced into a sell signal. Of course, by using only weekly data, the market may move by more than 4% before you get a change in signals. Occasionally, the market may make a big move in a given week and you may be buying 6% or 7% or 8% above a weekly high, or perhaps selling that much below a weekly low; but nonetheless, you're still in gear with the major trend.

The virtue of this Four Percent Model, or any trend-following model, is that if the market makes a very large move, you will be on the right side of the bulk of it. But there is no free lunch in the stock market. Although you are guaranteed of being on the right side of major moves, you may get whipsawed over very short-term movements. If the market were to zig and zag by moves only a little bit greater than 4%, you might be zagging when you should be zigging and zigging when you should be zagging. That

e money, but the long-run results of the Four
arly show that it is worth that cost.

all the signals from Davis's test of the Four
ing May 1966. In this table we have assumed
the sell signals (a comprehensive discussion
of short selling appears in chapter 14) and go long on the buy
signals. I don't necessarily advise that you do that, but I want to
show what the profits would have been had you sold the market
short on the sell signals. One could just as easily assume that a
luckless investor had always bought on the sell signals. The
results of those sells then would have shown considerable losses.
But of course that would be doing just the opposite of what the
wise speculator would do; namely, follow the trend.

TABLE 18

FOUR PERCENT MODEL
VS. VALUE LINE COMPOSITE INDEX:
MAY 6, 1966 to APRIL 12, 1985

Signal	Date	Value Line Index	Profit (%)	Days	$10,000 Growth
SELL	5/06/66	133.09	15.9	168	11,591
BUY	10/21/66	111.92	33.6	371	15,488
SELL	10/27/67	149.55	− 2.2	63	15,142
BUY	12/29/67	152.89	− 4.5	42	14,463
SELL	2/09/68	146.04	.3	56	14,510
BUY	4/05/68	145.57	12.3	112	16,300
SELL	7/26/68	163.53	− 2.9	42	15,831
BUY	9/06/68	168.24	5.2	126	16,653
SELL	1/10/69	176.98	3.1	119	17,172
BUY	5/09/69	171.46	− 8.0	35	15,798
SELL	6/13/69	157.74	8.3	126	17,114
BUY	10/17/69	144.60	− 3.2	35	16,564
SELL	11/21/69	139.95	8.8	105	18,022

(*TABLE 18 continued*)

Signal	Date	Value Line Index	Profit (%)	Days	$10,000 Growth
BUY	3/06/70	127.63	− 4.6	14	17,192
SELL	3/20/70	121.75	21.7	70	20,918
BUY	5/29/70	95.36	− 6.9	28	19,475
SELL	6/26/70	88.78	− 1.9	21	19,100
BUY	7/17/70	90.49	− 3.7	28	18,458
SELL	8/14/70	87.45	− 9.3	14	16,742
BUY	8/28/70	95.58	2.0	56	17,082
SELL	10/23/70	97.52	− 1.4	42	16,837
BUY	12/04/70	98.92	19.6	175	20,130
SELL	5/28/71	118.27	3.5	84	20,843
BUY	8/20/71	114.08	− 2.2	56	20,381
SELL	10/15/71	111.55	5.1	49	21,410
BUY	12/03/71	105.92	13.2	154	24,236
SELL	5/05/72	119.90	6.2	189	25,741
BUY	11/10/72	112.45	.6	42	25,899
SELL	12/22/72	113.14	25.3	203	32,460
BUY	7/13/73	84.48	1.6	28	32,986
SELL	8/10/73	85.85	− 1.2	28	32,595
BUY	9/07/73	86.87	3.6	56	33,754
SELL	11/02/73	89.96	12.1	63	37,821
BUY	1/04/74	79.12	− .9	84	37,501
SELL	3/29/74	78.45	9.1	70	40,914
BUY	6/07/74	71.31	− 6.5	14	38,263
SELL	6/21/74	66.69	20.2	91	46,003
BUY	9/20/74	53.20	− 6.3	14	43,115
SELL	10/04/74	49.86	− 11.8	7	38,039
BUY	10/11/74	55.73	− 5.5	42	35,957
SELL	11/22/74	52.68	1.1	42	36,340
BUY	1/03/75	52.12	45.2	203	52,766
SELL	7/25/75	75.68	5.8	112	55,813
BUY	11/14/75	71.31	− 5.0	21	53,019
SELL	12/05/75	67.74	− 5.7	28	49,982
BUY	1/02/76	71.62	19.7	98	59,808
SELL	4/09/76	85.70	− 1.4	77	58,992

(TABLE 18 continued)

Signal	Date	Value Line Index	Profit (%)	Days	$10,000 Growth
BUY	6/25/76	86.87	− 1.3	56	58,245
SELL	8/20/76	85.77	− 2.8	35	56,629
BUY	9/24/76	88.15	− 4.1	14	54,309
SELL	10/08/76	84.54	− 2.3	49	53,044
BUY	11/26/76	86.51	4.0	133	55,159
SELL	4/08/77	89.96	− 5.5	77	52,130
BUY	6/24/77	94.90	− 3.1	56	50,493
SELL	8/19/77	91.92	− .5	84	50,263
BUY	11/11/77	92.34	− 1.5	56	49,517
SELL	1/06/78	90.97	− 3.4	70	47,813
BUY	3/17/78	94.10	10.6	105	52,899
SELL	6/30/78	104.11	− 4.5	28	50,496
BUY	7/28/78	108.84	4.4	56	52,718
SELL	9/22/78	113.63	11.8	77	58,944
BUY	12/08/78	100.21	14.9	308	67,738
SELL	10/12/79	115.16	1.3	42	68,626
BUY	11/23/79	113.65	9.6	98	75,178
SELL	2/29/80	124.50	11.5	42	83,801
BUY	4/11/80	110.22	29.3	210	108,321
SELL	11/07/80	142.47	− 4.1	7	103,926
BUY	11/14/80	148.25	− 7.3	28	96,313
SELL	12/12/80	137.39	− 5.0	14	91,483
BUY	12/26/80	144.28	4.9	196	96,004
SELL	7/10/81	151.41	12.3	84	107,810
BUY	10/02/81	132.79	− .8	105	107,007
SELL	1/15/82	131.80	3.1	77	110,278
BUY	4/02/82	127.77	− 2.3	56	107,784
SELL	5/28/82	124.88	2.9	84	110,857
BUY	8/20/82	121.32	64.3	343	182,184
SELL	7/29/83	199.38	− 1.6	56	179,279
BUY	9/23/83	202.56	− 4.2	28	171,791
SELL	10/21/83	194.10	− 1.7	35	168,959
BUY	11/25/83	197.30	− 4.4	70	161,568
SELL	2/03/84	188.67	6.0	182	171,305

(*TABLE 18 continued*)		Value Line Index	Profit (%)	Days	$10,000 Growth
Signal	Date				
BUY	8/03/84	177.30	− .9	119	169,837
SELL	11/30/84	175.78	− 3.0	42	164,716
BUY	1/11/85	181/08	7.2	91	176,596

The fourth column in the table shows the percentage of profit on all of the signals, both the sells and the buys. Also shown are the calendar days during which each signal was open and, in the right-hand column, the cumulative value of an initial $10,000 portfolio. The results here are theoretical because no one could have actually bought and sold the Value Line Index over this period. Stock index futures began to trade on the Value Line Index in 1982. Since then, one could have closely approximated the returns on the actual Value Line Index. Over the span since 1966, you could have had some approximation of the Value Line Index by buying diversified mutual funds that had broad-based portfolios, or by buying a diversified portfolio of stock heavily weighted toward medium- and smaller-sized companies.

Graph I (pp. 98–99) shows the buy and sell signals on the Four Percent Model plotted against the Value Line Index back to 1978. The B's on the graph show the buy signals while the S's show the sell signals.

Table 19 sums up the results of the Four Percent Model. There were 42 buy signals, with the last one still open at the cutoff of this study, April 12, 1985. Of these 42 buys, only 20 were profitable, just 48%. However, those 20 profitable buys produced average profits of 15.3% per trade. Conversely, the 22 losing trades lost only 3.9% per trade. This is a perfect example of *cutting your losses short and letting your profits run*, the ideal strategy for the speculator... and not such a bad idea for the traditional investor either.

Taking the 42 buy signals together, they produced an average gain of 5.2% per trade. The buy signals were in effect for 94 calendar days on average, or something more than 13 weeks per trade. That's not really too many trades. It's within reason as far as commissions and portfolio turnover are concerned. When that 5.2% profit per trade is annualized, it works out to 17.9%. From

1966 to April 1985, had you merely bought and held the Value Line Index, you would have made only 2.0% per year. These calculations ignore dividends both on buy-and-hold and on trading. Obviously, the addition of dividends would add to the return in both cases.

The results on the sell side are similar. Assuming that you had sold short on the sell signals, you would have made money 22 times in 42 trades, a success rate of 52%. That may not sound like much, but on those 22 successful trades on the short side, the average gain was 8.9%. (Alternatively, had you insisted on buying in those 22 cases, you would have lost an average of 8.9%.) By contrast, of the 20 cases in which the short-selling speculator would have been wrong, his average loss would have been only 3.6%. It nets out to an average gain per trade on the short side of 2.9%, with an average holding period of 70 days, or 10 weeks. The annualized profit on the short side was 14.4%. That means that the investor who kept on buying during the sell signals would have lost 14.4% per year in those spans.

The third section of table 19 combines all trades, irrespective of whether they were buys or sells. Fifty percent of those trades lost money, but the average loss was only 3.8%. The 50 percent that made money showed average gains of 11.9%. The average gain per trade over 84 total trades was 4.1%. That equals an annualized return from trading with the Four Percent Model of 16.4%, far in excess of the 2.0% return that one could have garnered from merely buying and holding over nearly 19 years. Obviously, this very simple model works well.

Occasionally, the losses are somewhat more than I would prefer, mainly because of the drawback of using only weekly closing prices. However, there's a plus side, primarily its simplicity and the fact that you need not hover over a Quotron machine daily, worrying about whether the model will flip or not. Sometimes, by examining too many trees, one loses sight of the forest—not a good idea. Had you traded both the long and the short side since 1966, an initial $10,000 would have grown to $176,596, exclusive of dividends. That's not bad for an extremely simple model.

You can use this model just as presented. Or you can alter it to your own liking. There's no law that says you have to wait for a 4% change. For example, if you want fewer trades and fewer signals, you can increase the 4% rule to, say, 5% or 6%. You'll

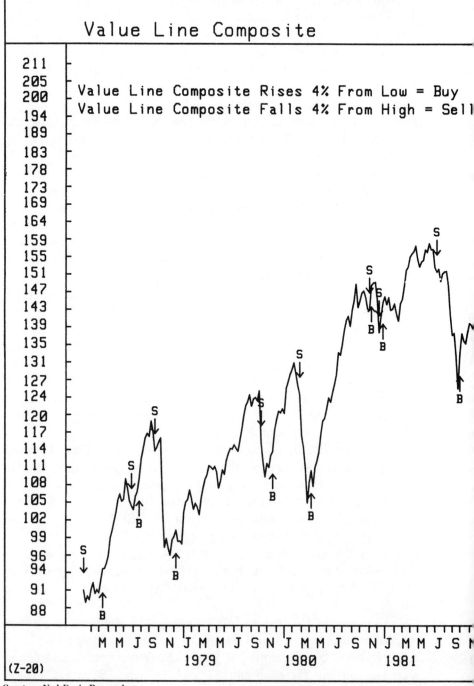

Value Line Composite

Value Line Composite Rises 4% From Low = Buy
Value Line Composite Falls 4% From High = Sell

(Z-20)

Courtesy Ned Davis Research

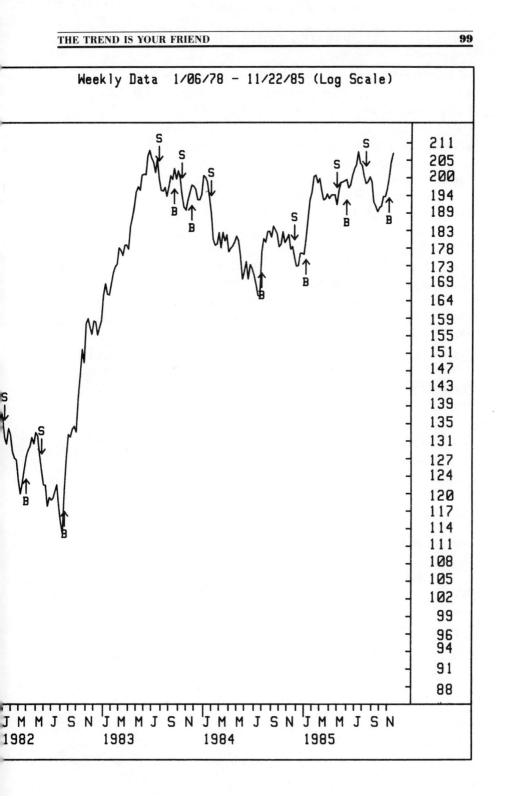

Weekly Data   1/06/78 - 11/22/85 (Log Scale)

probably have a slightly lower return on a gross basis, but you'll save something in transaction costs and avoid some of the signals. Conversely, if you are more short-term-oriented, you might cut the rule to, say, 3% or even 2½%, and have more trades, probably a higher gross return, but greater transaction costs. I feel the 4% rule is a nice trade-off between excessive turnover on the one hand and solid returns on the other.

You could also apply a similar rule to some of the other major averages such as the S&P 500, but it won't work as well as it does on the Value Line or on the Zweig Unweighted Price Index. That's because the major averages are not as volatile as the Value Line of ZUPI and generally don't go up as much in bull markets, nor fall as much in bear markets.

Let's sum up how the Four Percent Model works. All you need is the weekly close on the Value Line Index. If the index rises by 4% or more, it triggers a buy signal. If it drops by 4% or more, it's a sell signal. About half the signals will be unprofitable. However, the profits on the good signals overwhelm the losses on the poor signals. *As a result, you'll make solid profits in the long run by staying in gear with the trend.*

TABLE 19

SUMMARY OF FOUR PERCENT MODEL VS. VALUE LINE COMPOSITE INDEX: MAY 6, 1966 to APRIL 12, 1985

Type of Trade	Number of Trades	Profit per Trade	Average Days per Trade	Annualized Profit
Buys (long)				
Losses	22 (52%)	− 3.9%		
Gains	20 (48%)	+15.3%		
Net	42 (100%)	+ 5.2%	94	+17.9%
Sells (short)				
Losses	20 (48%)	− 3.6%		
Gains	22 (52%)	+ 8.9%		
Net	42 (100%)	+ 2.9%	70	+14.4%
Total				
Losses	42 (50%)	− 3.8%		
Gains	42 (50%)	+11.9%		
Net	84 (100%)	+ 4.1%	82	+16.4%

Results of all trades:

$10,000 became $176,596 in 18.9 years (+16.4% annualized return).

Annualized return for buy-and-hold = +2.0% ($10,000 became $14,587).

CHAPTER 6

Combining Monetary and Momentum Indicators— The Only Investment Model You Will Ever Need

*I*n chapter 4 we developed the Monetary Model using interest rate and Federal Reserve indicators to forecast the market. Its excellent results verify the rule "Don't fight the Fed." In chapter 5 we developed three momentum-type indicators, one of which, the Four Percent Model, gives continuous bullish or bearish signals. Its results are also excellent and honor the theory "Don't fight the tape." Given those solid results, it would be reasonable to combine both monetary and momentum indicators to obtain a superior model, one that will follow both the Fed and the trend of the tape. In this chapter we will develop such a model.

Once again I'll try to keep the model as simple as possible. We'll start directly with the Monetary Model from chapter 4 and use the gradings as described there. Recall that the model can run from zero up to 8 points. The Monetary Model gives a buy signal when the model hits 6 points or more, and stays on the buy until the model drops to 2 points or less, when it gives a sell signal. To that model we will add a weighting for the Four Percent Model, as developed in chapter 5.

When the Four Percent Model is on a buy signal, award it 2 points. When the Four Percent Model is on a sell signal, give it zero points. Then, add the points from the Four Percent Model to the points in the Monetary Model. Theoretically, the combined model, which we'll call the Super Model, can range from zero to 10 points. That is, if all three indicators in the monetary model were bullish, and if the Four Percent Model were on a buy signal, the Super Model would be +10. Conversely, if all three monetary indicators were bearish, with the Four Percent Model on a sell signal, the Super Model would read zero. You'll find the Super Model construction in table 20.

TABLE 20

SUPER MODEL
WORKSHEET

Date	ZUPI	S&P 500	Dow	Prime Rate	Fed	Install- ment Debt	4% Model	Super Model
12/31/79	112.33	107.94	839	2	0	0	2	4
2/19/80	117.09	114.60	876	0*	0	0	0*	0
4/11/80	100.52	103.79	792	0	0	0	2*	2
5/1/80	103.73	105.46	809	2*	0	0	2	4
5/6/80	105.52	106.25	816	2	2*	0	2	6 [BUY]
5/22/80	110.68	109.01	843	2	4*	0	2	8
6/16/80	117.46	116.09	878	2	4	2*	2	10
8/26/80	132.08	124.84	953	0*	4	2	2	8
11/7/80	133.15	129.18	932	0	4	2	0*	6
11/14/80	138.18	137.15	986	0	2*	2	2*	6
12/4/80	136.90	136.48	970	0	1*	2	2	5
12/12/80	128.32	129.23	917	0	1	2	0*	3 SELL
12/22/80	132.87	135.78	959	2*	1	2	0	5
12/26/80	134.98	136.57	966	2	1	2	2*	7 BUY
4/24/81	148.46	135.14	1020	0*	1	2	2	5
6/16/81	149.84	132.15	1003	2*	1	2	2	7
6/22/81	149.02	131.95	994	0*	1	2	2	5
7/10/81	144.14	129.37	956	0	1	2	0*	3 SELL
9/9/81	128.22	118.40	854	0	2*	2	0	4
9/21/81	127.04	117.24	847	2*	4*	2	0	8 BUY
10/2/81	126.78	119.36	861	2	4	2	2*	10
1/15/82	128.45	116.33	848	2	4	2	0*	8
2/1/82	128.68	117.78	852	0*	4	2	0	6

(*TABLE* 20 *continued*)

SUPER MODEL
WORKSHEET

Date	ZUPI	S&P 500	Dow	Prime Rate	Fed	Install- ment Debt	4% Model	Super Model
3/8/82	121.07	107.34	795	2*	4	2	0	8
3/16/82	120.96	109.28	798	0*	4	2	0	6
4/2/82	127.71	115.12	839	0	4	2	2*	8
5/28/82	127.76	111.88	820	0	4	2	0*	6
6/4/82	125.50	110.09	805	0	2*	2	0	4
7/19/82	124.03	110.73	826	0	4*	2	0	6
7/26/82	124.39	110.36	825	2*	4	2	0	8
8/20/82	126.35	113.02	869	2	4	2	2*	10
5/19/83	203.54	161.99	1191	2	2*	2	2	8
7/29/83	205.39	162.56	1199	2	2	2	0*	6
8/10/83	200.53	161.54	1176	0*	2	2	0	4
9/23/83	209.93	169.51	1256	0	2	2	2*	6
10/13/83	209.04	169.88	1261	0	2	0*	2	4
10/21/83	204.43	165.95	1249	0	2	0	0*	2 SELL
11/25/83	207.01	167.18	1277	0	2	0	2*	4
2/3/84	201.64	160.91	1197	0	2	0	0*	2
4/6/84	189.74	155.48	1132	0	1*	0	0	1
8/3/84	187.22	162.35	1202	0	1	0	2*	3
10/6/84	192.21	162.13	1178	0	2*	0	2	4
10/15/84	194.61	165.77	1203	2*	2	0	2	6 BUY
11/21/84	193.94	164.52	1202	2	4*	0	2	8
11/30/84	193.25	163.58	1189	2	4	0	0*	6
1/11/85	200.36	167.91	1218	2	4	0	2*	8

*Indicates change.

There are many complex ways you could use this model, including going fully invested above certain levels, or perhaps three-quarters invested at other levels, or half invested on certain values. To simplify matters, we'll just create a system for going either 100% invested or 100% in cash.

The rules are these: When the Super Model reaches 6 points or more, it gives a buy signal. We'll assume that at that point the investor goes 100% invested in stocks. The buy signal remains in effect until the Super Model drops to 3 points or less, at which time it gives a sell signal. Upon a sell signal, it is assumed that the investor goes out of stocks and 100% into money market instruments such as Treasury bills, CDs, or money market funds. We'll use the Treasury bill yield as a proxy for the interest rate one could have earned over the years.

Obviously, if all the indicators in the two models are bullish, the Super Model would be bullish, and vice versa. But the virtue of combining the monetary and tape indicators is that, if the monetary indicators were relatively neutral but the market's momentum was positive, it could be just enough to give us a buy signal. At such a time, it might make a bit more sense to be invested in stocks rather than in cash. Alternatively, if the Monetary Model were roughly neutral and the tape soured, it might be just enough to trip a sell signal, which is what we'd want under those circumstances. Obviously, our first choice is to have both the monetary and the momentum indicators on our side. But that's not always possible. The Super Model allows for some reasonable trade-off between the monetary and the tape indicators.

Table 21 shows how the Super Model performed when traded against the Zweig Unweighted Price Index between 1966 and the end of this study in April 1985. The left side of the table shows the dates of the Super Model's buy signals, the values of the Zweig Unweighted Price Index (ZUPI) at those points, the percentage changes in the ZUPI during the buy signals, and finally, the approximate number of months that the buy signals were in effect. For example, the first buy signal occurred on November 16, 1966, when the ZUPI was 108.75. That signal stayed in effect 20.5 months, finally ending with a sell signal on July 26, 1968, when the ZUPI was 156.34. During that span the ZUPI rose a mightly 43.8%.

TABLE 21

SUPER MODEL
VS. ZWEIG UNWEIGHTED PRICE INDEX:
1966 to 1985

BUY SIGNALS				**SELL SIGNALS**			
Date	ZUPI	% Change	No. of Months	Date	ZUPI	% Change	No. of Months
				3/10/66	125.43	−13.3	8.0
11/16/66	108.75	+43.8	20.5	7/26/68	156.34	+ 1.2	2.0
8/30/68	158.29	+ 9.4	4.0	12/31/68	173.15	−45.7	17.0
5/29/70	93.96	+32.2	13.5	7/16/71	124.17	−12.4	3.0
11/19/71	108.82	+11.2	7.5	6/26/72	121.02	−37.1	19.5
2/14/74	76.18	+ 2.4	1.5	3/29/74	78.02	−33.3	7.0
10/25/74	52.03	+76.0	31.0	5/31/77	91.57	+15.2	35.0
5/6/80	105.52	+21.6	7.0	12/12/80	128.32	+ 5.2	.5
12/26/80	134.98	+ 6.8	6.5	7/10/81	144.14	−11.9	2.5
9/21/81	127.04	+60.9	25.0	10/21/83	204.43	− 4.8	12.0
10/15/84	194.61	+10.5	5.5	4/5/85	215.01[a]		

$10,000 becomes: $96,238   122.0 mo. $1,780   106.5 mo.
Annualized return = +24.8%   −17.6%
Buy-and-hold return = +2.9% per year

[a] The latest date when table was prepared (not a signal).

The right-hand side of the table lists all the sell signals, the first of which was on March 10, 1966. By the luck of the draw, the first signal just happens to be a sell signal, which is why you do not see a prior buy signal. There would have been a buy signal sometime back in 1965, which would have led to the sell in March of 1966. The sell signal side of the table also gives the percentage changes and the number of months held. For example, the March 10, 1966, sell signal was in effect eight months until the subsequent buy on November 16, 1966. Over that time the ZUPI declined 13.3%.

To date there have been ten sell signals and ten buy signals, the last of which was still open when this study was concluded. At the bottom of the table you'll see that $10,000, invested only during the buy signals periods, would have become $96,238 in a total of 122 months, or roughly 10 years. That equals a healthy return rate of 24.8% a year. That does not include interest, dividends, or commissions. Conversely, had you fought the Fed and fought the tape and unwisely bought stocks during the sell signal periods, your initial $10,000 would have shrunk to only $1,780 in a cumulative period of 106.5 months, or roughly 9 years. That works out to an annualized loss rate of 17.6%.

During this 19-year period, had you purchased the ZUPI and held it over the entire span without trading at all, you would have earned 2.9% a year. So, the buy signals produced an annualized return more than 20 percentage points better than the buy-and-hold result, while the market during sell signal periods under-performed buy-and-hold by more than 20 percentage points a year. Those are excellent spreads against the market, especially for a relatively simple model that averages only about one trade per year.

It's also worth noting that of the ten buy signals, four of them were in place for more than one year—which was the minimum holding period for long-term capital gains. However, in mid-1984 the minimum time to establish long-term gains was reduced to six months. Seven of the first nine buy signals lasted more than the six-month period, and the tenth signal has gone beyond six months at this writing. *In other words, in eight of ten buy signal cases (80% of the time), you would have garnered long-term capital gains under current tax rules.*

Thus, this model incorporates relative simplicity in the calculations, only about one transaction a year on average, and it manages to capture long-term capital gains most of the time. In fact, the total gains in the two holding periods that were short-term (on the buy signals in August 1968 and February 1974) were relatively small. The overwhelming bulk of the profits over this test would have resulted in long-term capital gains.

The table shows that each of the ten buy signals produced profits. In seven of the ten cases, on the sell signals the market went down, and, in two of the three times it rose, the gains were minimal. The worst sell signal loss was a market rise of 15.2% on the sell given May 31, 1977. Note, though, that the sell stayed in effect for thirty-five months, nearly three full years. During that period interest rates were high, and had you invested your money in Treasury bills (not even the highest-yielding short-term instrument), you would have made a total return of 27.1%, nearly double the market's capital appreciation over that time (although I have not included dividends at this point).

Most of the buy signal gains are very substantial, such as the 43.8% gain beginning in 1966; the 32.2% gain from the May 1970 signal; the 76% profit on the October 1974 buy signal; and the 60.9% increase on the September 1981 signal. When the big bull markets arrived, the Super Model did its job by getting you in very quickly and staying bullish throughout the bulk of the advances that followed.

On the other hand, the model also worked very well on the sell signals, managing to keep the investor out of the worst bear markets during the period. In particular, the Super Model gave a terrific sell signal on the last day of 1968, after which prices crashed 45.7% in the next seventeen months. The Super Model also performed well by giving a well-timed sell signal in June 1972, following which prices skidded 37.1% over the next year and a half or so. After a very brief foray into bullish territory, the Super Model reversed course, giving an accurate sell signal March 29, 1974. The worst part of the worst bear market since the thirties ensued in the next seven months, during which prices plunged an additional 33.3%. The Super Model also helped avoid the greatest portions of the bear markets in 1966 and in 1981.

Graph J (pp. 110–111) plots the Super Model back to 1966 against the Zweig Unweighted Price Index. Crossings to above the upper dotted line correspond to the buy signals while crossings to below the lower dotted line correspond to sell signals.

Table 22 shows the same study when the Super Model is traded against the Standard & Poor's 500 Price Index. Here nine of the ten buy signals were profitable, with the tenth showing a modest loss of 5.3% in 1980–81. Seven of the ten sell signals led to market declines, with two of the three failures showing only very small advances. The largest market rally on a sell signal was 10.6% back in 1977–80, which was a skimpy return for a nearly three-year period considering, once more, that T-bills earned a total of 27.1% in the same time frame. At the bottom of table 22

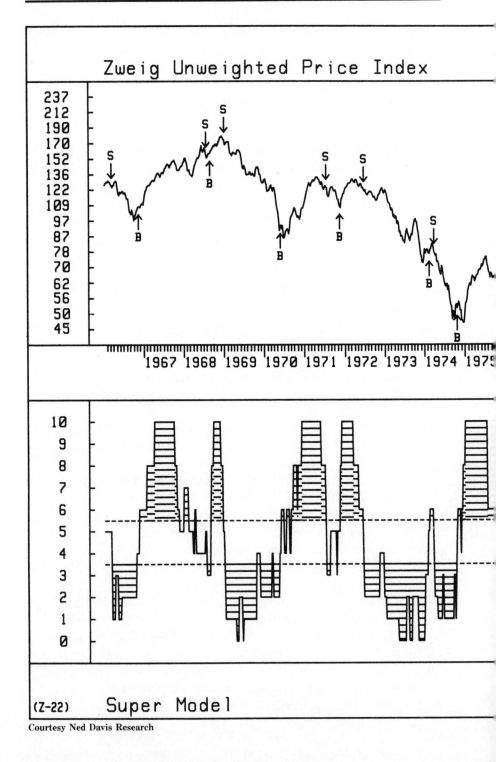

(Z-22)   Super Model

Courtesy Ned Davis Research

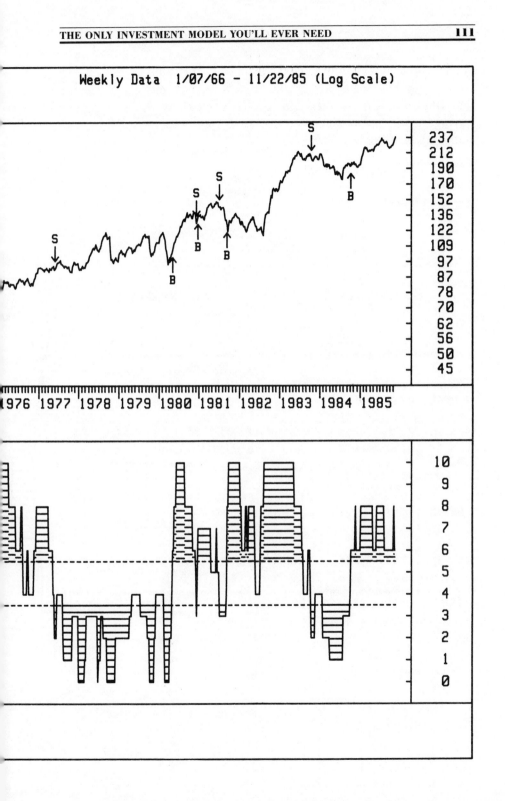

Weekly Data 1/07/66 - 11/22/85 (Log Scale)

you'll see that the annualized return on the buy signals when traded against the S&P 500 is 16.5% versus merely 3.7% for buy-and-hold. Conversely, the S&P declined by 9.2% per year during sell signal periods, or nearly 13 percentage points worse than buy-and-hold.

TABLE 22

SUPER MODEL
VS. STANDARD & POOR'S 500 INDEX:
1966 to 1985

BUY SIGNALS				SELL SIGNALS			
Date	S&P	% Change	No. of Months	Date	S&P	% Change	No. of Months
				3/10/66	88.96	− 7.4	8.0
11/16/66	82.37	+19.4	20.5	7/26/68	98.34	+ .5	2.0
8/30/68	98.86	+ 5.1	4.0	12/31/68	103.86	−26.3	17.0
5/29/70	76.55	+29.5	13.5	7/16/71	99.11	− 7.6	3.0
11/19/71	91.61	+17.3	7.5	6/26/72	107.48	−15.4	19.5
2/14/74	90.95	+ 3.3	1.5	3/29/74	93.98	−25.4	7.0
10/25/74	70.12	+37.1	31.0	5/31/77	96.12	+10.6	35.0
5/6/80	106.25	+21.6	7.0	12/12/80	129.23	+ 5.7	.5
12/26/80	136.57	− 5.3	6.5	7/10/81	129.37	− 9.4	2.5
9/21/81	117.24	+41.5	25.0	10/21/83	165.95	− .1	12.0
10/15/84	165.77	+ 8.0	5.5	4/5/85	179.03[a]		

$10,000 becomes: $47,509 122.0 mo. $4,232   106.5 mo.
Annualized return = +16.5%   −9.2%
Buy-and-hold return = +3.7% per year

[a] The latest date when table was prepared (not a signal).

How would you have fared had you used the Super Model since 1966? The question is answered in table 23, which shows the returns made by buying the Zweig Unweighted Price Index, or baskets of stocks roughly equivalent to it, when trading is guided by the Super Model. The approach assumes buying the ZUPI or its equivalent on the buy signals and selling it and going 100% into Treasury bills on the sell signals. *Dividends are included.* The first two columns list the dates and types of signal. On sell signals, the next three columns are deliberately left blank because they are irrelevant. How the stock market actually did during the sell signals was shown earlier anyhow, in tables 21 and 22. The next-to-last column on the right shows the interest you would have earned on the Treasury bills while staying out of the stock market during the sell signal periods. The right-hand column shows what would have happened to $10,000 when following the Super Model. For example, upon the sell signal of March 10, 1966, you would have gone into Treasury bills and earned 3.2% over the next eight months, until a buy signal was given on November 16, 1966. That meant that the initial stake of $10,000 would have grown to $10,320 in that time, as seen in the top entry of the right-hand column.

Next, the second line of table 23 shows what happened after the buy signal of November 16, 1966. Column 3 indicates that the ZUPI appreciated 43.8% over the next twenty months or so before the sell signal of July 26, 1968. During that span it is estimated that dividends earned on the stocks amounted to about 4.3%, as seen in column 4. Column 5 shows the total return on buy signals, which is the sum of the appreciation in column 3 plus the estimated dividends in column 4, in this case a nice 48.1%. When that return is earned on the $10,320 at the beginning of the signal, it brings the portfolio value up to $15,289. All the signals then follow through the remainder of the table.

Note in column 5 that the total return on the buy signals is profitable in every single case. The interest earned on Treasury bills on the sell signals in column 6 was also always profitable. So over the nineteen years during the test period, the investor was continuously earning money. Of course, there would have been short-run spans within a buy signal period where the market might have gone down for a while, but by the end of the signal the market was always higher, and dividends added another kicker.

TABLE 23

TOTAL RETURNS ON SUPER MODEL VS. ZWEIG UNWEIGHTED PRICE INDEX: 1966 to 1985

Date	Signal	% Appreciation on Buys	Estimated Dividends on Buys	Total Return on Buys	Interest Earned in Sell Periods	$10,000 Growth
3/10/66	Sell				+ 3.2	$ 10,320
11/16/68	Buy	+43.8	+ 4.3	+48.1		15,289
7/26/68	Sell				+ .9	15,421
8/30/68	Buy	+ 9.4	+ .7	+10.1		16,979
12/31/68	Sell				+ 9.8	18,643
5/29/70	Buy	+32.2	+ 3.7	+35.9		25,336
7/16/71	Sell				+ 1.4	25,690
11/19/71	Buy	+11.2	+ 1.5	+12.7		28,953
6/26/72	Sell				+10.0	31,849
2/14/74	Buy	+ 2.4	+ .3	+ 2.7		32,708
3/29/74	Sell				+ 4.2	34,082
10/15/74	Buy	+76.0	+11.2	+87.2		63,802
5/31/77	Sell				+27.1	81,092
5/6/80	Buy	+21.6	+ 2.6	+24.2		100,717
12/12/80	Sell				+ .7	101,422
12/26/80	Buy	+ 6.8	+ 1.9	+ 8.7		110,245
7/10/81	Sell				+ 3.1	113,663
9/21/81	Buy	+60.9	+ 9.8	+70.7		194,022
10/21/83	Sell				+ 9.2	211,872
10/15/84	Buy	+10.5	+ 1.6	+12.1		237,509
4/5/85	Last					

Total Super Model return:		$237,509
Annualized return on Super Model:		+18.0%
Buy-and-hold (including dividends):	$30,713	
Annualized return on buy-and-hold:	+6.1%	

At the bottom of the table you'll see that the total value of the portfolio grew from $10,000 to $237,509 in just over nineteen years. That equals an annualized return of 18.0%. Alternatively, had you purchased the ZUPI and held it ninteen years and received and reinvested all dividends throughout that period, $10,000 would have grown to only $30,713, an annualized return of just 6.1%. Thus, trading with the model produced a per annum gain approximately triple that of buy-and-hold. Furthermore, it did so while being out of the market and at zero risk almost half of the time. *So, on a risk-adjusted basis, the returns are even better since you would have earned three times the annualized return but taken on only about one-half the risk of the buy-and-hold investor.*

You may want to compare the $237,509 total return on the Super Model in table 23 with the $96,238 return on the buy signals in table 21. That latter sum is included in the total of table 23 since it represents the appreciation on the buy signals seen in column 3 of that table. The remainder of the gain is made up by the compounding effect of all the dividends earned in column 4 plus all of the interest earned in column 6.

Table 24 shows how the Super Model worked when traded against the S&P 500 Index. An investor would have earned money in the buy signal periods nine of the ten times, losing a small 2.9% in total on the December 26, 1980, buy signal. Of course, there would always be positive returns on interest during the sell periods. As seen at the bottom of the table, after nineteen years, $10,000 would have grown to $131,426, an annualized gain of 14.4%. Buy-and-hold on the S&P 500, including dividends, would have turned $10,000 into $43,359, a per annum return of only 8.0%. So, even on the far-less-volatile S&P 500, an investor would have beaten that benchmark by 6.4 percentage points a year over a nineteen-year stretch, and would have an ending portfolio about three times as large in dollars as would the buy-and-hold investor.

TABLE 24

TOTAL RETURNS ON SUPER MODEL VS. STANDARD & POOR'S 500 INDEX: 1966 to 1985

Date	Signal	% Appre-ciation on Buys	Estimated Dividends on Buys	Total Return on Buys	Interest Earned in Sell Periods	$10,000 Growth
3/10/66	Sell				+ 3.2	$ 10,320
11/16/68	Buy	+19.4	+ 6.1	+25.5		12,952
7/26/68	Sell				+ .9	13,068
8/30/68	Buy	+ 5.1	+ 1.0	+ 6.1		13,865
12/31/68	Sell				+ 9.8	15,224
5/29/70	Buy	+29.5	+ 4.9	+34.4		20,461
7/16/71	Sell				+ 1.4	20,748
11/19/71	Buy	+17.3	+ 2.1	+19.4		24,733
6/26/72	Sell				+10.0	27,250
2/14/74	Buy	+ 3.3	+ .5	+ 3.8		28,286
3/29/74	Sell				+ 4.2	29,473
10/15/74	Buy	+37.1	+14.0	+51.1		44,534
5/31/77	Sell				+27.1	56,603
5/6/80	Buy	+21.6	+ 3.2	+24.8		70,641
12/12/80	Sell				+ .7	71,135
12/26/80	Buy	- 5.3	+ 2.4	- 2.9		69,072
7/10/81	Sell				3.1	71,214
9/21/81	Buy	+41.5	+12.0	+53.5		109,313
10/21/83	Sell				+ 9.2	119,370
10/15/84	Buy	+ 8.0	+ 2.1	+10.1		131,426
4/5/85	Last					

Total Super Model return: $131,426
Annualized return on Super Model: +14.4%
Buy-and-hold on S&P 500 (including dividends): $43,359
Annualized return on buy-and-hold: +8.0%

These tests on the Super Model, recall, use a buy rule of 6 points and a sell rule of 3 points on a scale from zero to 10. You could modify the trading rules, if you choose, so that the entire portfolio is not necessarily moved on any one signal. For example, you might be fully invested in stocks if the model were, say, 7 points or higher. If the model then fell to 5 or 6 points, you might sell off one-third of your portfolio, and remain two-thirds invested in stocks. If the Super Model then fell into the 3-to-4-point range, you might sell off a second third of the portfolio, leaving yourself one-third invested in stocks and two-thirds in Treasury bills. Finally, if the Super Model were to drop to 2 points or less, you could then go 100% into cash equivalents and be totally out of the stock market.

You could devise similar schemes for being, say, 0%, 50%, or 100% invested. Or you could get even more complicated and have ranges of 0%, 25%, 50%, 75%, and 100% invested. The point is, you don't have to move from 0% invested to 100% invested in one fell swoop. *You should use the model in the way that makes you most comfortable. Remember, the odds are best for the market when the model is highest, and worst when the model is lowest.*

If the Super Model were on a buy signal, launched at 6 points or greater, but had deteriorated later down to 4 or 5 points, the buy signal would still be in effect, but the risk-averse investor might feel a bit queasy about remaining 100% invested when the model was in neutral territory and falling. If so, that investor ought to do a bit of selling. There's an old saying that one should "sell down to the sleeping point." That's not a bad idea in a situation like this.

On the other hand, say that the Super Model had previously given a sell signal at 3 points, but over some period there had been some improvement in the model up to the 4- or 5-point region. Some investors at that time might feel uneasy about being 100% invested in Treasury bills and might rationally want to own a stake in the stock market. I wouldn't advise, of course, going 100% invested, but going one-third or one-half into stocks at that point might be sensible. *Again, choose the alternative that makes you comfortable, as long as it makes sense according to the Super Model.*

CHAPTER 7

Fighting the Tape— An Invitation to Disaster

I *can't overemphasize the importance of staying with the trend in the market, being in gear with the tape, and not fighting the major movements. Fighting the tape is an open invitation to disaster.* Let me give you an example. As an investment advisor I live in a glass house, so I'm not about to throw stones at any of my competitors. Therefore, I'd rather not mention this other advisor's name. We'll just call him Sam. Sam writes a market letter and, on a few occasions in the 1960s and early 1970s, had gone haywire by fighting both major bull and bear markets. But like many of us, he has had his share of successes and, beginning in 1975, got on a hot streak. For several years Sam called numerous market turns correctly, most of them intermediate swings. He picked up a large following and his business boomed.

During the early eighties Sam turned bearish. In the summer of 1981 the Dow fell about 200 points and Sam looked like a genius. As prices fell, Sam grew ever more bearish. In an interview in a major financial publication in early 1982 he predicted vastly lower prices for the Dow Industrials and for the market. A reporter asked Sam how he would know if he had been wrong in his prediction. Sam answered, "If the Dow were to rally one hundred points I would be wrong and I would change my prediction."

Sam's thinking was actually pretty good at that time. A 100-point Dow advance then would have been roughly 12%. That's much higher than our 4% rule, but Sam was looking for the major trends, and giving up that much in a possible forthcoming bull market wouldn't have been bad at all. Sam could have turned bullish just 100 points from the bottom and would have gotten back in gear with the tape, even though he would not have called the precise low. A noted trend follower, Sam had said on many occasions, "The market is like a train and I am the caboose: I simply follow the train." Again, excellent advice.

In August 1982 interest rates fell sharply and suddenly the market bolted ahead, rising some 38 points on August 17. In just six market days, from its low of 777 on August 12, 1982, the Dow had surged to 891, a whopping 114-point advance. That was the sign for Sam to follow his own advice. Had he done so, he could have told the world later that he turned bullish just six days after the bear market bottom. True, he would have missed the first 100 or so points, but that was small potatoes compared to what followed.

By October 1983, less than fourteen months later, the Dow hit a temporary top of 1285. By following the trend, as Sam had once planned to do, he would have made about 400 Dow points. Moreover, the average stock during that period went up far more than the Dow. In fact, in the year or so that followed August 1982, stock prices had their greatest advance in a relatively short period since the twin bottoms of the worst bear market, way back in 1932 and 1933. But Sam did not follow his own sound advice. As prices soared, Sam stayed bearish. He fought the tape and failed to remember that he was the caboose and the market was the train. Sam ran off the tracks.

Sam's fatal flaw in this case is that he had a preconceived idea of where the market would go, and for a time he was right. When conditions changed—and they changed quickly—Sam refused to accept the new evidence and to alter his outlook accordingly. Instead, Sam began to search for shreds of evidence to support his bearish case. This is a very common trait of stock market investors. Psychologists would call it "selective perception." One sees only what one wants to see.

Unfortunately, in the stock market, there is always some bearish evidence and some bullish evidence. You never have difficulties in unearthing clues to back your viewpoint. If there were a hundred stock market indicators out there, it would be highly unusual to have even eighty of them bullish at one time. In fact, if 80% of all the indicators were bullish at once, it would be an overwhelmingly bullish case. But a bear could hang his hat on any or all of the twenty indicators still giving negative signs. Sam chose the latter and made a mistake that just about every stock market player makes once or more in his lifetime.

It's the kind of mistake that you should never make more than once. I've been there, too, having made the opposite error back in the bear market of 1974. I had turned bearish in the spring of 1972, virtually at the top of the bull market for most stocks. For two years I remained bearish most of the time, going bullish only on a short-term basis here and there and catching a few rallies. But in June 1974, for whatever the reason, I turned all-out bullish and had my head handed to me over the next three months.

I could argue that a year after I had turned bullish the market was higher. I could argue that I was not wrong, just "early." I could stubbornly insist that I was right and the market was wrong. These are all common rationalizations among those who err. The fact is, I was just plain wrong. In the weeks that followed I sensed that I was wrong, I knew deep in my bones I was wrong, but my ego got the best of me and I was convinced that the bottom was close at hand anyhow. Instead of staying in gear with the tape and flipping back to the bearish side, I searched out indicators that backed my bullish stance. There were many of them at that time, and I was hooked on them. But the weight of the evidence was still bearish and I blew it.

My main mistake then was in ignoring the very bearish monetary conditions that prevailed. Determined not to go that route again, I then constructed several new monetary indicators that have since served me well. Even so, I made one more major mistake a year and a half later, in January 1976. This time I fought the tape on the upside, staying neutral and in a 100% cash position while the market rallied smartly for a couple of months. My mistake here was ignoring the powerful momentum of the market, and soon I did something about it. After in-depth research, I developed improved momentum and tape-following indicators, first using them individually and then, by 1978, putting them together into a model.

Since those days I absolutely and utterly refuse to fight a major trend in the market. I'll simply move with the tape even if it means being whipsawed every now and then. As a result, I have not missed a major move since that time. Mind you, I'm not bragging, because I know I'm going to be wrong at times, but by following the tape I know I will not blow a major move. So, I've been there before, and I've learned from my lessons the value of staying in gear with the tape.

By contrast, Sam—and probably millions of other investors— had made those mistakes more than once and yet continued to fall into the same trap of fighting the trend. The market just doesn't allow you that many mistakes before it brutalizes your pocket- book. Ignorance (yes, I plead ignorance for my earlier mistakes) can cause you to fight the trend the first time and perhaps the second, but to do so a third or fourth or fifth time is no longer ignorance when you have already suffered the consequences.

What causes the subsequent failures is ego. When you take the attitude that you're right and the market is wrong or that your preconceived idea must be right no matter what the tape shows, you're headed for big trouble. The market can humble any and all of us at any time. Your best protection is to stay in gear with the trend. *In other words, don't fight the tape.*

CHAPTER 8

Sentiment Indicators— When to Part Company with the Crowd

*T*here's an old story about the promotional genius P. T. Barnum. He was staging one of his famous sideshows and the crowd kept growing, finally reaching far beyond the limits of the relatively small tent. He couldn't simply ask people to leave— that would be a faux pas equivalent to a waiter requesting someone to vacate a table in a restaurant. Finally, his brilliant mind came up with a solution. He put up a sign with an arrow saying: "This way to the egress." Many in the crowd, anxious to view the egress, suddenly found themselves exiting the tent. Instead of enjoying more of the show, those who departed wound up outside looking in.

This is approximately what happens in the stock market when the crowd gets too large. The crowd tends to follow the wrong signs near the market tops and bottoms. Consequently, many investors find themselves outside looking in when the market surprises them and changes direction.

Here's roughly how it works. Let's start in the depths of a bear market. The economy is usually in a recession or worse, business profits are tumbling, and investors are punch-drunk from suffering huge losses during a year or two of falling prices. Bad news is making headlines; good news is not even a dream at this point. Conditions have been so awful for so long that most people can see nothing else but the downtrend continuing. It's amid such doom and gloom that bear markets bottom and bull markets begin, meaning that the vast majority is wrong, precisely at the bottom.

123

Why? Well, with the economy collapsing, the Federal Reserve will usually begin loosening credit, and interest rates will start to fall precipitously. This gives stocks additional value as the competition from yields on cash equivalents falls. Typically, though, the economy has another six months or more left on the downside, and the worst results for corporate earnings usually lie ahead.

Even if Wall Street is correct in anticipating these lower profits, it can hardly equate them with higher stock prices. *There seems to be some inborn reasoning in Wall Street that better profits mean higher stock prices, but this simply is not true in the aggregate.* The best gains made in bull markets, as seen in chapter 5, tend to come in the first six months of a fresh bull market, when profits are usually declining. So, it's difficult for investors to be optimistic when they're staring at a terrible outlook for corporate earnings.

At this point investors and speculators have built up extraordinary cash reserves on the sidelines, partly because of the higher interest rates during a bear cycle and partly because the outlook is so gloomy that they prefer to hold cash rather than stock. Individuals and institutions have high levels of cash and little or no willingness to purchase stocks. Pessimism reigns. But when rates start to decline, that acts as a catalyst in generating buying power because cash coupled with lower rates is not as attractive as cash coupled with higher rates. Moreover, the sharp drop in interest rates will usually stimulate the economy six to twelve months down the road. The stock market is a discounting mechanism, always looking ahead. So the *current* profit scene is not nearly as important as that anticipated.

With declining rates the usual stimulus, prices begin to rally as a new bull market is born. Not only is there tremendous pessimism before this initial rally, but that first rally traditionally is not believed. During the previous bear market, several rallies started, only to bite the dust, leading to lower and lower prices later. So why trust the new rally in the new bull market, especially since it tends to be the most vigorous rally seen in the cycle? The thinking is that if prices rally even more than usual in a short period, they have that much more to fall back.

So, the shrewd investor, going against crowd behavior, has two clues near a bear market bottom: first, extraordinary pessimism among the crowd at the bottom, and second, continued skepticism and pessimism during the first sharp rally in the bull market. In bear rallies the pessimism usually fades rapidly since investors are very eager to want to believe in the rally, hoping that the old bull market is resuming. But at the bottoms of bear markets the crowd has been hammered too many times and regards the first true rally in the new bull market as an opportunity to sell. The crowd tends to be wrong at exactly the wrong time.

As a bull market proceeds and the rally fails to give way to a major decline, many investors find themselves shut out. Slowly they begin to believe that the move might be for real, and the thinking is, "I'll buy on the next decline." The problem is that the declines are never large enough to make people feel comfortable about buying. That's because there are too many bears on the sidelines eager to get in.

When prices back off just a couple of percent, several of these bears begin to buy, prematurely ending the decline and not allowing the bulk of the bears the opportunity to buy at lower prices. This trend continues as the market goes higher and higher with only small sell-offs. Eventually, the number of bulls becomes greater than the number of bears and, to some people studying the behavior of crowds, that becomes a signal to sell.

The idea is that if you use contrary opinion, you should go against the majority. But that's an oversimplification and certainly not true in the middle of a bull market. Just because 51% of the crowd is bullish and 49% bearish is no reason the market cannot go higher. In fact, it probably will advance at that point. The time to be wary of crowd psychology is when the crowd gets extraordinarily one-sided.

As the bull market continues to move higher, more and more people turn bullish. The flash point is really hit when the crowd has gotten so optimistic that it has used up the bulk of its cash. Cash represents firepower in the stock market. When it's depleted, the ammunition to blast stocks higher is gone. About the best the market can do then is hold the line. If interest rates climb or some other undesirable fundamental factor appears, the market would be in serious trouble if the cash levels were low.

Near the top of the market, investors are extraordinarily optimistic because they've seen mostly higher prices for a year or two. The sell-offs witnessed during that span were usually brief. Even when they were severe, the market bounced back quickly and always rose to loftier levels. The crowd anticipates higher prices, and it "knows" that even if a sell-off comes, it will only be another buying opportunity and eventually will lead to still further advances.

At the top, optimism is king, speculation is running wild, stocks carry high price/earnings ratios, and liquidity has evaporated. A small rise in interest rates can easily be the catalyst for triggering a bear market at that point. On the first decline, pessimism does not pick up very much. Remembering the lessons of the bull market, people rush to buy on the decline, figuring that prices will bounce right back to new highs. But the first rally falters, doesn't get very far, and fails to make a new high. The next decline comes and carries prices even lower.

Now people begin to get a bit nervous and the pessimism slowly rises. It takes numerous sell-offs over many months before the pessimism really picks up speed. At some point in the midst of a bear market, business conditions worsen and the pessimism grows and grows. It finally reaches the depths of pessimistic thinking when business conditions are terrible. Then we're right back to the beginning of the cycle at the bottom of the bear market, when pessimism is at a peak.

Some people call the idea of monitoring the crowd and going against it the art of contrary opinion. It's okay to use that term, but just remember that you don't always want to go contrary to the crowd—you only want to do so when the crowd is extremely one-sided. It's not easy to define *extremely*. There are many ways to measure the sentiment of a crowd, but the exact percentage of bulls or bears on any one indicator needed to give a buy or sell signal varies considerably from cycle to cycle. There is no magic level of optimism or pessimism that gives precise signals. That may be frustrating but it's a fact of life.

Nonetheless, by measuring a significant sample of crowd sentiment, ranging from the cash positions of individuals and institutions to the amount of speculative activity in short selling or option trading or the purchase of new issues, you can get a rough gauge of the degree of optimism or pessimism prevailing. When the crowd does get extreme, you should at least be wary. You can then integrate the sentiment readings, as crude as they might be, with monetary and tape conditions and have a fairly good sense of the major direction of the stock market.

MUTUAL FUNDS' CASH/ASSETS RATIO

Let's start with the first example of crowd behavior. Institutions are the most important investors today because they dominate the market, doing the majority of the trading. Mutual funds that deal in stocks control well over one hundred billion dollars' worth of assets. Although that's only a small fraction of the total represented by institutions, it's a pretty big sample. More important, accurate data on the cash and assets holdings of mutual funds have been available since 1954.

The optimism or pessimism among mutual funds can be measured by constructing a simple ratio of cash divided by assets. If the funds are very optimistic, they will use up their cash to buy stocks, and the ratio of cash to assets will decline. If the funds are pessimistic, they'll sell stocks, allow their cash holdings to jump, and the cash-to-assets ratio will rise.

To be sure, there is a problem in determining just how low is a "low" ratio or how high is a "high" ratio. But, with the benefit of 20/20 hindsight, we can observe when the cash/assets ratio hit various peaks and troughs throughout the last three decades. Recall, a peak in the ratio would show excessive pessimism, and a trough would indicate extreme optimism.

Table 25 shows the "forecasting" record of mutual funds since 1954. The second column lists the times when the funds reached extremes of optimism as signified by the various low points in the cash/assets ratio. For example, in July 1956, the cash/assets ratio bottomed at a low of 4.7%. The third column shows the extremes of pessimism as calculated by the various highs in the cash/assets ratio. After reaching an optimistic extreme in July 1956, the mutual funds became more pessimistic as stock prices declined. Finally, in June 1958 the cash/assets ratio reached a maximum at 7.2%, the high for the cycle.

TABLE 25

"FORECASTING" RECORD OF MUTUAL FUNDS BASED ON CASH/ASSETS RATIO: 1954 to 1985

Date		Cash/Assets Ratio Extreme Optimism	Extreme Pessimism	Dow[a]	Dow Change to Next Funds' Extreme	Funds "Predictions" Right	Wrong
July	1956	4.7%		516	− 29 points		X
June	1958		7.2%	487	+148		X
April	1959	4.4%		635	− 57		X
September	1960		6.6%	578	+123		X
December	1961	4.3%		701	−128		X
September	1962		7.0%	573	+296		X
November	1964	4.5%		869	− 60		X
October	1966		9.7%	809	+ 70		X
September	1967	5.2%		897	+ 1	X	
March	1968		9.2%	898	+ 38		X
December	1968	6.1%		936	−191		X
July	1970		11.8%	745	+217		X
April	1972	4.6%		962	−307		X
September	1974		13.5%	655	+282		X
September	1976	4.9%		937	−124		X
March	1978		11.3%	813	+ 25		X
September	1978	6.9%		838	+ 32	X	
May	1980		10.4%	870	+136		X
March	1981	8.0%		1006	−177		X
June	1982		11.7%	829	+430		X
December	1983	7.5%		1259	−158		X
June	1984		10.3%	1101	+166		X
March	1985 (Last)			1267			

Dow points gained on funds' predictions:	+33	
Dow points lost on funds' predictions:		−3,162
Net points lost on funds' predictions:		−3,129

[a]Dow price is third Friday of following month when cash/assets data are available.

As seen in the fourth column, the Dow Industrials had been 516 when the optimistic extreme was reached. About two years later, when the pessimistic extreme was hit, the Dow was 487, down 29 points from the high. In other words, the extreme optimism in July 1956 was unjustified. Instead of prices rising as the funds had anticipated, they fell.

In mid-1958, when the funds were at their most pessimistic level in several years, the market was just coming off a bottom. In less than a year the Dow ran up 148 points, reaching 635 in the spring of 1959. At that time, data for the month of April 1959 showed that the funds had reverted to an extreme of optimism once again, as their cash/assets ratio had fallen to 4.4%. Thus the funds, by having become extremely pessimistic in 1958, were wrong.

The table continues in this fashion, showing how the Dow performed between the extremes of optimism and pessimism on the cash/assets ratio. To date there have been twenty-two such extremes in the last thirty-one years. In twenty of these cases the Dow Jones Industrials moved in the opposite direction from that which the funds had expected.

After the extreme of optimism in September 1967, the Dow managed to move up a single point prior to the pessimistic extreme in March 1968, a tiny win for the funds. After the optimistic extreme in September 1978, the market once again managed to move higher by a small 32 points before the funds reached a pessimistic extreme in May 1980. Even here that was a very dubious victory, because the market collapsed in October 1978. However, the Dow managed to go higher later, so it was somewhat above the 1978 levels at the next pessimistic extreme, in May 1980.

The two "correct" forecasts from the funds produced a net profit of 33 Dow Jones points. By contrast, there were twenty "wrong" predictions by the funds, which totaled to a loss of 3162 Dow points. The net loss on the funds' predictions was 3129 Dow points!

The data on mutual fund activity are available from a trade organization called The Investment Company Institute, in Washington, D.C. Approximately three weeks after the end of a month, the institute releases a report on the cash and assets of the various groups of funds. Please note, the Dow Jones prices in

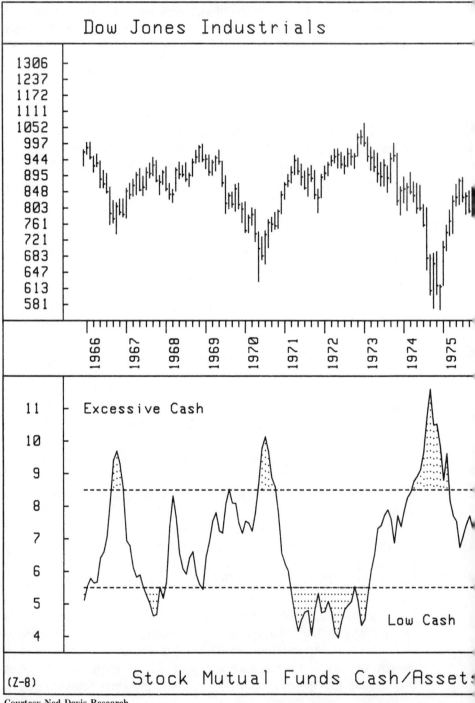

Courtesy Ned Davis Research

Monthly Data 12/31/65 - 9/30/85 (Log Scale)

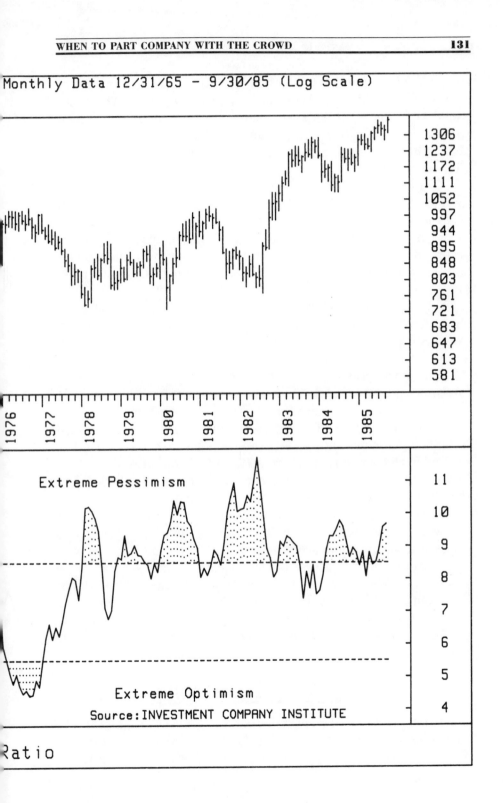

1306
1237
1172
1111
1052
997
944
895
848
803
761
721
683
647
613
581

1976 1977 1978 1979 1980 1981 1982 1983 1984 1985

Extreme Pessimism

11
10
9
8
7
6
5
4

Extreme Optimism

Source:INVESTMENT COMPANY INSTITUTE

Ratio

table 25 reflect the delay in getting the data; they are the prices on the third Friday of the month following the data. The funds would have looked even worse had I used the month-end prices that corresponded to the data, but since the public did not know about the cash/assets ratios for roughly three more weeks, I allowed for that delay.

Graph K (pp. 130–131) shows the mutual funds' cash/assets ratio plotted back to 1966. There is no magic number that leaps out and tells you the ratio is so high that prices might go up, nor is any so low that it indicates prices might fall. However, by glancing at the graph you can see vividly that high ratios tend to coincide with bottoms and that low ratios, more often than not, lead to trouble. For example, near bear market bottoms in 1966, 1970, 1974, 1978, spring 1980, and 1982, the ratio got up much higher than its norm for the past few years, and prices, indeed, bottomed. Conversely, when the cash/assets ratio got low in 1967, 1971–72, and in 1976, prices moved sideways to lower.

One of the problems with the cash/assets ratio is that it tends to rise as interest rates climb because cash is more valuable at higher rates. The ratio also tends to be lower when interest rates are lower. In the late 1970s interest rates began to move upward to higher plateaus, and, as you can see, the cash/asset ratio has roamed in the range roughly from 7% to 12% in that period. Prior to the late seventies the cash/assets ratio frequently dipped into the 4% region when interest rates were substantially lower.

If you like, you can work out sophisticated adjustments for the level of interest rates; indeed, I have done so myself. But even these adjustments are no sure thing. The point here, as with other sentiment indicators, is that when you can see excessive pessimism—when anyone can observe it—it's time to start thinking about a bull market. Or, when the optimism is overripe—and it's easy to see it in the marketplace—you ought to begin preparing for a bear market. *The idea is: Beware of the crowd when the crowd is too one-sided.*

INVESTMENT ADVISORS

Next to the institutions, the biggest group of players in the stock market is the general public. Many individual investors rely on investment advisors for advice, so the opinions of the advisors are often influential. Moreover, even if the opinions are not followed, they are important since a sample of advisors is really a good cross-section of the crowd in general.

An advisory service called Investors' Intelligence, of Larchmont, New York, has been monitoring other services since 1963. At present they rate approximately 140 advisory services weekly, making a determination—sometimes difficult because of the haziness of the writing—of whether the advisor is bullish, bearish, or neutral. The neutral category might include long-term bulls looking for a short-term sell-off, or some other vague classification. I find it best simply to ignore the neutrals.

I prefer making a calculation of bulls divided by the total of bulls plus bears. For example, if 60% of all advisors are bulls, 20% bears, and 20% neutral, my calculation would be 60% (bulls) divided by 80% (60% bulls plus 20% bears), which equals 75%. In other words, of those advisors clearly expressing an opinion (80% of the total), 75% are bullish.

Table 26 shows the "forecasting" record of investment advisors for the twenty-year period from 1965 to 1985. The table is prepared the same way as table 25, on the mutual funds. The second column searches, with perfect hindsight, the optimistic extremes reached by the advisors, while column 3, again with hindsight, looks for the pessimistic extremes.

TABLE 26

"FORECASTING" RECORD OF ADVISORS: 1965 to 1985

| | % of Advisors Bullish | | | Dow Change to Next Advisors' | Advisors' "Predictions" | |
Date	Extreme Optimism	Extreme Pessimism	Dow	Extreme	Right	Wrong
4/23/65	89.7		911	− 48 points		X
7/30/65		41.4	863	+125		X
1/26/66	90.9		988	−217		X
10/19/66		28.0	771	+158		X
9/20/67	70.6		933	− 93		X

(*TABLE 26 continued*)

"FORECASTING" RECORD OF ADVISORS:
1965 to 1985

Date	% of Advisors Bullish		Dow	Dow Change to Next Advisors' Extreme	Advisors' "Predictions"	
	Extreme Optimism	Extreme Pessimism			Right	Wrong
4/3/67		13.7	840	+ 74		X
6/12/68	69.8		914	− 18		X
9/4/68		31.6	896	+ 70		X
12/25/68	68.8		966	− 62		X
3/21/69		25.7	904	+ 57		X
5/16/69	61.0		961	−143		X
8/1/69		19.6	818	+ 42		X
11/14/69	63.1		860	−142		X
5/15/70		31.2	718	+195		X
3/26/71	85.0		913	− 55		X
8/6/71		50.0	858	+ 55		X
9/10/71	82.1		913	− 96		X
11/26/71		50.0	817	+167		X
12/15/72	85.0		1027	−127		X
6/8/73		38.8	920	+ 59		X
10/12/73	69.4		979	−157		X
11/30/73		35.9	822	+ 56		X
3/22/74	64.4		878	−191		X
8/23/74		29.1	687	+ 63		X
2/21/75	79.1		750	+ 76	X	
8/15/75		46.4	826	+146		X
1/14/77	94.6		972	−196		X
2/10/78		27.6	776	+121		X
8/1x/78	79.7		897	− 74		X
11/3/78		29.2	823	+ 57		X
8/24/79	60.3		880	− 74		X
11/9/79		22.1	806	+ 75		X
2/1/80	62.1		881	− 69		X
3/14/80		27.1	812	+128		X
9/26/80	67.6		940	− 4		X
2/20/80		35.9	936	+ 71		X
4/3/81	61.0		1007	−171		X

(*TABLE 26 continued*)

"FORECASTING" RECORD OF ADVISORS:
1965 to 1985

Date	% of Advisors Bullish Extreme Optimism	% of Advisors Bullish Extreme Pessimism	Dow	Dow Change to Next Advisors' Extreme	Advisors' "Predictions" Right	Advisors' "Predictions" Wrong
9/18/81		28.7	836	+ 20		X
11/13/81	59.7		856	− 51		X
6/4/82		27.0	805	+437		X
6/24/83	82.9		1242	−118		X
6/1/84		36.6	1124	+175		X
3/1/85	82.0		1299			

Dow points gained on advisors' predictions:	+76
Dow points lost on advisors' predictions:	−4,457
Net points lost on advisors' predictions:	−4,381

Source: Advisory data courtesy of Investors' Intelligence,
Larchmont, N.Y.

For example, on April 23, 1965, an extreme of optimism was hit when 89.7% of the advisors became bullish. Column 4 shows the Dow Jones Industrial Average at 911 at that time. The market then trended lower to 863 on July 30, 1965, the second entry on the table. On that date, pessimism had risen to where only 41.4% of the advisors were still bullish, the extreme of pessimism at that time. In the three months after April 1965, when nearly 90% of the advisors were bullish, the Dow dropped 48 points. The advisors were wrong, as signified by the "X" in the far-right column. From the pessimistic extreme in July 1965, the market began to rally, reaching 988 in January 1966. At that point 90.9% of the advisors had turned optimistic, one of the highest readings in history. On January 26, the Dow was only 7 points under its bull market peak and had gone up 125 points from extreme pessimism six months earlier. The advisors had been wrong in their pessimism in mid-1965, and were about to be wrong in their extreme optimism in early 1966. Thereafter the

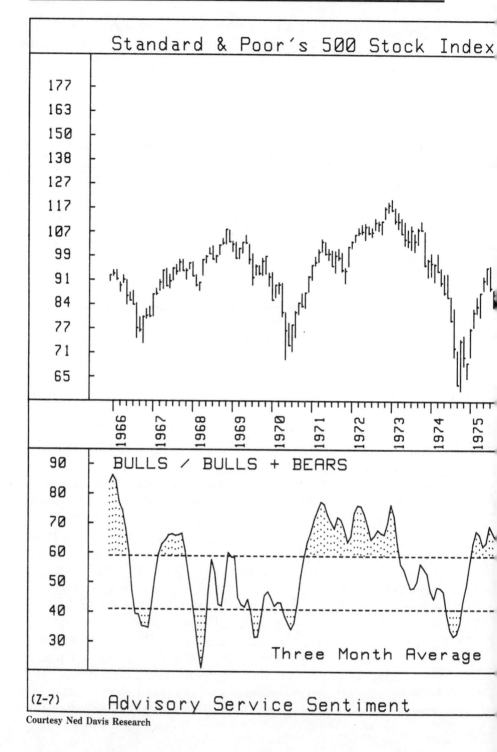

(Z-7)   Advisory Service Sentiment

Courtesy Ned Davis Research

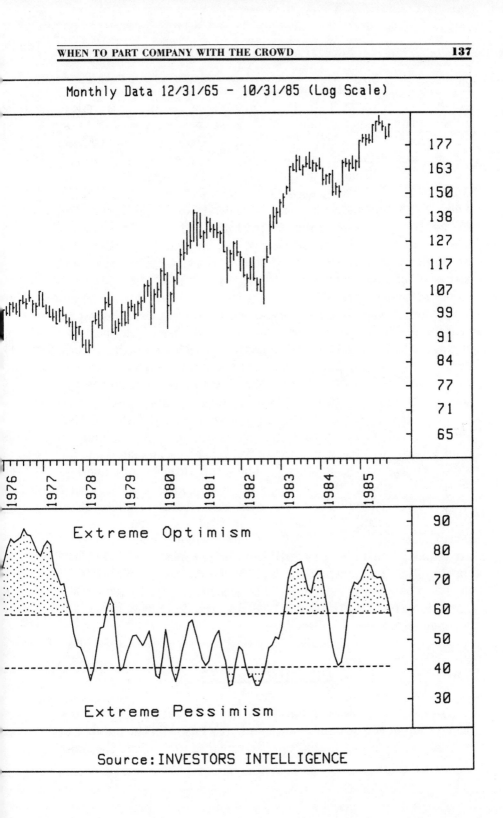

Monthly Data 12/31/65 - 10/31/85 (Log Scale)

Extreme Optimism

Extreme Pessimism

Source:INVESTORS INTELLIGENCE

Dow declined more than 200 points as a bear market unfolded.

The table shows 42 times when advisors reached extremes of either optimism or pessimism in the past two decades. Only once, in February 1975, when 79.1% of the advisors were bullish, did the market move in the predicted direction before the next extreme of sentiment. In that case the Dow rose 76 points by August 1975, when only 46.4% of the advisors were on the bullish side. Using hindsight to measure the advisors' "predictions" in the aggregate, the group was wrong 41 of 42 cases, or a success rate of just 2%—a failure rate of 98%. Had you known the extremes of the advisors' sentiment at exactly those times, and had you followed their advice, you would have lost 4381 Dow points in twenty years!

Graph L (pp. 136–137) shows the ratio of bulls to bulls plus bears going back to 1966. In this graph I've used a three-month average (thirteen weeks) of the sentiment. This smooths out the number so that you get a much longer-term picture. For the calculation of the thirteen-week average you simply add up the last thirteen weekly ratios and divide by thirteen. That's it.

The graph shows, more or less, what table 26 shows, that when the bullish percentage gets too high, the market tends to head for trouble, and when it gets too low, as pessimism rises, it's often the time to buy stocks. When the three-month average drops below about 40% bulls, it's often a good long-term buying spot. This occurred near bear market bottoms in 1966, 1970, 1974, 1978, spring 1980, and 1982. The ratio also reached 40, or thereabouts, around the spots of intermediate-type bottoms in early 1968, late 1978, late 1979, September 1981, and mid-1984. On the other hand, when the bullish percentage reaches 75% or so, it's often a warning sign. This occurred in early 1966, 1971 through early 1973, 1976, and 1983. Intermediate or bear market declines ensued.

BARRON'S ADS

In the early 1970s I developed a new indicator that is the first cousin of the advisory sentiment. It's based on the number of bullish and bearish ads that appear weekly in *Barron's*, the most popular medium for advisory advertisements. During a roaring bull market you will find far more bullish ads there than is normal. There are two reasons: First, advisors, as we saw in the previous section, tend to be trend followers. So, when prices have been shooting upward for some time, the optimism among advisors grows, and it eventually shows up in the type of ads they run. In other words, a large number of bullish ads would reflect a great deal of optimism among the advisors themselves. And, as noted in the previous section, this can be the kiss of death for stocks. Second, advisors are business people. They tend to run the ads that pull the best. In a strong bull market, advisors find that bullish ads pull while bearish ads don't.

This is a reflection of the optimism among the public that buys subscriptions to these services. Advisors don't like to run ads that lose money, so when they find that the public wants to hear the bullish side of the market, the advisors will tend to run bullish ads. Thus, the number of bullish ads reflects the public sentiment as a whole as well as the advisors' own preferences.

Just the reverse is true deep into bear markets. In those dreary times, very few bullish ads appear. First, it's an indication that the advisors themselves have turned more pessimistic. Second, it is evidence that the public has also become gloomier. Generally, once the public accepts the fact that a bear market has been established, investors are not particularly interested in reading the bullish side since most are convinced that the market has nowhere to go but down. Of course, they tend to be wrong in their negative outlook when that pessimism becomes too thick.

I count both the number of bullish ads and the number of bearish ads. However, I've found that the number of bullish ads is a more effective indicator since bearish ads tend to be fewer in number and are not as good a sample size. Graph M (pp. 140–141) shows the four-week average of bullish ads in *Barron's* since 1974. The most striking factor is that back in 1974 there were periods in which there were actually no bullish ads whatsoever. That also marked the bottom area of the worst bear market since the Depression. By contrast, near market peaks in 1976, 1978, early 1980, and 1981, the number of bullish ads increased to about 20 per week on a four-week average. In 1976 prices moved sideways for the rest of the year, while in the other three cases the market plunged. In

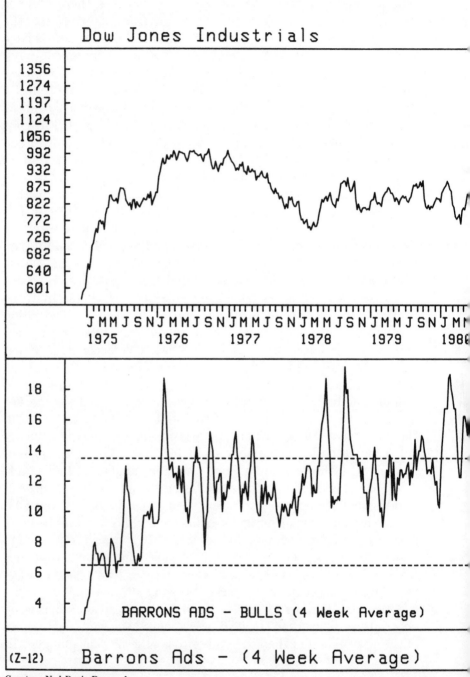

Weekly Data 12/06/74 - 11/15/85 (Log Scale)

mid-1980 the indicator also reached the 20 area, but the market went higher for a few more months, primarily because monetary conditions were still positive.

In 1983, before the market went into an intermediate decline, the peak of bullishness among the *Barron's* ads was about 16 per week on a four-week basis. That was pretty high, but not ultrahigh as seen in the earlier cases. Of course, that range was reached as early as late 1982, but the market still kept on rising because monetary conditions were excellent and most other factors were still quite good. But, by the middle of 1983, as the other evidence began to turn more negative, stocks couldn't buck that trend much longer and began to fade.

Note that, as with all indicators, one must use *Barron's* ads as part of a bag of tools. It's too much to expect one indicator always to be correct. What you look for are tendencies. When enough indicators are showing tendencies in the same direction, it's time to believe that those indicators, working in concert, will be correct.

Now look back at graph M and review the cases when the four-week average of bullish *Barron's* ads dropped to about 7 or less. This was seen in fall 1975, mid-1982, mid-1984, and late 1984. In 1982 stocks embarked on their greatest bull market advance in more than fifty years. In the other three cases, intermediate declines ended and bull market advances renewed.

As a rough guide, I would suggest getting cautious when the number of bullish *Barron's* ads reaches about 13 per week on a four-week basis, and I would tend to get more bullish when the figure drops to about 7. If monetary conditions are bullish—say, according to our model in chapter 4—I would raise the range toward about 16 on the negative side and perhaps 10 on the positive side. When monetary conditions are bearish, I would drop the range a few points. In that case somewhere around 10 to 11 might be considered dangerous, while 4 or fewer might be positive. Again, these are only rough guides, not absolutes.

As for the data, I'm the only one I'm aware of who actually takes the time and trouble to count these ads—I've been doing it since about 1972. Whenever the number becomes too extreme, I mention it in my advisory service, *The Zweig Forecast*. Other than subscribing to my service, about the only way to obtain these figures is to count the ads in *Barron's* yourself. Of course, if you count them, you might come up with a slightly different number than I would. The reason is that some of the ads are vague, and some interpretation is necessary to determine whether they are bullish, neutral, or bearish. By the way, I ignore the neutral ads. Whatever biases I may have have been consistent for the thirteen or so years during which I've been keeping count.

The consistency of any bias is important in an indicator such as this. For example, if you were to start counting the number fresh, you might average 3 more bullish ads per week than I would. That might lead you to an opinion that optimism is too heavy, while I would take more time to reach that same conclusion. It's just a fact of life that whoever counts these ads will have some bias in the interpretation.

The same is also true for Investors' Intelligence's survey of the advisory services. But only two people, the late Abe Cohen and the present editor, Michael Burke, have been doing the counting there. So once again, their biases have been consistent. If I tried to count the sentiment among the 140 or so advisors, I would surely come up with a different figure than they do. It's not the absolute figure that's important, but rather the deviation from whatever is normal, and normal includes the bias of the counter.

SECONDARY OFFERINGS

I'm trying to give you a flavor of various sentiment indicators, and, as with most endeavors in this book, I'm trying to keep it simple. I am deliberately avoiding indicators that deal with short-selling statistics and puts-and-calls option trading, for example, because they are too complex, and they have been subjected to great distortions in recent years for various reasons, primarily the advent of options trading in the 1970s and of futures trading in stock indexes in 1982. Besides, there are usually a lot of calculations involved in these particular sentiment indicators. I'd rather talk about indicators that need very little computation. In this vein, a worthy indicator, especially for calling market tops, is the number of secondary distributions, or secondary offerings.

A secondary offering is an issue of stock being sold by a company that is already public. It is *not* an initial public offering, or new issue as it's commonly called. Because there already is stock out, this subsequent distribution of additional shares is classified as "secondary." Another type of secondary distribution is when a very large block of stock, held by an insider or possibly another corporation, is marketed through a brokerage house in the form of a secondary distribution because it may be easier to sell that way than to have it hit the floor of the exchange. In such a secondary, a whole network of brokers at different brokerage firms is able to drum up interest in the distribution, much as with an initial public offering. It makes no difference whether the secondary is being sold by the company itself or by an individual or other corporate holders. A secondary is a secondary. You'll find them listed in a table in the back pages of *Barron's* each week.

Very few secondary distributions are seen once a bear market gets rolling. People are not interested in buying more stock at those times; moreover, if prices are depressed there is less interest by corporate or individual holders in selling such blocks. However, when bull markets heat up and speculative froth is in the air, the number of secondaries increases markedly.

This is so for two reasons: First, it's a lot easier to sell such blocks when the market is roaring, because the public's speculative appetite is whetted and it's willing to bite. It's easy to sell secondaries in a hot bull market, just as it's easy to sell initial public offerings. Second, it's more enticing for the selling company or selling shareholders to dump such blocks when prices are high. After all, everyone would rather sell stock when prices are high rather than when they are low.

I track both the number of secondary offerings and the total dollar amount involved. The dollar figures involve too many complications, but the absolute number of offerings, which is simpler, works even better. Graph N (pp. 146–147) shows the three-month average of secondary offerings going back to 1958. When the number of secondaries fades to about 5 per month or less, it indicates very little speculative activity and not much overhanging supply of stock—a relatively bullish condition. Such scores were seen at the bottoms or near-bottoms of bear markets in 1960, 1970, 1974, early 1980, and mid-1982. It is interesting that after the devastating bear market of 1973–74, the number of secondaries fell to just about zero. After that it took many years before secondaries increased in number toward the norm of the 1960s and early 1970s.

Generally, when secondaries are averaging fewer than 10 per month on a three-month average, and monetary conditions are favorable, it is bullish. But when monetary conditions are negative, secondaries ought to drop to between zero and 5 per month before the implication is positive.

The number of secondaries is even more valuable in suggesting that speculation has gone too far and that a top is being formed. As seen on the graph, the total of secondaries rose to above 25 per month in 1959, 1961, 1965, 1968–69, 1971–72, and 1983. Bear markets ensued in four of these cases. In 1965 there was an intermediate decline, the worst sell-off in three years. After a rally of several months, stocks finally buckled and went into a moderate bear market in 1966. In the 1983 case, stocks peaked in midyear, and entered into an intermediate decline that lopped 200 points off the Dow Industrials in less than one year.

As a rule, when monetary conditions are very favorable, I would not get too nervous about the number of secondaries until it rises to approximately 30 per month on a three-month average. But when monetary conditions are bearish, even a figure of 15 or so would be a poor sign.

In sum, the number of secondaries is an excellent barometer of excessive speculation near tops when the figure gets quite high. The indicator is best used for determining such tops. However, when the number of secondary offerings dips to extremely low numbers, it's a sign of lack of speculative enthusiasm in the market, which implies pessimism. And that is often the harbinger of a market bottom.

ZWEIG'S SENTIMENT INDEX

You would not be able to calculate my Sentiment Index on your own. But I will present it here so that you can see how you might combine numerous measures of crowd psychology into a workable indicator. You could construct your own index, if you wish to take the time, by using even the four simpler indicators discussed earlier in this chapter. You can, of course, add more indicators on your own.

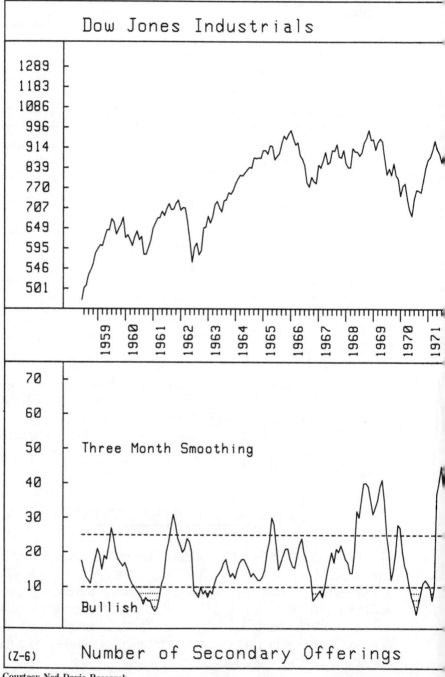

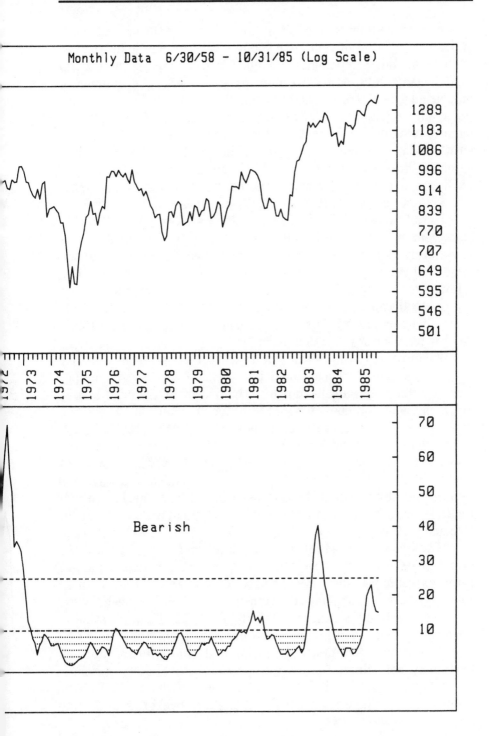

Monthly Data 6/30/58 - 10/31/85 (Log Scale)

I regularly maintain a list of approximately thirty sentiment indicators, several of them overlapping to form one indicator out of three or four components. Included in this index is the mutual funds' cash/assets ratio, the advisory sentiment, the number of bullish ads in *Barron's,* and the number of secondary distributions, all of which I've covered in this chapter. Others that I monitor include the puts/calls ratio, which I invented and first wrote about in *Barron's* in 1970–71; half a dozen different measures of short-selling activity; odd-lot buying and selling; insider trading; margin debt trends; initial public offerings; and speculative volume on the AMEX and OTC markets.

I grade most of these indicators on a scale where +2 points is extremely bullish, +1 moderately bullish, 0 is neutral, −1 is moderately bearish, and −2 is extremely bearish. On some of the lesser indicators the scale would only range from +1 to −1. For a few, such as the advisory sentiment, the scale can range from +3 to −3 because these indicators are more telling than the rest. I then convert the ratings to an aggregate reading where 100 is dead neutral on my Sentiment Index.

Theoretically, the Sentiment Index can range from +200 at the bull extreme—which would imply that every single component is extremely bullish—down to the bearish extreme of zero—in which every component would be extremely bearish. There has never been a reading at the extremes. The bullish record was 183 at the bear market bottom in mid-1970. The bearish extreme was a score of 26 in the spring of 1976, when the Dow was a couple of points away from its high. After that it trended sideways for several months and then finally eased into a bear market, which took the industrials down about 250 points before bottoming in February 1978.

Graph O (pp. 150–151) shows my Sentiment Index back to its origin in 1965. Scores above 140 show excessive pessimism and are rated extremely bullish. Scores between 120 and 139 are bullish. Readings between 100 and 119 are neutral to slightly bullish. When the Sentiment Index ranges between 76 and 99 the implication is moderately bearish. Finally, when my Sentiment Index is 75 or less it signifies too much optimism and the interpretation is extremely bearish.

Of course, as I've indicated before, one should use sentiment numbers in conjunction with the monetary background. Lower numbers than normal are needed for tops when monetary conditions are good, but only moderately low numbers might mark peaks in prices when monetary conditions are poor. Conversely, extraordinarily high scores such as those in 1966, 1970, and 1974 are required to pinpoint bottoms in times when monetary conditions are unfavorable. Readings in the moderately bullish range between 120 and 139 can be sufficient to herald excellent buying opportunities when monetary conditions are favorable, such as the intermediate bottom in the fall of 1975 or the buying juncture at the tail end of 1984, prior to a very spirited rally in January 1985.

The main thing to remember about measuring sentiment is to use several measures and not to value it too much when the numbers are relatively neutral. But when so many of your indicators show excessive pessimism that your index rises toward a high extreme, it's probably a pretty good sign that the pessimism is overdone and that prices are near a bottom. Likewise, when too many folks are optimists and most of your readings indicate this, it's time to start thinking about selling stocks. It's quite useful to know when the crowd is extremely one-sided in its opinion. It is not as helpful to know that 55% are bulls, 45% are bears. The extremes are what really matter.

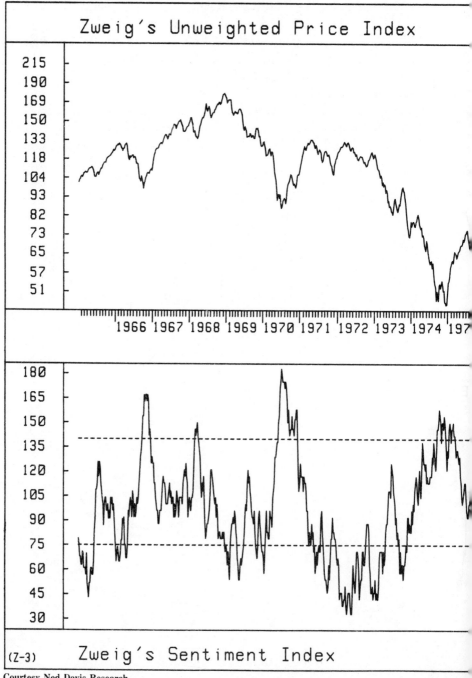

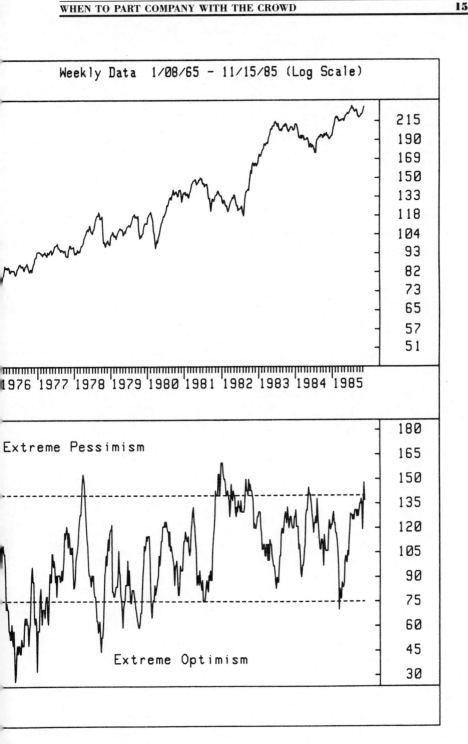

Weekly Data 1/08/65 - 11/15/85 (Log Scale)

CHAPTER 9

Seasonal Indicators—
A Year-Round
Forecasting Guide

I suppose I was destined to be interested in the intriguing
seasonal tendencies of the stock market. My youngest son was
born on an Easter weekend and my eldest on Memorial Day
weekend. My birthday usually falls on the July 4th weekend and
my wife's near Labor Day. Moreover, my mother found out she
was pregnant with me on December 7, 1941—Pearl Harbor Day.
To be sure, December 7 is not exactly a holiday, but my personal
history on that day was just one more reason for me to be
interested in the calendar and, more precisely, how it might
affect stock prices.

I'll cover six types of calendar tendencies in this chapter,
starting with the most interesting, the market's action around
holidays. Later we'll cover days of the week, months, month-end
tendencies, the presidential cycle, and finally, the effects of
year-end tax selling.

If the market were a truly unemotional mechanism, there
would be no reason to expect any aberrant behavior around
holidays, except conceivably late in the year, around Christmas
and New Year's, when transactions made for taxes—truly an
economic purpose—might have some effect. But there is no
economic reason to account for abnormal trading patterns around
the other holidays. I have gone back and inspected the market's
action around the holiday periods back to 1952, giving us thirty-
three to thirty-four observations per holiday. If trading had been
normal at these times, the number of days that the market was
up would be slightly more than one half, the long-run average for

the market. What I found, however, is anything but normal. Rather, price trends near holidays are extraordinarily bullish, shattering the myth espoused by many academicians that stock price movements are random. Moreover, it's nearly certain that these patterns are attributable to the emotionalism of investors.

There are seven major holidays during the year in which the stock market is closed, and two others that can be dismissed. We'll throw out Election Day right off. First, a national election day occurs only once every two years, and in those years when only the congressional elections were at stake, the stock market remained open. The exchanges used to be closed only for presidential elections, but even that tradition was ended in 1984. So there is no longer an election holiday as far as stocks are concerned. The borderline case is the so-called presidential holiday in February, a sort of combination of both Washington's and Lincoln's birthdays celebrated on a Monday. Years ago, the exchange would sometimes close for both presidents' holidays, other years only for one. Beginning in 1969 the new holiday format was adopted.

Actually, the market has done very well on the day prior to President's Day. Of the seventeen occasions of this "newer" holiday, the Zweig Unweighted Price Index has risen 12 times prior to the holiday, declined 3, and was unchanged twice. Ignoring the unchanged days, that's an 80% success rate. The ZUPI gained an average of .17% per holiday period, for an annualized gain of 28.3%. That's way above random, although, as we'll see, it's not up to snuff vis-à-vis other holidays. Moreover, since this holiday's history is relatively brief, I've decided to ignore it in the forthcoming discussion.

We'll focus on the seven remaining holidays: Easter, Memorial Day, July 4th, Labor Day, Thanksgiving, Christmas, and New Year's. In all cases, I measured the market's activity around the holiday season using my Zweig Unweighted Price Index. The most startling observation is that on the last trading day prior to the holiday, the market had an exceptional tendency to rise, no matter which holiday was involved.

Table 27 shows the price action on the day preceding each of the seven holiday periods. For example, in the 34 observations prior to Easter, the market rose 26 times, fell only 5, and was unchanged 3 times. The ZUPI gained an average of .26 of a percent per day, an annualized pace of 68% a year. As seen in the middle column, had you invested $10,000 on only the one day preceding the Easter holiday over the past thirty-four years, the money would have grown to $10,906. Similar data follow for each of the other holidays.

The holidays with the most bullish tendencies are Labor Day and New Year's. Labor Day produced the best percentage gains, with the ZUPI up .64 of a percent for the day, an annualized rate of a whopping 180.4%. The market was up 31 times and down only twice on the day before Labor Day. New Year's had the best percentage of winning days, with the market up 31 times, down only once, and even once. The ZUPI rose .53% on the day, or a per annum rate of 146.3%.

As seen in the top summary line of table 27, there were a total of 223 pre-holiday trading days. Of these, the market rose in 193 cases, or 83% of the time. Only 28 times, or in 12% of the cases, did the market fall; the market was even 12 times, which is 5% of the cases. If you ignore those dozen cases of a flat market, the market rose 193 times out of 221 cases, a phenomenal 87% success rate. Again, ignoring the unchanged cases, it means that the odds of the market rising on the day before a holiday are about seven out of eight.

TABLE 27

PRE- AND POST-HOLIDAY PRICE ACTION
ZWEIG UNWEIGHTED PRICE INDEX:
January 1952 to June 1985

Holiday	Direction of Market			$10,000 Investment	Return per day	Annualized Return
	Up	Down	Unchanged			
Pre-holiday:						
Easter	26	5	3	$10,906	+.26%	+ 68.0%
Memorial Day	25	4	5	$11,402	+.39%	+111.7%
July 4	28	5	0	$11,644	+.46%	+127.0%
Labor Day	31	2	0	$12,335	+.64%	+180.4%
Thanksgiving	27	4	2	$11,325	+.38%	+102.4%

(*TABLE 27 continued*)

Holiday	Direction of Market			$10,000 Investment	Return per day	Annualized Return
	Up	Down	Unchanged			
Christmas	25	7	1	$11,302	+.37%	+100.6%
New Year's	31	1	1	$11,893	+.53%	+146.3%
Post-holiday:						
Thanksgiving	30	2	1	$12,286	+.63%	+176.6%
Christmas	22	10	1	$10,967	+.28%	+ 74.7%
Total 7 pre-holiday days only:	193 (83%)	28 (12%)	12 (5%)	$27,188	+.43%	+189.7%
Total of all 9 days:	245 (82%)	40 (13%)	14 (5%)	$36,633	+.44%	+179.6%

Had you invested an initial $10,000 on the pre-holiday trading strategy back in 1952, you would now have $27,188, despite having been in the market a total of only 233 days, which is actually less than the equivalent of one full year (there are about 255 trading days in a normal calendar year). The result shows an average gain by the broad market of .43% on the day prior to all these holidays. That works out to an extraordinary annualized gain of 189.7%. *Indeed, the major drawback with holiday trading is that there aren't enough holidays! If you could somehow invent a holiday for each trading day of the year, you could roughly triple your money in a year, and after a few years could retire. Of course, if every day were a holiday, the market would never open!*

I unearthed a second fact concerning two of the holidays, namely that the day *after* both Thanksgiving and Christmas showed a very bullish bias as well. As you'll note in table 27, the market rose 30 times after Thanksgiving, fell twice, and was unchanged once. The annualized gain of 176.6% is the second highest for all of the holiday cases. On the day after Christmas the market was up 22 times, down 10, and unchanged once.

That's the worst of the cases, but it still produces a nifty 74.7% annualized gain.

Over a total of 299 holiday trades, the market rose 245 times, declined 40 times, and was unchanged on 14 occasions. Ignoring the unchanged instances, this means that the market was up 245 out of 285 days, a success rate of 86%. A $10,000 investment would have grown to $36,633, a gain of .44% per day, or 179.6% per annum. Had you traded around these holidays over the years, you would have been in the market 9 days per year, and in those 9 days would have made 3.99%. In other words, by being in the stock market only about 4% of all trading days, you would have made roughly 4% on your capital. The other 96% of the time you could have earned the normal interest rate. Thus, by taking on only 4% of the market's overall risk, you could have increased your return over that of a normal T-bill or a money market portfolio by nearly 4 percentage points a year. Of course, that assumes no transaction costs, which is not necessarily the case.

The question, then, is how to trade around the holidays without seeing most of your profits eroded by transaction costs. One way is to trade no-load mutual funds, especially since it's easy to tell the funds in advance exactly which day you want to buy or sell. The drawback is that very few funds will be amenable to such in-and-out activity.

The second way is to trade stock index futures. Since the Value Line Index is nearly identical to my Zweig Unweighted Price Index, you could opt to trade Value Line futures on the Kansas City Exchange. Transaction costs are nominal. The drawback, however, is that the futures can trade at various premiums over the actual market index ... or occasionally even at discounts. If the premium stays at the same relative level during the day that you trade, it would not be a factor. However, you might run into the disheartening situation where the premium shrinks and essentially wipes out your profit.

For example, suppose that on the day before a holiday the Value Line Index itself is at 200 and the future is trading at 204, a four-point premium. Suppose on the strong holiday the Value Line Index advances one point, equal to one-half of a percent, and closes at 201. It's possible that the future may simply stagnate and stay at 204 on that day, not giving you any profit at all, as the premium shrinks from four points down to three points. Of course, if the future goes up in line with the actual index, it would rise a point to 205 and you would earn your profit.

Over the long haul, it's probable that the futures will produce roughly the same amount of change as the actuals, but there's no guarantee. Moreover, in some of the cases, you're bound to feel the negative effects of premium shifts, but at other times the shifts in premiums may work for you. You could also trade futures on the New York Composite Index, the Standard & Poor's 500 Index, or the Major Market Index, a composite of twenty blue chip stocks, traded on the AMEX.

There are other ways to benefit from the holiday tendency. *If you are going to buy stock anyhow, it would not be a bad idea to buy it a day before the holiday in order to increase your odds of getting off to a good start. If you are thinking of selling a stock, don't sell the day before the holiday.* Rather, wait until the close just prior to the holiday, or even hold over the holiday and sell on the opening the day after the holiday . . . except, of course, for Thanksgiving and Christmas, when you should hold on for at least one more day.

In addition, if you are willing to risk the transaction costs and the lack of diversification, you might want to trade a few large market-type stocks around the holiday period. Such active market leaders as IBM, Digital Equipment, Merrill Lynch, or Texas Instruments might make good trading vehicles at that time. However, the price tendencies of these stocks might not show the equivalent performance of my broadly based Zweig Unweighted Price Index.

The obvious question in light of these seasonal tendencies is, why do they occur? As noted, it has nothing to do with economics, except possibly for some biases created by tax transactions around Christmas or New Year's. The most compelling explanation I've come across is that people are affected emotionally around holidays. Most of us feel better prior to a holiday. Why not? It's nice to know that a three- or even a four-day holiday is at hand. You can look forward to relaxation, time with the family, a visit to the country, or whatever. Under those circumstances, it would not be unreasonable for people to be more optimistic and thus more prone to buy than to sell stocks, thereby creating an upward bias in prices. If this tendency is true prior to holidays, it should also be true on Fridays. That is, people should be in a more upbeat mood approaching a regular weekend than they would otherwise normally be. We'll see that this is, indeed, the case.

223 WINS VERSUS 8 LOSSES

We've seen that there's an overwhelming tendency for stock prices to rise the day prior to a holiday. The day after Thanksgiving also has a tremendous upward tendency, possibly because it's really part of a four-day holiday period for most people. On that day, which is always a Friday, people still have the weekend to look forward to. The day after Christmas is more difficult to categorize, in part because the day of the week will vary. However, Christmas is usually the most upbeat of all holidays, and usually there's still a dose of good cheer right after the holiday itself. Even so, as noted, the tendency on the day after Christmas is not nearly as strong as the pre-holiday days or the day after Thanksgiving.

Given these holiday tendencies, I have added a few new wrinkles to devise an even more potent trading strategy. It's based on the premise that the market should go up during the aforementioned holiday periods—indeed, it does so seven-eighths of the time. But if the market does not do what it's supposed to do prior to the holidays (or immediately after Thanksgiving and Christmas), then that in itself is a negative sign and increases the probability that stocks will fall in the short run. Thus, the general trading strategy is to observe prices during the pre-holiday period, and if, at the close of the day, the market is unchanged or down—defying the normal tendency—then one should sell short the market for the day after the holiday. This rule would apply to Easter, Memorial Day, July 4th, Labor Day, and New Year's.

Obviously, the strategy would be somewhat different around Thanksgiving and Christmas, because we want to be long on the market on the day after those two holidays. For Christmas, though, we'll adopt a rule similar to the other holidays. Namely, if the market is flat or down on the day following Christmas, then at the close of that day we would short the market for one day following—that is, the second day after the Christmas holiday.

For Thanksgiving, the rule is slightly different. Overall, the two days around Thanksgiving—that is, Wednesday and Friday—have extraordinarily strong seasonal tendencies. In only six of the past thirty-three years has the market failed to advance by at least one-half of one percent for the two days combined. Thus, I would consider a gain of less than one-half percent over that two-day stretch to be "inferior." If the Zweig Unweighted Price Index rises by less than .50% during the Wednesday and Friday around Thanksgiving combined, then we'll short the market at the Friday close and hold that short position for one more day.

Table 28 shows the results of this expanded trading strategy, which calls for the use of short sales—or negative bets—for one day following subpar performance if it occurs during the normally strong holiday period. For example, the first line of the table shows the 34 cases since 1952 involving Easter. As noted earlier in table 27, there were 5 cases when the market went down prior to Easter and 3 cases in which it was unchanged. In those eight years, you would have shorted the market just at the close prior to the Good Friday holiday and held through the close of Monday following the Easter holiday. Had you done so, you would have made money on the short side in *all* 8 cases.

The good results, for the short seller, on these Mondays would have given you a total trading profit for the Easter period in thirty-three of thirty-four years. You *never* would have lost money, and you would have broken even once. You can't do much better than that. In a total of forty-two trading days (of which eight were on the short side) a $10,000 investment would have appreciated to $11,634, a gain of .45% per holiday, or an annualized gain of 99.2%.

The results for the other holidays are similar. The addition of 9 short-selling attempts around Memorial Day winds up producing a holiday profit in thirty-two of thirty-four years, with only two losing periods. For July 4th, Labor Day, and Thanksgiving the returns become truly spectacular as each holiday escapes with a perfect 33-to-0 record. *In other words, in 99 holiday spans encompassing those three holidays, you would have made money 99 times and never lost!* At Christmas time there were 27 winners, 5 losers and 1 tie, but that still works out to a nice 88.8% annualized profit around that holiday. New Year's checks in with 32 wins and 1 loss.

TABLE 28

OPTIMAL HOLIDAY STRATEGY
ZWEIG UNWEIGHTED PRICE INDEX:
January 1952 to June 1985

Holiday	Total Days Invested[a]	Direction of Market			$10,000 Investment	Return per Day	Annualized Return
		Up	Down	Unch.			
Easter	42	33	0	1	$11,634	+ .45%	+ 99.2%
Memorial Day	43	32	2	0	$11,767	+ .48%	+104.8%
July 4	43	33	0	0	$12,481	+ .67%	+147.1%
Labor Day	35	33	0	0	$12,657	+ .72%	+193.6%
Thanksgiving	72	33	0	0	$14,564	+1.15%	+161.6%
Christmas	77	27	5	1	$12,680	+ .72%	+ 88.8%
New Year's	35	32	1	0	$11,857	+ .52%	+135.3%
Total:	347	223 (96%)	8 (3%)	2 (1%)	$47,353	+ .45% + .67% per period	+184.5%

[a] Total days invested includes the days after Thanksgiving and Christmas plus all days with short positions according to formula described. Direction of market refers to trend for that particular holiday period, which can vary from one to three days.

The number one holiday on an annualized basis is Labor Day, sporting a 193.6% per annum profit. However, the best total gain per holiday comes at Thanksgiving, when the market is up 1.15% per holiday, thanks in part to the fact that one is always long for two days at Thanksgiving. But the annualized gain for Thanksgiving is "only" 161.6%.

Since 1952 there were a total of 347 days when one would have traded the market around holidays, of which 48 days were spent on the short side of the market after the original holiday period turned in subpar performances. In that span, a $10,000 investment would have appreciated to $47,353, a gain of .45% for every day one was invested, or a profit of .67% per holiday period (there were 233 such holiday periods). This works out to an annualized gain of 184.5%. It is also equal to a gain of 4.78% per calendar year. In other words, had one engaged in this holiday trading strategy over the last thirty-three years, you would have made about 4.75% in the average year, despite being invested only about 4% of the total time. *You would never have had a losing year!*

Of the 233 holiday periods, 223 were winners, only 8 produced losses, and 2 were ties. Eliminating the ties, that works out to a 97% success rate. Some would argue that these returns are only theoretical and that they would be difficult to achieve in practice. If you tried to enhance the overall holiday strategy by selling short at the appropriate times, you could not use no-load mutual funds for this purpose. However, you could trade stock index futures. Again, though, you might encounter problems with the vagaries of movements in the premiums on the futures relative to the underlying stock index. *But even if you do not trade stocks actively around the holidays, it must be acknowledged that the price behavior at these times is truly extraordinary and anything but random.*

DAYS OF THE WEEK

One of the early studies on the effects of days of the week was by Art Merrill (Merrill Analysis, Box 228, Chappaqua, NY 10514). Between 1952 and 1974 he checked to see the proportion of days that were up or down on the Dow Jones Industrial Average. For all days together, the Dow was up 52.5% of the time. There was no significant difference during midweek. Tuesdays rose 51.8% of the time, Wednesdays 55.5%, and Thursdays 53.5%. However, Mondays lagged the normal tendency quite a bit, rising only 41.6% of the time, while Fridays were up 59.8% of the time. That strong Friday tendency is consistent with the behavior of prices seen prior to holiday weekends.

In other words, investors ought to be in better-than-normal moods prior to a weekend, although that tendency should not be as strong as it is prior to longer holiday weekends, which is, indeed, the case. By contrast, if emotions have any negative effect on any day of the week, it ought to be the first day of the business week, thanks to the "blue Monday" syndrome. It's safe to say that most of us—if we're going to get the blahs—are more likely to get them on Mondays.

Another early study, by Frank Cross (*Financial Analyst Journal*, November–December 1973), verified Merrill's work on the strong Friday and poor Monday results. Cross used the S&P 500 Composite as his market index and found that, between 1953 and 1970, Fridays were up 62.0% of the time, whereas Mondays rose only 39.5%. The average percentage change was +.12% on Fridays and −.18% on Mondays.

In a somewhat more recent test by Michael Gibbons and Patrick Hess (*Journal of Business*, 1981, volume 54, number 4), they checked returns by days of the week from 1962 through 1978. They found that the S&P 500 declined .13% on Mondays and rose .08% on Fridays. Moreover, they found that an unweighted price index (somewhat similar to my own Zweig Unweighted Price Index) fell an average of .11% on Mondays but rose a substantial .22% on Fridays.

So, the Friday and Monday effects on stock prices are interesting, but they probably don't offer great profit opportunities for investors because of transaction costs. *However, other things being equal, if you were going to sell late in the week, you would probably want to wait until Friday's close or even Monday's opening. If you were going to buy, you should not do so late Friday or during the day Monday. You are probably better off waiting until Tuesday.* Of course, these tendencies might be overwhelmed by more important indicators such as those discussed in earlier chapters.

MONTHS

Table 29 shows the results of another Art Merrill study, this one on seasonal tendencies for months of the year from 1897 to 1974. The table shows the percentage of the months in which the Dow Jones Industrial Average advanced. It is seen that there are two significant times in which the months do the best: at year's end, with December the top month with a 71.8% success rate and January at 64.1%; and then during the summer, with July up 64.6% of the time and August up 68%. By contrast, the average for all months to rise was only 57.1%. At the other end of the spectrum, September had the worst tendency, rising only 44.9% of the time, with June the second worst, up only 46.8%.

A more recent study, by Anthony Tabell of the brokerage firm Delafield, Harvey, Tabell, substantiates Merrill's earlier findings. Covering the span from 1926 to 1982, Tabell found that once again December was up more than any other month, with the S&P 500 rising 42 times and falling only 15. There was a three-way tie for second among January, July, and August, with each rising 36 times and falling 21. Those were the same months that Merrill found to be the best on the Dow during a somewhat earlier span.

In the far-right column of table 30, you'll see Tabell's calculations for the actual percentage changes on the S&P 500 during the various months. On this basis, July comes out ahead, having risen an average of 1.84%. August was next at 1.44%, followed by December at 1.21%, April at 1.12%, and January at 1.00%. Consistent with Merrill's study, Tabell found September to be the worst month, with only 22 gains versus 35 losses and a total average return of −1.36%.

Once again, human emotions probably account for the bulk of the patterns of these returns. Indeed, the days before and after Christmas and the day before New Year's account for almost all of December's 1.21% average gain. January's advance is attributable to the end of tax selling, as is explained in the last section of this chapter. A portion of July's excellent performance is accounted for by the pre–July 4th holiday pattern. The rest of the solid results for the July–August period are, in my book, attributable to the fact that, on balance, people generally feel better in the summer vacation periods than they do at other times of the year. That's in sharp contrast to the dreary short days of winter when, in many sections of the country, you are apt to feel miserable fighting snowbound traffic.

Both Tabell and Merrill found that September was the worst month of the year, which is not surprising if you monitor mood swings. September's that time when vacation is over and people begin to think about the winter that lies ahead. It's also a time for those back-to-reality blahs, when days off are fewer and the work load increases.

I suppose that if one follows mood swings, February would

TABLE 29

MONTHLY TENDENCIES OF DOW JONES INDUSTRIAL AVERAGE:
1897 to 1974

Month	% of cases in which Dow rose in the month
January	64.1
February	48.7
March	57.7
April	53.9
May	50.0
June	46.8
July	64.6
August	68.0
September	44.9
October	56.4
November	57.7
December	71.8
Average all months over 78 years:	**57.1%**

Source: Arthur A. Merrill; Merrill Analysis Inc., Box 228,
        Chappaqua, NY 10514

also figure to be a poor month since it generally produces the
most rotten weather of the year. Indeed, Tabell found that
Februarys declined an average of .19% on the S&P versus an
average gain for all months of .45%. Merrill also found February to
be a subpar.

For trading strategies involving months of the year, the best

TABLE 30

MONTHLY SEASONAL TENDENCIES:
S&P 500 INDEX 1926 to 1982

Month	Direction of S&P 500 Index Advances	Declines	Average % Change in S&P 500 Index
January	36	21	+1.00
February	29	28	− .19
March	31	26	− .06
April	32	25	+1.12
May	28	29	− .83
June	28	29	+ .86
July	36	21	+1.84
August	36	21	+1.44
September	22	35	−1.36
October	30	27	− .37
November	35	22	+ .70
December	42	15	+1.21
Total:	385	299	+ .45%

Source: Anthony W. Tabell; Delafield, Harvey, Tabell,
600 Alexander Road, Princeton, N.J. 08540.

would be to buy stocks at the end of May, hold them throughout June, July, and August, and sell after the Labor Day holiday. This would produce an average gain of 4.2% on the S&P through August, plus another fraction in the first days of September prior to the Labor Day holiday. Even that decent return in the summer, though, might be swamped by the more traditional monetary, sentiment, and momentum indicators. But if these measures are bullish and summer pops up on the calendar, you might buy a bit more aggressively than you otherwise would.

END-OF-MONTH PATTERNS

In still another study, Art Merrill found that the market tended to be stronger than normal in the last three days of a month and the first six days of the subsequent month, while the rest of the time the market performed below its average. In a more comprehensive study a decade or so ago, analyst Norman Fosback (Institute of Econometric Research, Ft. Lauderdale, Florida) found a slightly tighter month-end tendency in which the market performed abnormally well in the last trading day of the month and the first four trading days of the following month, a total span of five "seasonal" days.

Some of these good returns are accounted for by the pre–July 4th holiday and the pre–New Year's holiday, which *always* fall within this five-day pattern, and the pre–Labor Day trading day, which usually falls within that period. Occasionally, Easter and Memorial Day might contribute a seasonally strong day as well to this five-day pattern. However, the upward bias of this five-day seasonal trend goes well beyond what can be explained by a few holidays.

Fosback studied 568 such month-end periods from 1928 to April 1975. He noted that a $10,000 investment in the S&P 500 only on those five trading days at month's end would have grown to $569,135, a gain of .71% per trading period, or an annualized profit of 43.8%. By contrast, the "nonseasonal" days—those from the fifth day of the month up through and including the next-to-last day of the month—would have withered a $10,000 investment to only $844, an annualized loss of 6.6%.

I recently updated Fosback's idea from April 1975 through June 1985. The upward bias when tested against the S&P 500 has not been as strong in the most recent decade, but there still is such a tendency. A $10,000 investment over the month-end seasonal period in the past decade would have appreciated to $13,322, a gain of .24% per period, or 12.8% a year, roughly only one-third the returns that Fosback found in the prior thirty-seven years.

I next went back to Fosback's starting date of 1928 and tested the month-end tendencies against my own Zweig Un-weighted Price Index through June 1985. The results were somewhat more consistent, although once again not quite as good in more recent years. For the entire 57½ years from 1928 through mid-1985, a $10,000 investment in the Zweig Unweighted Price Index during the month-end seasonal periods would have appreciated to $495,300, a gain of .57% per period, or an annualized pace of 33.4%. That breaks down, by the way, to a gain of just over 7% in each calendar year, given that one has invested in only sixty trading days in that year.

It's unfortunate that the 33.4% annualized rate cannot be earned over a complete calendar year since there are only sixty days in which you can trade with the month-end seasonal tendency. Nonetheless, that 7% per annum is gained in less than one-quarter of all trading days, and it leaves you free with cash to invest at prevailing interest rates over the rest of the time. Moreover, you would not want to be in stocks during the nonseasonal days if you could avoid all transaction costs. In the ten years from April 1975 to June 1985, a $10,000 investment in the ZUPI at month-end periods would have grown to $17,659, a rate of .46% per month's end, or an annualized pace of 26.3%.

Once again, if you trade at month's end you have the problem of transaction costs. However, here the strategy of buying no-load funds just prior to the last trading day of the month, and selling them after the fourth trading day of the next month, is somewhat more palatable since it involves only twelve switches a year with mutual funds. Some mutual funds are willing to accept that level of trading. You could also combine the effects of holiday periods and month-end periods, or even of the strong Friday tendency.

For example, if the fifth trading day of the month is a pre-holiday period—say the Thursday before Easter—you could hold stocks for one more day. Likewise, if the next-to-last trading day of the month is a holiday or a Friday, you could buy one day earlier before the month-end period. In the long run, this would enhance returns and enable you to stay in the market a bit longer to generate more profits.

Outside of those months such as December, when the holiday effect coincides with the month-end seasonal effect, I can offer no reasonable explanation for this month-end behavior. It's doubtful that it derives from any economic origin, and I cannot explain it on emotional or "mood" grounds. I doubt that people feel more "up" at month's end or month's beginning than they do at other times. So, the causes of this effect remain a mystery. But what is fact is that this market pattern has persisted for decades, even though the impact in the most recent decade has not been quite as strong as in earlier spans.

THE PRESIDENTIAL ELECTION CYCLE

There is a theory that presidential elections make a difference to more than just the candidates involved; that they also greatly affect the stock market. This belief is based on the premise that the party in power will attempt to do whatever it can economically to stay in power. The implication is that the incumbents will take positive economic action in the year or two before an election, which normally might translate into better-than-average results for stocks. Of course, the piper must eventually be paid, and this would lead to rather poor stock market returns in the year or two following the election. Let's check the actual results to see if there's any validity to this theory.

I've gone back and matched stock market performance against the election cycle since 1872. Since the election itself comes at the beginning of November, I measured a year's performance on an October-to-October basis using average prices for the Octobers. In other words, for the year 1984, the market's performance is measured on the basis of the average price of October 1984 relative to the average price of October 1983. After 1926 the S&P 500 Index was used. Prior to that, I used the most appropriate available stock index, such as that compiled by the Cowles Commission.

Table 31 basically backs up the presidential theory. The pre-election years, each of which starts two years before an election and ends one year before an election, show the greatest gains, with average returns of 6.6% per annum. The market rose 68% of the time, climbing 19 times and falling 9. An investor would have increased his initial stake six-fold in those 28 pre-election years.

TABLE 31

THE STOCK MARKET AND THE ELECTION CYCLE:
1872 to 1984

Year	No. of Cases	$10,000 Investment	Annualized Return (%)	Direction of Market: Up Down	% of Years Market Was Up
Pre-Election	28	$60,010	+6.6	19 - 9	67.9
Election	29	$35,822	+4.5	20 - 9	69.0
Post-Election	28	$17,840	+2.1	14 - 14	50.0
Midterm	28	$ 9,512	− .2	15 - 13	53.6
All years	113	$365,788	+3.2%	68 - 45	60.2%

Note: Market is measured by October-to-October change, with average S&P or Cowles Commission prices used for the Octobers.

The next-best returns were made in the election years them-selves, that is, in the years ending on the eve of the election. The market rose 20 times and fell 9, for a 69% success rate. The annualized rate of gain was 4.5%, which was slightly better than the market's overall return of 3.2% for the 113 years through 1984.

Once the elections were over, the stock market did, in fact, do a bit worse than was normally the case. In the post-election years, stocks appreciated by only 2.1% per year, more than a full percent worse than buy-and-hold. Year-by-year results were a standoff, with 14 winners and 14 losers.

Finally, in midterm years, beginning one year after the end of the election and ending two years after the election, the market on average actually fell slightly, declining at an annualized rate of − .2%. Stocks rose 15 times and declined 13 times, a 54% success average.

Thus, the results show that there is something to the election cycle, but clearly not enough to dominate strategy. For example, the pre-election year is the best of the four-year cycle, but on occasion the results have been far less than satisfactory. In 1903 stocks plunged 26.9%, in 1907 they fell 33.4%, and in 1931 the market was blasted for a 42.8% loss. In the election year itself, another supposedly strong period, the market suffered losses of 16.8% in 1920, 30.5% in 1932, and 16.8% in 1940. More recently, the market dropped a modest 1.9% in the election year of 1984. Obviously, one should not bet the deed to the ranch on the stock market's going up in pre-election or election years, even though there would be small odds in your favor.

Conversely, don't bet against the market just because an election was recently over. In 1933 stocks soared 31.4% on the heels of an election; in 1945 they moved up 27.8%, and in 1961 they rose 26.6%. Likewise, in the midterm year stocks on average do their worst, but there have been many cases of exceptionally large gains, including 1950, up 25%; 1954, with a 34.3% gain; and 1958, with a nice 23.5% appreciation. Stocks didn't do all that badly in the two most recent midterm years either, showing a 5.8% gain in 1978 and an 8.9% profit in 1982.

YEAR-END TAX SELLING

Late in the year, investors holding depressed stocks frequently sell them to take advantage of the tax loss. By establishing the loss before the calendar is over, it can be used to offset capital gains that the investor might have on other stocks, real estate, or any other asset. Thus, in the first few weeks of December, the market is often artificially depressed by tax selling, at least in those stocks that haven't done well during the year. Such selling is minimal in stocks that have acted well, since few investors have losses in them. But stocks that, in the month of December, are wallowing near their lows for the year are prime targets for tax selling. However, by Christmas time or so, these stocks tend to bounce.

Ben Branch (*Journal of Business*, April 1977) has examined the eleven year-end periods from 1965 through and including 1975. His objective was to purchase stocks making new lows during each year's last full week of trading. The stocks were arbitrarily sold four weeks later, in late January. He found that, on average, these depressed stocks had rebounded a full 9.0% in just one month, whereas the New York Stock Exchange Composite Index—a weighted measure of some 1700 Big Board stocks—had climbed only 2.6%.

A similar study in a doctoral dissertation by Robert McEnally (University of North Carolina, 1969) examined the tax-selling effects from 1946 through 1959. Starting with a sample of 650 stocks, he planned to buy the 10% that had performed the worst during the calendar year. He bought them at year's end and held those 65 worst stocks for one month, selling them at the end of January. On average, the artifically depressed stocks gained 5.9% in the following month versus a rise of only 2.8% for the sample of all stocks.

Other studies in more recent years have confirmed the tendency for stocks at or near their lows in December to outperform the market over the next several weeks. This approach, by the way, works best in years where the market as a whole is relatively near its own low in December, implying that many more stocks are making individual lows. In very strong market years, such as 1976 or 1982, when stocks finished the year virtually at their highs, you'll find few individual issues at or near their lows. In those years, the tax-selling game is not worth playing—especially since the handful of stocks that are down-and-out is likely to have some very real problems.

If you want to play this tax-selling game, review *Barron's* or one of the daily newspapers in the month of December and search for stocks that have made new lows sometime around late December. As long as there are at least several dozen stocks from which to choose, I would advise buying equal dollars' worth of at least several issues. Buy them and hold them for a few weeks. The sell date is quite arbitrary, but if the market acts well in January, I would continue to hold the stocks until late in that month. If by the second week of January the stock market as a whole is no longer acting well, I would jettison them.

CHAPTER 10

Major Bull and Bear Markets— How to Spot Them Early

The big money is made or lost in stocks during the most violent bull and bear markets. The bad news for those who crave action is that the market does not behave dynamically all that often. Even within the great bull market advances, there are periods of lull. I would estimate that stocks spend only about 20% of the time in the most active phases of the bull trend and only about 10% in the severe downward periods of major bear markets. Roughly 70% of the time stocks either meander in a neutral trading range or undergo minor rallies or declines within their various bull and bear cycles. During that 70% span—let's call it the neutral area—your overall market strategy doesn't matter all that much. You could be fully invested, partially invested, or all in cash. If you have a broadly diversified portfolio while the market hovers in these neutral ranges, you are not likely to make or lose a lot of money.

The other 30% of the time, when dynamic phases of major bull and bear markets are in progress, is another story—and it's worthwhile to examine the chief characteristics of these periods. *The good news is that you can watch for a few key signals that offer exceedingly high probabilities of catching the best portion of the great bull markets while avoiding the devastation of the worst phases of major bear markets.* The first part of this chapter will focus on the bull market signals, and the last part on the bearish indications.

TWO BASIC INGREDIENTS FOR BULL MARKETS

There is no official way to define or measure the greatest bull markets in history. To keep things simple, I have arbitrarily selected the ten times since 1926 when the Standard & Poor's 500 Index recorded the greatest maximum percentage gains within an eighteen-month period. I'm using 1926 as the base date because that is when the S&P Index began.

In many cases stock prices continued to rise after eighteen months, but I figured a year and a half was appropriate for determining a truly robust bull market—especially since the greatest percentage gains come in the early months of such markets. Occasionally the S&P peaked well before eighteen months. For example, if the market was, say, 100% higher in twelve months and only 50% higher eighteen months after the bull cycle began, I used the 100% gain as the yardstick.

Table 32 lists the ten such greatest bull markets from 1926 to 1985, in chronological order. By the way, the great bull market of the 1920s is not included here. First, the last portion of it, from 1926 (when this study began) to 1929, never had an eighteen-month period where the gain was large enough to make this listing. Second, any dynamic gains from 1921 to 1926 preceded the beginning of this research effort.

Leading off the table is the all-time greatest advance, which began June 1, 1932. It took only three months for the S&P to rise an incredible 154.5%, soaring from 4.40 to 9.31 in September. It's worth remembering, however, that that enormous gain restored prices only to where they had been in December 1931 on the S&P. Unfortunately for investors in those days, the 1932 bull market was short-lived. By February 1933 the S&P had plunged to 5.53, a decline of 41.6%. A few days later the new president, Franklin D. Roosevelt, ordered a bank holiday (over five thousand banks had failed during the Depression). The stock market was closed for about two weeks, giving people time to reflect on the situation.

TABLE 32

GREATEST S&P 500 ADVANCES:
1926 to 1985

Date of Low	Maximum % Gain Within 18 Months of Low
6/1/32	+154.5
2/27/33	+120.6
3/31/38	+ 62.2
4/28/42	+ 69.2
6/13/49	+ 50.0
9/14/53	+ 65.2
10/22/57	+ 49.2
5/26/70	+ 51.2
10/3/74	+ 66.1
8/12/82	+ 68.6

On March 15, the first trading day after the bank holiday, the S&P spurted 16.6% above the previous closing prices. Despite some backing and filling after that for a few weeks, that really marked the beginning of the second great bull market of the 1930s. By July 18, just 4½ months after the February bottom, the S&P had risen a tremendous 120.6%. We have never seen anything quite like the two bull markets of the early 1930s, which ended the worst crash in history, from 1929 to 1932.

The most recent bull market to make the top ten (as of this writing) started in August 1982. It achieved the third-greatest advance within the first two to three months of any bull market since 1926, and its maximum gain within eighteen months, a sparkling 68.6%, comes in fourth place on our list, barely edged out by the 69.2% gain of the 1942 bull market.

Alas, only geniuses and/or fibbers buy smack at the lows and hold all the way up. The rest of us mere mortals can only hope to develop indicators that might catch the bulk of the big moves. And to have a fighting chance, we must be resigned to giving up a fair number of points at the start in order to detect the type of tape momentum that makes buying safe, such as the buy spots generated by the advance/decline 2-to-1 ratio described in the momentum chapter. Indeed, that's a good place to start.

The Advance/Decline Indicator is one of two ingredients that, when combined, have had an outstanding record in calling the bull market advances listed in table 32. Recall, from chapter 5, that when the number of stocks advancing leads the number of stocks declining by a 2-to-1 ratio over a ten-day period, it is a rare and very bullish event. Just three months after such instances in the past, the Zweig Unweighted Price Index rose an additional 12.3%. The existence of a 2-to-1 advance/decline figure (for ten days) is the first condition necessary to herald a major bull advance. For illustrative purposes, let's call this factor a Super-Advance/Decline Ratio.

The second condition involves the Fed Indicator, which was fully explained in chapter 4. The Fed Indicator gains points when the Federal Reserve lowers either the discount rate or reserve requirements, and loses points when the Fed does the reverse. To verify the early stages of a powerful bull advance, the Fed Indicator must rise from a rating of zero points or less to a score of +3 points or more. (It requires a score of just +2 for the Fed Indicator to rate "extremely bullish," but the requirement here is even more demanding.) If the Fed Indicator is +3 or higher, and then dips to scores of +2 or +1, and subsequently returns back to +3 or higher again, that would *not* produce the signal we are seeking. What we need is a move in the indicator from a negative or zero condition to a very, very positive condition. This usually requires at least two successive cuts in either the discount rate or reserve requirements. Let's call this condition a Super-Bullish Fed Indicator.

What we would like to find is a Super-Advance/Decline Ratio and a Super-Bullish Fed Indicator reading simultaneously. It is sufficient if the two occur within a relatively brief span of one another. Testing has found that a three-month time frame is reasonable. Now, let's put the two pieces—the Fed and the tape—together and hopefully load the shotgun. I'll call the pair a double-barreled buy signal.

Table 33 lists all the double-barrel buy signals since 1926. Prior to 1985, there were only ten such potent signs. Carefully examine the dates of the double-barreled buy signals and compare them to the dates in table 32, which show the beginnings of the ten greatest bull markets since 1926. The respective pairs of dates fit very closely. For example, the first double-barreled buy came on July 21, 1932, just two weeks after the Dow Industrials bottomed and about six weeks after the S&P 500 made its low. *Without exception, all the double-barreled buys came early enough in the respective bull markets to catch a significant portion of the subsequent advances.*

The second column of table 33 shows how the S&P 500 Index performed one month after the dates of the double-barreled buy signals. In the 1932 case the S&P rose a sensational 49.7% in just a month. That, of course, is unlikely to be duplicated. But the market was higher in seven of the other nine cases through 1982, and the compounded return for the S&P showed a gain of 8.2% just one month after the double-barreled buys.

The other columns in table 33 show how the S&P fared three months, six months, twelve months, and eighteen months after the double-barreled buy signals. Three months after the buys, the compound return for the S&P was up 13.9%, six months later up 21.1%, twelve months later 28.7%, and a year and a half later it had risen a solid 40%.

Now let's consider that eighteen-month performance following the first ten double-barreled buy signals. A $10,000 investment in the S&P 500 would have grown to $252,005 in a total of 14.3 years (the holding period is adjusted for the 1932–33 overlap). The 40% return per eighteen-month period is equal to a very healthy 25.2% annualized profit. By contrast, from January 1926, when the study began, to January 1985 a buy-and-hold investor would have seen $10,000 grow to only $138,942. And, because he had his money invested for over 59 years, his annualized rate of return (not including dividends) would have been only 4.6%, not even one-fifth the annualized return following the double-barreled buys. Moreover, in the 44.7 years that did not fall within eighteen months after double-barreled buys, $10,000 would have actually

TABLE 33

DOUBLE-BARRELED BUYS VS. S&P 500:
1926 to 1985

Date of Buy	% Change in S&P 500				
	1 Month	3 Months	6 Months	12 Months	18 Months
7/21/32	+48.7	+35.0	+40.6	+85.5*	+85.0*
5/26/33	+16.4	+20.8	+ 7.5	+ 4.4	+ 1.9
4/16/38	− 5.1	+14.1	+25.0	+ 4.1	+ 1.9
9/14/42	+10.3	+10.2	+29.4	+39.1	+42.9
7/13/49	+ 3.7	+ 8.1	+12.8	+12.9	+42.8
2/15/54	+ 2.0	+10.6	+18.0	+41.7	+61.9
1/24/58	− 2.5	+ 3.4	+11.8	+34.3	+43.0
12/4/70	+ 1.9	+ 9.5	+13.2	+ 8.5	+22.7
1/10/75	+ 7.9	+15.4	+30.6	+30.8	+44.6
8/23/82	+ 6.6	+14.5	+26.4	+40.2	+32.9
1/23/85	+ 1.2	+ 2.6	+ 8.6	—	—

$10,000 becomes:

         $22,047 $36,677 $67,984 $119,557 $252,005

Return/period =

         + 8.2%   +13.9%   +21.1%   +28.7%   +40.0%

*12- and 18-month returns for 1932 buy signal are cut off on 5/26/33 in order to avoid overlap with the latter signal. Returns for the 1985 signal are not included in the totals.

shriveled to $5,513, an annualized loss of 1.3% *In other words, one could rightfully say that all of the gains and then some that the market has seen since 1926 have occurred in the eighteen-month spans following double-barreled buy signals, and that the rest of the time one would have actually lost money in the stock market.*

Table 34 shows how the Zweig Unweighted Price Index fared after the double-barreled buys. The bottom line on the table shows that the ZUPI rose 12.4% one month later, 20.4% three months later, 28.5% six months later, 46.2% twelve months later, and a big 62.9% after eighteen months. Following the approach above, had you invested $10,000 in the ZUPI (or an approxima-

TABLE 34

DOUBLE-BARRELED BUYS VS. ZWEIG INDEX:
1926 to 1985

Date of Buy	% Change in Zweig Index				
	1 Month	3 Months	6 Months	12 Months	18 Months
7/21/32	+64.3	+54.5	+39.6	+189.6*	+189.6*
5/26/33	+27.1	+31.2	+ 4.3	+ 48.9	+ 22.4
4/16/38	− 2.6	+28.8	+37.9	+ 10.3	+ 49.8
9/14/42	+12.5	+12.3	+57.4	+ 77.1	+ 96.1
7/13/49	+ 5.7	+12.5	+20.2	+ 18.5	+ 58.3
2/15/54	+ .8	+ 5.5	+19.2	+ 44.2	+ 49.3
1/24/58	− 1.4	+ 4.4	+15.4	+ 48.9	+ 58.2
12/4/70	+ 4.8	+19.8	+21.8	+ 7.6	+ 19.6
1/10/75	+12.1	+18.2	+38.9	+ 34.6	+ 59.6
8/23/82	+ 8.1	+24.2	+38.4	+ 57.1	+ 47.1
1/23/85	+ 3.7	+ 2.9	+11.0	—	—

$10,000 becomes:

| | $32,158 | $63,894 | $122,352 | $411,141 | $1,093,184 |

Return/period =

| | +12.4% | +20.4% | +28.5% | +46.2% | +62.9% |

*12- and 18-month returns for 1932 buy signal are cut off on 5/26/33 in order to avoid overlap with the latter signal. Returns for the 1985 signal are not included in the totals.

tion of it) and held for eighteen months after these potent signals, you would have run your bankroll up to $1,093,184, a superlative annualized return of 38.6%.

Conversely, one who had bought and held the ZUPI for over 59 years would have seen $10,000 grow to only $388,603, an annualized gain of 6.3%. That's about one-sixth the annualized return made by following the double-barreled buys. In the 44.7 years not falling within eighteen months of the double-barreled buys, a $10,000 ZUPI investment would have shrunk to $3,555, an annualized loss of 2.3%.

So, prior to 1985 there were only ten double-barreled buy signals in history, and incredibly, each one corresponded with the early stages of the ten most powerful bull markets in the past six decades. The double-barreled buy signals produced terrific profits, with both the S&P 500 and the ZUPI going higher in every single holding period from three months to eighteen months.

As I was writing this book, the eleventh double-barreled buy signal appeared on January 23, 1985. I have added to the tables the returns for the holding periods realized up to the time this book went to press. The one-, three-, and six-month returns are all positive. I have not factored these returns into the cumulative returns at the bottom of the tables. *Whether the 1985 advance will prove to be one of the eleven greatest bull markets in history remains to be seen, but that is not the real question. What is important is whether the market generates above-normal gains over the months following the buy signal.*

THREE CRUCIAL CONDITIONS FOR BEAR MARKETS

I've now given you a method, using two indicators, that helps call major bull markets. Now, let's talk about bear markets. First, in order to avoid confusion, I'll define a bear market as a decline of at least 15% in *each* of three important stock averages: the Dow Jones Industrials, the S&P 500 Index, and the Zweig Unweighted Price Index (or the Value Line Index, if you prefer). There are declines in which one or even two of these three averages have gone down by 15%, but not all three. Those might be borderline bear markets, intermediate declines, or just mixed markets in which some segments are in bear trends and others are not. But in this section I'm just concerned about the really significant bear moves; therefore, I'm insisting that all three averages decline substantially in order to reach our benchmark.

There's one minor exception to my definition, and that is the period from the mid-1920s to the mid-1930s. That span was extraordinarily volatile, and in the context of normal trading in those days, a 15% decline was no big deal. For example, in just three trading days, from July 18, 1933, to July 21, 1933, the Dow Industrials plunged 18.4%, declining from 108.67 to 88.71.

Prior to that nasty spill the market had been extraordinarily strong. Gigantic speculation was fueled at that time by the so-called alcohol stocks and by shares of those companies involved in agriculture that stood to benefit by the end of Prohibition. The state legislatures around the country were voting one by one to repeal the Eighteenth Amendment prohibiting the sale of alcohol or liquor in the United States. As the vote to repeal mounted, so did share prices on the anticipation that the liquor and related companies would make enormous profits.

In July 1933, two southern states broke away from the hard-core prohibitionist sentiment in that area of the country and voted for repeal. That was good news for the end of Prohibition, but it had been anticipated by the stock market, which had rallied with a frenzy prior to the announcements. When the "good news" struck, speculators began to sell their stocks to nail down profits. (Wall Street professionals often operate on the old adage, "Buy on the rumor; sell on the news.") As the leading speculative stocks—the alcohols—broke down, most other stocks fell along with them. Simultaneously, commodity markets also collapsed as speculators tried to cash in their profits on rye, corn, and other grains that might have benefited from the end of Prohibition.

Still, that was not much of a decline in July when one considers that in February the Dow had been 50.16—less than one-half mid-July prices—or that within several weeks most of that sell-off had been recouped. There were a few other less extreme examples of these quick sell-offs during that time.

There have been fourteen bear markets since 1919 that meet the above criteria. They are listed in table 35. Although there is no single common thread among all of them, at least one of three critical conditions was present near the beginning or during a fair portion of each of the bear markets. These three conditions all have highly negative implications for the market. The presence of any single one does not necessarily guarantee that a bear market will commence right away, but *there has not been a bear market in the past seven decades that did not have a least one of these conditions.*

The first is *extreme deflation.* I measure extreme deflation by looking at the Producer Price Index (previously called the Wholesale Price Index), which the government publishes month-

TABLE 35

MAJOR BEAR MARKETS:
1919 to 1985

Bear Markets	Extreme Deflation	Very High P/E Ratio	Inverted Yield Curve	% Decline in Dow Industrials
1919-1921	yes		yes	−47.6
1923			yes	−18.6
1929-1932	yes	yes	yes	−89.2
1933	yes			−37.2
1937-1938	yes			−49.1
1938-1942		yes		−41.3
1946-1949		yes		−24.0
1956-1957			yes	−19.4
1962		yes		−27.1
1966		yes	yes	−25.2
1969-1970		yes	yes	−36.1
1973-1974		yes	yes	−45.1
1978-1980			yes	−16.4
1981-1982			yes	−24.1
Average:				−35.7%

ly, and I check for major declines. Such a decline would be a 10% drop in producer prices on a six-month average of annualized month-to-month changes.

I know that sounds like a mouthful, but here's how I calculate it. To keep it relatively simple, suppose that January's Producer Price Index is 100 and February's is 99. That's a 1% drop for the month, which annualized (without bothering to compound) would be −12%. In other words, multiply the monthly change by 12 (that's not exactly correct when compounding, but it's close enough for our purposes). You would then take the last six months of such changes, add them up, and divide by six to get the average change for the six months. If that number is −10% or worse, then you have extreme deflation. This condition has not been present for several decades.

Recall, from chapter 3, that extreme deflation is a sign of an economy in dire trouble. When manufacturers and retailers cannot sell their goods, they cut prices. When even the price cuts fail to stimulate sales, additional reductions are made. The end result is collapsing prices and lousy sales, the norm during depressions. Stocks, of course, have not done well during depressions, nor during periods of extreme deflation. Graph P (pp. 184–185) shows the Producer Price Index plotted back to 1948.

As seen on the graph, extreme deflation was present during four of the bear markets, 1919–21, 1929–32, 1933, and 1937–38. The first of these coincided with the 1920 Depression, and the other three with the Great Depression of the thirties, which actually was divided into two economic phases, one in the early thirties (encompassing two bear markets) and then a relapse in 1937.

The second very bearish condition for stocks is *ultrahigh price/earnings ratios*. The price/earnings ratio is the market price of the stock divided by the last twelve months of earnings per share. For the market averages, the P/E ratio would be the value of the average itself divided by average earnings for the stocks in that average. Dow Jones and Standard & Poor's regularly calculate the P/E ratios for their respective averages. For the market as a whole, P/E's in the 10–14 area are roughly normal. Very low P/E's, in the 6–8 zone, tend to be bullish for the long run, while P/E's in the upper teens and twenties generally reflect excessive speculation, gross overvaluations, and poor future stock price performance.

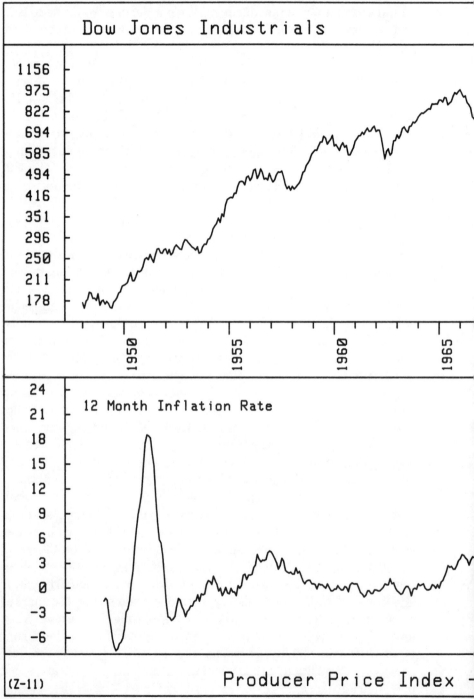

Dow Jones Industrials

12 Month Inflation Rate

(Z-11)   Producer Price Index -

Courtesy Ned Davis Research

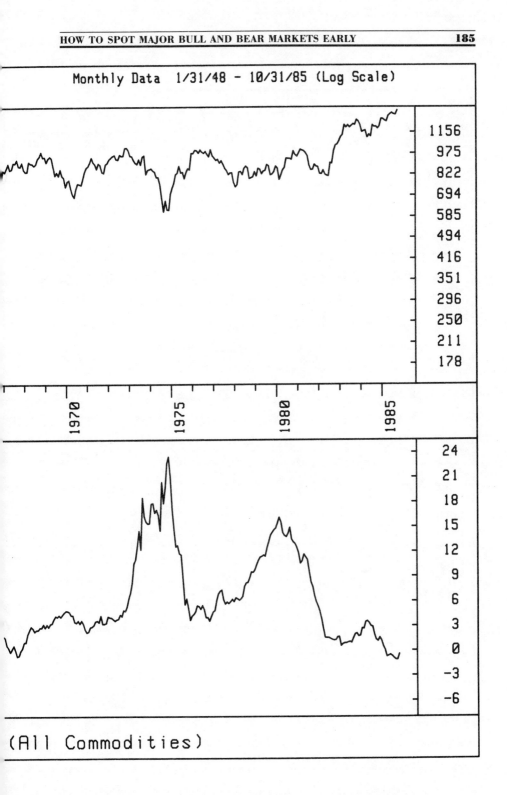

Monthly Data 1/31/48 – 10/31/85 (Log Scale)

(All Commodities)

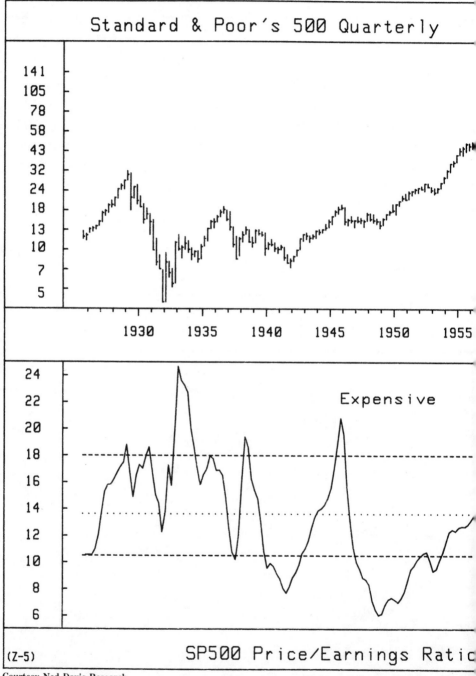

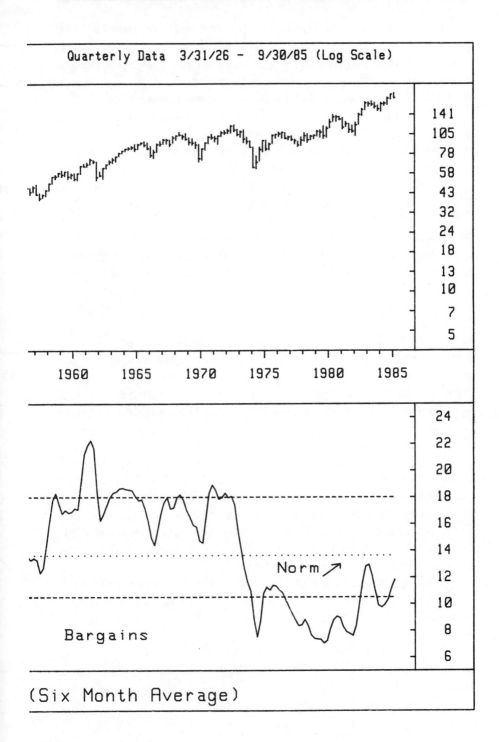

Quarterly Data 3/31/26 — 9/30/85 (Log Scale)

(Six Month Average)

Graph Q (pp. 186–187) shows the P/E ratio on the S&P 500 plotted back to 1926. I have found that when the S&P 500's P/E reaches 18 or greater, or if the Dow Industrials' P/E reaches 20 or more, that is sufficient to trigger a bearish indication. The exception to this rule would be during a severe business downturn, when corporate profits have been hacked so low that P/E ratios are high only because earnings are down.

For example, suppose that during a bear market the price of a major stock average falls from 100 to 50, a very large 50% decline. Suppose that at or near the bull market high, when the price average was 100, earnings for that average were $5. The P/E at that time would have been 20, tripping a warning signal for stocks. But suppose that during the bear market, the economy collapsed and earnings for the stock average were unusually depressed at just $1. The P/E ratio for the average at that point would be 50, but that is not a very stable or meaningful P/E ratio, because the earnings are underwater. If one normalized earnings over the previous several years, they certainly would have been much greater than recession-eroded earnings. In other words, the average earnings for several years would give a much more meaningful P/E ratio during those rare periods when earnings are abnormally depressed.

This situation actually happened with the Dow Jones Industrial Average in 1983. The economic recession, which ended shortly before then, had devastated the earnings of some of the Dow's major components, especially steel companies. Some of these firms took huge write-offs, and the Dow's total earnings at one point were less than $10 a share. With the Industrials somewhere over 1200, the P/E ratio at one point was over 130. That, of course, is absurd, not because of gross speculation but because of temporarily microscopic earnings. As profits came back to more normal levels in 1984, the Dow's P/E settled back into a more normal range of 11 to 14. A similar condition existed in 1932, when corporate profits for the entire nation were negative and profits for the Dow Jones Industrials were barely positive.

As you see in the third column in table 35, seven of the bear markets suffered from extremely high P/E ratios. The most noteworthy of these was 1962, when both monetary conditions and economic conditions were reasonably favorable. The only thing really wrong with that market was the market action itself, because speculators drove prices up to insane heights, with the Dow Industrials reaching a record twenty-three times earnings in late 1961 (excluding, of course, those times when the Dow's earnings were depressed).

The third extremely bearish factor is an *inverted yield curve*. This is the condition when short-term interest rates rise to levels above longer-term interest rates, an inversion of the normal situation. Usually bond yields, which are long-term rates—say fifteen to thirty years to maturity—carry higher interest rates than such short-term instruments as Treasury bills or money market funds because bonds are much riskier. Thus, investors usually demand an interest rate premium to entice them into accepting the added risk of buying bonds.

However, during a money crunch, in which the Federal Reserve is tightening money conditions, or when a financial crisis is brewing, short-term rates can jump sharply, sometimes to way above long-term rates, thereby generating a negative yield curve. To measure the yield curve I use Moody's Aaa Corporate Bond Yields as the long-term rate, and six-month commercial paper rates as the short-term rate. You can find these figures in government publications, *Barron's*, and other financial periodicals.

Graph R (pp. 190–191) shows the yield curve back to 1960. The shaded area below the zero line shows the times when the yield curve was inverted. For example, in late 1980 short-term rates were as much as four percentage points greater than long-term rates. Conversely, the yield curve was between three to four percentage points positive in 1971–72, 1975–76, and periods in the early 1980s. When the yield curve is negative on a monthly basis (the graph is plotted monthly), I consider that an extremely unfavorable condition for stocks.

Sometimes the negative yield curve will last only a month or two and a bear market might not develop. But if the spread between commercial paper rates and bond yields keeps widening in the negative direction, the odds for stocks get worse and worse. Table 35 shows that nine of the last thirteen bear markets came when the yield curve was negative for at least a fair chunk of the decline and/or near the top of the prior bull market.

As seen in table 35, only one bear market, 1929–32, had all three extremely negative conditions, and not so coincidentally it

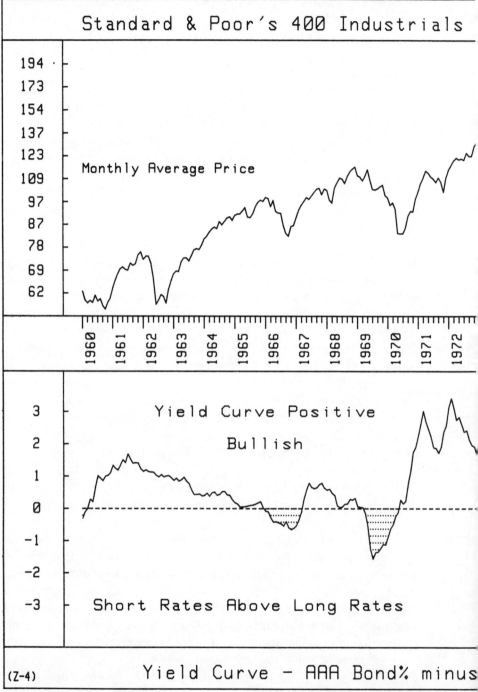

Standard & Poor's 400 Industrials

Monthly Average Price

194
173
154
137
123
109
97
87
78
69
62

1960 1961 1962 1963 1964 1965 1966 1967 1968 1969 1970 1971 1972

Yield Curve Positive

Bullish

3
2
1
0
-1
-2
-3

Short Rates Above Long Rates

(Z-4)   Yield Curve - AAA Bond% minus

Courtesy Ned Davis Research

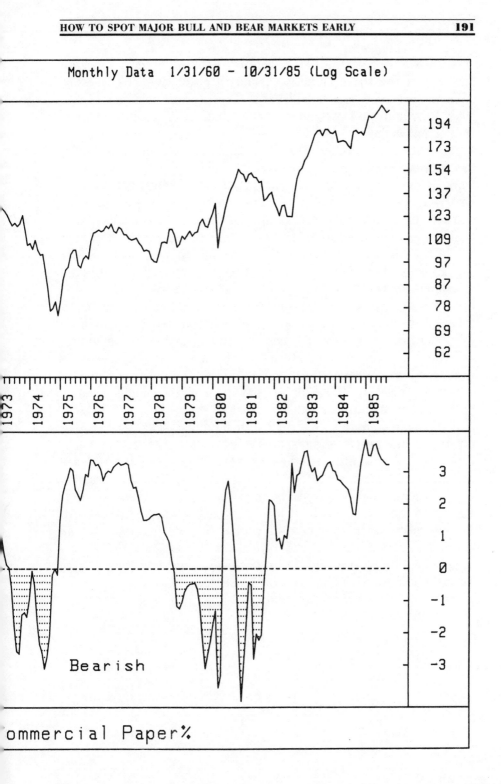

Monthly Data 1/31/60 - 10/31/85 (Log Scale)

Bearish

ommercial Paper%

was the worst bear market in history. Four other bear markets had two of the three conditions, and three of those bears were devastating: 1919–21, in which the Dow Industrials fell 47.6%; 1969–70, when the Dow plunged 36.1%; and 1973–74, in which the Industrials collapsed 45.1%. In the other case, 1966, the Dow fell a more moderate 25.2%. However, that was the beginning of a much greater long-term bear market, which took the Dow downward in real terms all the way into 1982 as described in chapter 3 on the stock market averages. The average of these four bear markets showed a decline of 38.5% on the Dow Industrials, well in excess of the average of the nine bear markets that had only one of the three negative conditions and fell an average of 28.6%.

In sum, there is no guarantee that a bear market will begin when one of the three extremely bearish market conditions is first present. But the longer such a condition persists, or the more severe it becomes, or when a second or third negative condition joins the first, the odds on a bear market become overwhelming. On the other hand, should the major averages experience a decline of, say, 10% or more with *none* of these three negative conditions present, the odds of that decline's becoming a major bear market are quite small.

It would generally pay to begin buying stocks after a 10% decline in all three averages, assuming that the three big negatives are *not* present. The odds of that decline's reaching 15% are remote, and except for a few meaningless cases in the extraordinarily volatile period from the mid-1920s to the mid-1930s, it simply has not occurred in at least the past seven decades. *So, if the background environment is reasonably decent—that is: no extreme deflation, normal P/E ratios, and a positive yield curve— then a decline of 10% sets in motion a buying opportunity with overwhelming odds that you won't lose more than 5% before the market begins to rally once more.*

CHAPTER 11

How to Pick the Winners— The "Shotgun" and "Rifle" Approaches

There are clearly a number of wrong ways to play the stock market, but there is no single right way. Many approaches can work. By work, I mean achieving a long-term rate of return better than the market's own performance. Rate of return, of course, would include capital appreciation plus dividends.

We can divide stock-picking methods into two extremely broad categories. First, there's the "shotgun" approach, with which you systematically compile publicly available data on any number of stocks. You then screen this massive amount of information by predetermined criteria and select the desired stocks more or less mechanically. With this broad approach you can cover nearly the entire stock universe while spending very little time on any one stock. By diversifying your portfolio—say, by buying ten, twenty, or even thirty stocks—you can protect yourself against the normal number of mistakes. The drawback is that no one company is investigated deeply and this may lead to some unwanted results.

The second broad method is the "rifle" approach, in which only a small number of firms are studied, with each carefully selected and analyzed fully. With this procedure you need not rely on the face value of publicly available data. You might dig further into various accounting methods, changes in management, trends in the underlying business, tax law changes, or virtually any other economic variable that might affect the company. Then, if you are capable of synthesizing all of this diverse information, you might be able to pick stocks that would beat the market.

This is really more of an investment approach relying heavily on underlying values. Its disadvantage is that it requires full-time study of the market and is not suitable for the part-time investor. Many Wall Street analysts and some money managers follow this technique. Even so, the investment returns from this rifle method vary enormously according to the analytical ability of the practitioners.

I don't think this rifle method is suitable for most readers of this book. Frankly, I'm not even that comfortable with it myself. I prefer the shotgun system, where I can systematically study thousands of companies. With this approach, my built-in error rate is about three-eighths. That is, out of eight stocks that I pick, three, or 38%, will underperform the market. Alternatively, it means that I may be right five out of eight times, which is not a bad batting average at all. I doubt that the rifle approach would do any better.

However, both of the stock-picking methods have their various advantages, and, in a limited partnership (called Zweig Partners) that I run with my partners, Joe DiMenna and Carol Whitehead, we integrate the two approaches. Basically, I do the broad market forecasting and some of the shotgun-type screening. Because he is more comfortable with the rifle technique, DiMenna handles this method of stock targeting, spending nearly all his time poring through financial documents and talking to analysts and company officials. So, working as a team, we are able to get the best of both worlds. But if I were operating strictly on my own, I would use the shotgun method, the approach I will outline in this chapter.

My stock-picking procedure involves a search for the following variables: strong growth in company earnings and sales; a reasonable price-to-earnings ratio given the company's growth rate; buying by corporate insiders, or at least the lack of heavy selling by insiders; and relatively strong price action by the stock itself. In other words, I tend to favor buying strength and selling weakness. I will go into detail about each of these general areas and provide specific examples of stocks I've recommended and tell you exactly where to find the data you will need. All the information for this method is publicly available.

SCANNING THE FINANCIAL SECTION

Step number one is to obtain the latest quarterly figures on company sales and earnings, and the best place is in the daily financial section of *The Wall Street Journal, The New York Times*, or any other paper that lists all the earnings reports daily. I prefer the *Times* myself, but whichever paper you use, stick with it, because a company's earnings might be reported in, say, the *Journal* on Monday and not hit the *Times* until Tuesday, or vice versa. So, if you skip from paper to paper, you might miss a report. One enormous advantage, by the way, of using the earnings reports in the papers is that it enables you to scan *every* report that comes out. By the end of a quarter you will have seen the earnings of four thousand or more companies. It is not as much work as it seems because in most cases you'll merely glance at a report and reject it immediately.

The illustration on page 196 shows some of the earnings reports as found on a typical day in *The New York Times* (June 18, 1985). You'll find that I circled four of the reports with a felt-tipped pen, my first step. What I am looking for are reasonable gains in both sales (revenues) and earnings per share. Take the first company listed in that day's earnings—Amcast Industrial Corp. The little "O" in the brackets after the company's name stands for over-the-counter, where that stock trades. An "N" in the brackets means the company is listed on the New York Stock Exchange, an "A" signifies the AMEX, and *no* letter at all means that the common stock either is not traded or does not even appear in the regular over-the-counter listings.

In the case of Amcast we see the results for the quarter ending June 2, 1985. The sales of a bit over $67 million were more than $2½ million below the previous year's quarter, not indicative of growth. Likewise, earnings per share were 50¢ versus 53¢ in the year-ago quarter. That, too, shows lack of recent growth. Since growth is a key variable, I eliminated Amcast.

Now skip down to Clabir Corp. on the NYSE. Revenues of $10.9 million were up roughly 43% from a year ago, a plus. Unfortunately, as we move down to the earnings per share, we see a net of only 2¢ versus a loss the previous year. While that is

THE NEW YORK TIMES, TUESDAY, JUNE 18, 1985

COMPANY EARNINGS

For periods shown. (N) indicates stock is listed on the New York Stock Exchange, (A) the American Stock Exchange and (O) Over-the-Counter.

AMCAST INDUSTRIAL CORP. (O)

Qtr to June 2	1985	1984
Sales $	67,084,000	69,676,000
Net inc	3,312,000	3,490,000
Share earns	.50	.53
9mo sales	182,770,000	212,483,000
Net inc	6,830,000	6,938,000
Share earns	1.03	1.05

BRINKMAN (L.D.)

Qtr to April 30	1985	1984
Revenue $	60,695,000	66,798,000
Net loss	b3,062,000	cd2,528,000
Share earns	—	.37
9mo rev	188,126,000	194,279,000
Net inc	b1,870,000	c7,361,000
Share earns	.22	1.08

b-Reflects losses from discontinued operations of $4,267,000 for the quarter and $4,551,000 for the nine months.

c-Includes income from discontinued operations of $11,000 for the quarter and $348,000 for the nine months.

d-Net income.

CAMBRIAN SYSTEMS INC.

Qtr to April 30	1985	1984
Revenue $	1,103,300	1,704,300
Net loss	495,800	133,600
9mo rev	3,346,000	4,428,900
Net loss	1,470,100	270,500

CLABIR CORP. (N)

Qtr to April 30	1985	1984
Revenue $	10,937,000	7,599,000
Net inc	b204,000	c796,000
Share earns	.02	—

b-After a tax credit of $531,000.

c-Net loss.

COGENIC ENERGY SYSTEMS (O)

Qtr to April 30	1985	1984
Revenue $	1,319,088	1,122,116
Net loss	766,954	367,630

CONTINENTAL HEALTHCARE SYS.(O)

Qtr to March 31	1985	1984
Revenue $	3,728,000	2,218,000
Net inc	486,000	261,000
Share earns	.16	.08
6mo rev	6,869,000	4,019,000
Net inc	575,000	b403,000
Share earns	.19	.13

b-Includes a gain of $30,000 from the cumulative effect of an accounting change.

CULLINET SOFTWARE INC. (N)

Qtr to April 30	1985	1984
Revenue $	52,728,000	35,149,000
Net inc	6,856,000	4,812,000
Share earns	.22	.16
Yr rev	184,100,000	120,036,000
Net inc	24,688,000	16,494,000
Share earns	.81	.54

The share earnings reflect a 2-for-1 stock split paid Jan. 21.

DATAPOWER INC. (O)

Year to March 31	1985	1984
Sales $	15,231,000	15,042,000
Net loss	b968,000	c506,000
Share earns	—	.24

b-After a gain of $258,000 from the cumulative effect of an accounting change.

c-Net income

DIGITECH INC.

Qtr to April 30	1985	1984
Revenue $	4,522,000	5,817,000
Net loss	331,000	392,000
6mo rev	9,018,000	10,706,000
Net loss	750,000	1,243,000

DIVI HOTELS

Qtr to April 30	1985	1984
Revenue $	12,702,953	8,363,826
Net inc	3,683,294	3,064,925
Share earns	1.98	2.52
Shares outst	1,858,338	1,219,862
Yr rev	29,098,500	20,155,485
Net inc	2,117,162	1,908,283
Share earns	1.38	1.59
Shares outst	1,530,595	1,200,949

EAGLE-PICHER INDUSTRIES (N)

Qtr to May 31	1985	1984
Sales $	174,646,965	180,866,737
Net inc	7,330,899	7,747,486
Share earns	.77	.80
6mo sales	329,358,506	335,415,217
Net inc	11,780,920	12,881,936
Share earns	1.23	1.33

ENNIS BUSINESS FORMS INC. (N)

Qtr to May 31	1985	1984
Sales $	27,255,000	25,305,000
Net inc	2,162,000	1,806,000
Share earns	.63	.51

EQUION CORP.

Qtr to April 30	1985	1984
Sales $	9,974,873	10,767,728
Net inc	b882,201	c1,438,948
Share earns	.16	.34
9mo sales	35,665,147	29,983,289
Net inc	b4,624,193	c2,928,918
Share earns	.90	.69

b-After tax credits of $436,419 for the quarter and $2,286,007 for the nine months.

c-After losses from discontinued operations of $195,305 for the quarter and $518,381 for the nine months and tax credits of $686,566 for the quarter and $1,397,051 for the nine months.

FEDERATED GROUP INC. (O)

Qtr to June 2	1985	1984
Sales $	74,320,000	40,537,000
Net inc	2,758,000	1,706,000
Share earns	.25	.19

Share earnings reflect a 3-for-2 stock split.

Results for the latest period are for 13 weeks.

GENERAL AUTOMATION

Qtr to April 27	1985	1984
Sales $	13,606,000	19,056,000
Net loss	4,542,000	b1,364,000
9mo sales	43,657,000	55,616,000
Net loss	6,742,000	c859,000

b-Reflects a loss of $50,000 from the reversal of a tax credit.

c-After a tax credit of $80,000.

KETTLE RESTAURANTS INC.

Qtr to April 30	1985	1984
Revenue $	11,556,000	12,578,000
Net loss	35,000	b703,000
Share earns	—	.30
6mo rev	23,156,000	25,915,000
Net inc	539,000	1,469,000
Share earns	.23	.62

b-Net income.

LEVI STRAUSS & CO. (N)

Qtr to March 31	1985	1984
Sales $	615,686,000	659,824,000
Net inc	32,059,000	b6,358,000
Share earns	.86	.17
6mo sales	1,133,855,000	1,193,677,000
Net inc	45,641,000	17,246,000
Share earns	1.23	.43

b-Reflects a charge of $24,500,000 for plant closings.

LEXICON CORP. (O)

Qtr to May 31	1985	1984
Revenue $	2,477,414	1,202,827
Net inc	457,852	315,125
Share earns	.04	.03
9mo rev	5,780,683	3,069,144
Net inc	686,847	366,282
Share earns	.06	.04

MCCORMICK & CO. (O)

Qtr to May 31	1985	1984
Sales $	209,232,000	186,872,000
Net inc	3,454,000	b7,696,000
Share earns	.28	.62
6mo sales	400,100,000	358,857,000
Net inc	7,070,000	c34,062,000
Share earns	.58	2.72

b-Includes a gain of $1,000,000, or 8 cents a share, on the sale of property.

c-Includes a gain of $22,200,000, or $1.77 a share, on the sale of property.

MEDICAL ELECTRONICS CORP.

Qtr to April 30	1985	1984
Revenue $	1,749,995	940,824
Net inc	239,642	b304,515
Share earns	.04	—
6mo rev	3,346,031	1,638,893
Net inc	380,654	b443,684
Share earns	.07	—

b-Net loss

NEWBERY ENERGY CORP. (A)

Qtr to March 31	1985	1984
Revenue $	21,895,000	21,214,000
Net inc	785,000	1,038,000
Share earns	.47	.61

Cont'd on Page D14

clearly an improvement, the earnings are rather insignificant and probably more indicative of a potential turnaround situation than true growth. That's not what I'm looking for. In addition, notice the lowerbase "b" in front of net income for the April 30, 1985, quarter. The footnote under the report says that that net income is after a tax credit of $531,000. In other words, without that extraordinary item, Clabir would have reported a loss of more than $300,000 for the quarter. So, we'll forget about that stock.

The next issue, Cogenic Energy Systems, reported a net loss, so I cross that one out too. Finally, we reach the first stock that I have circled, Continental Healthcare Systems, traded over-the-counter. Revenues for the March 31 quarter were up 68% to $3.7 million, a good sign. Next, earnings per share doubled from 8¢ to 16¢ in the quarter, an excellent trend. However, if you read further, there is a negative.

Except for the first quarter in a company's fiscal year, the other three quarterly reports will have the cumulative total of revenues and earnings for the current fiscal year. In Continental Healthcare's case, the March quarter was the second of its fiscal year, so the six-month report is also shown. We see on the last line of the report that six-month earnings are 19¢ versus 13¢ a year ago. With a little subtraction (the six-month figure less the second quarter), we can then calculate what the earnings were for the first quarter, the one ending December 31, of the current fiscal year. It works out to 3¢ this year versus 5¢ a year ago. Obviously, that was not such a great quarter. I am not only looking for growth in the current quarter, but I prefer steadier growth over a longer time frame. Continental Healthcare failed to show that in the first quarter of the current fiscal year. So, I would eliminate the stock by simply x-ing it out in that day's newspaper.

I have also circled the next stock, Cullinet Software on the New York Stock Exchange. Revenues were up a nifty 50% to more than $52 million, and earnings per share jumped over 37%, from 16¢ to 22¢. So far, so good. As it turns out, this April 30 quarter was the fourth and last quarter in Cullinet's fiscal year. The results for the entire year are found below. They show revenues of $184 million, up 53% from a year earlier, and earnings of 81¢, up 50% from a year ago. Cullinet's sales increase for the current quarter was only a tad below the increase for the full year, which is reasonable, but its earnings growth was only 37% for the quarter. By subtracting, we can see that for the first three quarters of the year, Cullinet earned 59¢ versus 38¢ a year ago, an increase of 55%. So earnings growth for the quarter was slowing, a cause for at least a touch of suspicion on our part. Still, that's a mighty high rate of growth, and if it were to continue at a rate of 30% or so, it would give us a potentially good stock. At this point I would leave Cullinet circled and go on to the rest of the list.

Later, as we move on to studying the price/earnings ratios, we will see that Cullinet's is much too high at roughly 30, so I would eliminate it on those grounds. But for the earnings report itself, the only negative is a slowdown in the growth in the most recent quarter, but not by enough to eliminate the stock at this point.

The next interesting stock is Ennis Business Forms on the New York Stock Exchange. Ennis, for its May 31 quarter, showed sales growth of about 8% to better than $27 million. As an aside, we know it is Ennis's first quarter of its fiscal year because there is no entry for the cumulative six months, nine months, or full year below the quarterly figures. An 8% sales increase is not robust; however, earnings per share are up over 23% to 63¢ for the quarter. That's not bad and it's worth another look. As it turns out, Ennis was already on my potential buy list, a list I keep on more than a hundred stocks at any point, always updating it by eliminating those with poor reports or some other negative, and adding to it for any new stock that comes along.

To make this potential list relatively easy to keep by hand I use index cards. (I do *not* use a computer in this part of my approach, nor will you need one.) I separate the cards into three groups, one for each exchange—NYSE, AMEX, and OTC. I then alphabetize each group. When you see a report in the paper on a stock that is already on your list, you will probably remember the name of that company, although occasionally you might not recall it. In any case, when in doubt, shuffle through your cards to see if the stock is already there, as it was for me in the case of Ennis.

Using Ennis as an example, here is a sample card with the information I keep:

EBF   ENNIS BUSINESS FORMS   37½   10m SHS

INSIDERS 0-4

EPS   .63 v.51 ($2.85) +8% YS. +21%   MAY '85
P/E   13X

MAKES BUSINESS FORMS
1.30, 1.56, 1.72, 1.80, 2.21

My first notation is the ticker symbol, EBF in this case, so that I can recall the stock on my Quotron machine if I want a current quote. Next I write out the name of the company, Ennis Business Forms, and the price at the last time I've updated the stock. In this case, it would be Ennis's price of 37½ on the day of the earnings report. I also note the approximate trading volume—about 10,000 shares for Ennis—because I don't like to recommend stocks that are too thin. However, you would not have that problem if you are dealing with a normal-sized account for yourself. I also note insider trading, which I'll get to later, but which, in Ennis's case, showed no buyers and four sellers, not good news. But that can change over time, so the stock remains on my potential list.

Next I erase the old quarterly earnings (always update your cards in pencil) and put in the new quarterly comparison, 63 versus 51. After that, in brackets, you'll see $2.85, which is the total earnings over the last four quarters. (I'll show you later in this chapter where to come up with that number.) Now you'll see

+ 8 after the brackets, which is the percentage increase in sales for the quarter as gleaned from *The New York Times*, after which you'll see + 21. When I culled the report on Ennis three months earlier, that latter number was the percentage increase in sales for the prior quarter. So, the not-so-good news for Ennis was that the rate of growth in sales declined from 21% to 8%. I next have the P/E ratio, which is 13, a brief description of the firm's business, and yearly earnings for the last several years.

Finally, there's a notation for the month, in this case May, which indicates the latest quarterly report. I keep that record so that, as I go through the cards searching for the stocks, I know whether I have an up-to-date report or a stale one. If we're already in, say, June, and I find that my latest quarterly report on a company is December, I figure that I probably missed the first-quarter report and will consult financial records to update that. In other words, putting the date of the last report is a check-off method for you. So, based on the day's earnings reports, Ennis maintains its place in my index file although it's *not* an immediate candidate for purchase.

The last stock circled for this particular day is Federated Group, traded over-the-counter. Sales were up sharply from about $40 million to over $74 million, an 83% increase. However, earnings per share, while up 32%, did not keep pace with sales. In some industries the failure of earnings to grow as rapidly as sales could mean heavy competition and price cutting and a subsequent thinning of profit margins. In other cases, it might be a reflection of expenses created by introducing new products, whereby the jump in sales may lay the foundation for much greater future increases in earnings. We simply don't have enough information to weed the stock out, so it remains a candidate for more investigation on this day.

Let's recap what we've done so far. We have searched through the day's earnings reports looking for reasonable growth in *both* revenues and earnings per share. Most stocks failed the test. Four of them were worth at least a second glance and have been circled. Continental Healthcare was quickly eliminated when, through a bit of subtraction, it was seen that the previous quarter's growth was negative, not consistent with our goal of solid long-term growth. The other three stocks remain with circles at least until the next step.

Once you get the hang of it, it will take only a few minutes a day to filter out the candidates from the also-rans, with the exception of the period roughly from the second through the fourth week of a calendar quarter. That's when an unusually large number of companies report their earnings, so the task will take you longer. But with experience, even during the heavy reporting seasons, it should not take more than fifteen minutes on a given day to screen the reports.

Please realize there is no substitute for experience. Although it may be slow going at first, your speed will gradually increase and, in a relatively short time, you'll become an expert at skimming the reports. By the way, always keep a calculator handy so that you can quickly compute the percentage changes in sales or earnings or do the subtraction required to isolate earnings from the previous quarter, six months, or nine months.

We have three stocks left with circles on this day, but so far we don't even know their prices. The next step, then, is to check the stock tables to get the previous day's closing prices. Cullinet and Ennis would be found in the listings for the New York Stock Exchange, and Federated Group in the NASDQ over-the-counter listings. For stocks on the New York and AMEX, the stock tables also give the P/E ratios (though they may not include the newest quarterly figures), so you might want to note those down as well. I scribble the prices and the P/E ratios in the margins of the stock tables near these stocks.

In addition, I always look for the change in price on that day. Most of these earnings reports appear either before the market opens or during trading that day. Not too many of the reports come out after 4:00 P.M., when the market is closed. Thus, a stock's action of that day is often a reflection of how the market absorbed the news of the particular earnings report. The worst thing the stock can do on news of earnings is to drop sharply. That usually indicates the market was disappointed with the earnings report—that it came in less than anticipated. Academic studies have shown conclusively that when earnings are significantly below expectations, such stocks, on average, will underperform the market over the next one to two quarters.

Therefore, if I see a stock down rather sharply percentage-wise—say, a point or more on a stock selling above $30, or three-quarters of a point or more on stocks in the $15–$30 range—I'll take a rather dim view of that action and probably eliminate the stock right then. *Remember that the tape is your best friend. Rotten tape action on the heels of an earnings report—no matter how good that report might seem to you—is often the kiss of death.* It's better to be safe than sorry.

None of the four circled stocks this day had significant changes in price, the largest change being only three-eighths of a point. I do not bother writing down the daily change unless it's significant. Indeed, you need not even bother with the most negative ones unless you are searching for short sales. I would simply cross out the stock at once. On the other hand, if the stock is up sharply on the heels of the earnings report, say a point and a half or two, it is a very hopeful sign and often means the market was pleasantly surprised by the report. Those same academic studies have found that stocks that report surprisingly good earnings tend to do better than the market as a whole over the next three to six months. So, if you find a big jump in price on the day of an earnings announcement, make a positive notation for yourself.

We can eliminate some stocks based on poor tape action the day a report comes out. The next means of elimination is an unreasonably high price/earnings ratio. The P/E ratio is simply the price of the stock (which you have found in your newspaper) divided by the total of the last four quarters of earnings. You won't have that figure available in the newspaper unless, by chance, the quarterly report was the last of its fiscal year, as was the case with Cullinet. Cullinet showed its earnings for the fiscal year of 81¢. By dividing its price of 24⅞ by 81¢ of earnings, we see that the P/E ratio is a lofty 31. That's enough for me to run for the hills. Cross out Cullinet. We don't know the last four quarters' earnings for Ennis or Federated, so we'll have to dig further. At this point, we've taken all there is worth getting out of the daily newspaper.

Now we'll need a new source of data, preferably a good chart service that also maintains decent figures on earnings. My own preference is the charts published by Harry Lankford Co. (P.O. Box 213, Wichita, KS 67201; 316-262-2111). There are three volumes, *Quote New York, Quote American,* and *Quote Over-the-Counter,* which correspond to each of these exchanges. The volumes are published weekly, but you may find that buying issues once a month is sufficient. Other possible services include William O'Neil & Company's *Long-Term Values* (P.O. Box 24933, Los Angeles, CA 90024; 213-820-2583), Standard & Poor's (25 Broadway, New York, NY 10004; 212-208-8769), Mansfield (2973 Kennedy Blvd., Jersey City, NJ 07306; 800-223-3530), or services heavier on financial data and less so on graphics, including Value Line, Inc. (711 Third Avenue, New York, NY 10017; 800-633-2252).

I prefer the Lankford charts because the book is pocket-sized and I can carry around all three editions and have access to some three thousand or more stocks. The Lankford charts generally include about five years of annual earnings and dividends plus the last five to eight quarters of earnings. The earnings per share are also graphed along with the price and volume in the stock. I also like the Lankford graphs because they are in semilog scale, which means that equal percentage changes in price are given equal distance on the graph.

For example, a move from 20 to 40 in a stock is the same . distance on the graph as a move from 40 to 80. That's the way it's supposed to be. Many of the other chart services plot prices in arithmetic scale, which can greatly distort the magnitude of price moves. On those arithmetic charts a move from, say, 80 to 100 can look like a straight-up advance in which an investor would have made tons of money. Actually, it's only a 25% gain and no different from an advance of 8 to 10, which might seem micro-scopic on those charts. The drawback of the Lankford charts is that you'd better have good eyes because they are very small. I don't mind that at all, but some people have trouble because of the tiny numbers. Shown on page 204 is an example of the Lankford chart for Ennis Business Forms.

Once you are in possession of a good chart or financial service you'll be able to check the earnings for the last twelve months. Take Ennis for example. The earnings report in *The New York Times* showed the quarter through May 31, its first quarter of the fiscal year, at 63¢. Checking the Harry Lankford *Quote New York* charts, we can see what the last three quarters were prior to that report. They total 67¢, 66¢, and 89¢. Added to the more recent report, the four quarters total $2.85. A second way to derive that figure is to take the difference between the current quarter and the year-ago quarter, which in this case is 63¢ minus 51¢, or 12¢. In other words, Ennis's earnings increased by 12¢

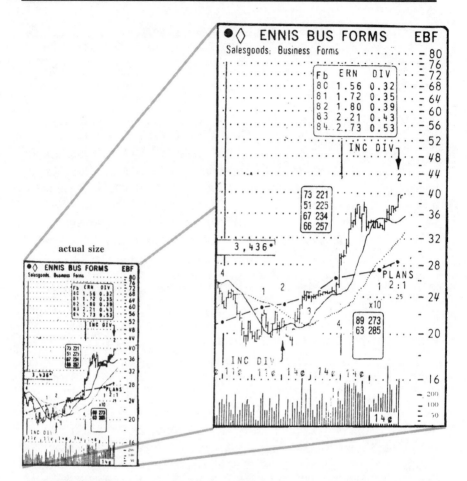

Reprinted Courtesy of Harry Lankford, Box 213, Wichita, Ks. 67201

above the year-ago quarter. All you have to do is add that 12¢ to the previous four-quarter total of earnings, which, in the Lankford charts, was $2.73. That would give you the $2.85 figure.

If you use the Value Line or Standard & Poor's or the Mansfield or O'Neil charts, you can do the same with the quarterly figures to get the last twelve months of earnings. In deriving your calculation you can briefly glance to see how the previous several quarters compared with their respective year-ago numbers. If you find that several earlier quarters were lower or the growth was skimpy, you'll probably want to ignore the stock. Remember, we're looking for reasonably steady growth.

PRICE/EARNINGS RATIOS

Earlier, in the case of Cullinet, I commented that we are trying to avoid very high price/earnings ratios. It's important now to describe in detail what we're looking for with respect to price/earnings ratios. It would be helpful to examine several decades' worth of academic studies involving these key relationships. In summary, *the data going all the way back to the 1930s show conclusively that stocks with low price/earnings ratios outperform stocks with high price/earnings ratios over the long term.* Specifically, then, how can we use the ammunition in our stock-picking method?

Here's how I go about it. I try to avoid the highest P/E ratios. Of course, the absolute level will vary considerably over the years as the market's P/E as a whole drifts higher or lower. The Dow Jones Industrial Average itself reached a ghastly 23 times earnings in 1961, an all-time record, barely beating out the prior mark set in 1929 before the crash. But P/E ratios again soared in 1968 and in 1972. It was not unusual in those years to find many stocks selling at 40 or more times earnings, including quite a number that got as high as 80 to 100 times earnings, truly an absurdity.

At the other end of the spectrum, the Dow Jones P/E ratio was not much over 6 at the 1974 and 1982 bear market bottoms. It wasn't easy at those points to find many stocks with P/E ratios of 20 or more. But whatever the high end of the range, I try to avoid those P/E's. As for, say, Cullinet, at 31 times earnings, the stock may go higher, but that's of no interest to me. What is of interest is an ultrahigh price/earnings ratio, nearly triple that of the market as a whole as of mid-1985. That tells me the situation is much too risky.

If Cullinet's future earnings work out as expected by Wall Street in general, or perhaps better than expected, the stock might do okay. But a disappointment could be devastating. Once P/E's get to ultrahigh levels, there's no room for error. If the growth is expected to be, say, 30% and the earnings come in up 20–25%, the stock might be hit hard. If the growth comes in at, say 10%, the stock could easily be mauled and, if the worst happens, with earnings slumping, a stock with a high P/E could easily fall 70–80%. Thus, stocks with very high P/E's can on occasion do well, but from a risk-reward standpoint they're poison.

Shifting to the opposite end of the field, the academic studies, as previously noted, have shown that very low P/E's perform the best. However, there are a few technical biases with the studies that can call into question some of the results, particularly the fact that companies that went bankrupt were often excluded from the studies, therefore giving the results somewhat of an upward bias.

There are generally two types of stocks that you'll find with extremely low P/E's, say in the 3, 4, or 5 range, as of 1985. The first is the company in extreme financial difficulty. It still has earnings but investors are not willing to put much of a multiple on them because of the danger that the company could go bust. You are not getting a bargain buying a stock at 3 times earnings if its balance sheet is terrible and if the company itself is going to go under in the next year or two. Of course, there is no certainty what will happen. I suggest, though, that if you are going to buy a stock with an extremely low P/E ratio, you first carefully investigate the balance sheet and other financial facts about the firm. I generally ignore this type of stock because it doesn't fit my shotgun-type approach.

The other type of stock with a very low P/E ratio is a firm in an industry suffering from general neglect, probably because of some bad news overhanging the group. For example, in the last year or two, public-utility stocks that have nuclear plant construction under way have sold at very low P/E's because of the risk that construction might be halted or that the companies might run out of funds to finance these ventures. Some current examples include Public Service of New Hampshire, Maine Public Service, and Long Island Lighting. These companies might even be borderline cases for the first category; that is, they could go bankrupt if they run into continued troubles with their nuclear construction.

Other recent examples of stocks with low P/E's include the motors, especially Ford and Chrysler. Chrysler itself did flirt with bankruptcy a few years ago but has made a financial comeback. Ford is a more solid firm, and yet it was carrying a P/E ratio of less than 3 in mid-1985. There's no reasonable prospect of bankruptcy in the case of Ford. Rather, the extremely low P/E is a function of record earnings, which Wall Street does not expect to continue because of the cyclical nature of the auto business and the threat of foreign competition.

Ford would be the type of stock that would mesh perfectly with those academic studies that show that low-P/E stocks perform the best. That's not to say I am recommending Ford. However, a group of stocks similar to Ford, held for a year or two, probably would outperform the market, especially if one's portfolio were reevaluated once or so a year to weed out the stocks that have gone up to higher P/E's and replace them with reasonably solid stocks that have drifted down to low P/E's.

Since my approach emphasizes stable and reasonable growth, I am very unlikely to find an extremely low P/E associated with that. For if a company does have stable and solid growth, that is likely to be recognized at least to some degree, and the P/E ratio is more prone to be in the normal or higher end. Indeed, if I come across a stock with excellent growth that has a very low P/E, I immediately get suspicious. I will check further to see if there is a problem on the balance sheet or if the backlog of orders has dropped off, or if there is some other outstanding negative; there often is. Thus, I usually don't go for the very low P/E's because they generally don't mesh with my approach. However, with caution, there's nothing wrong with using the low-P/E method of investing exclusively.

I also avoid the very-high-P/E stocks. Most of the stocks I select have P/E's near the average for the market or somewhat above it. If the market's average P/E is, say, 10, and I find stocks with better growth and more stable growth than the market as a whole, I would expect that the fair value of these stocks would warrant a higher-than-market P/E, say an arbitrary 14 or 15. If I can find such a stock with a P/E of 11 or 12, other things equal, it would be a bargain. If the P/E were up to, say, 16 or 17, it would be less of a bargain, although if the growth rate were high enough and if the company had a significant competitive advantage, giving the higher probability of stable growth, it still might be worth the price. This is a judgment I base on my experience and instinct.

To make some sense out of what might be a reasonable P/E, you'll have to go back and study the earnings trend for the past several years. Look at the little box in the Lankford chart, for Ennis Business Forms, on page 204. You'll see that for its 1980 fiscal year, earnings were $1.56. They then trended up in the subsequent years to $1.72, $1.80, $2.21, and $2.73. Using my trusty calculator, I find that that works out to a four-year compounded growth rate of 15% per annum. By the way, it is *very* useful if you have a calculator that can easily do compounded rates of return. I find the Hewlett-Packard 12C calculator to be excellent in that respect. A great financial calculator, it's small, easy to carry around, and runs on batteries. Texas Instruments also makes a good one, and there are several other satisfactory ones on the market.

Back to Ennis. A 15% per year growth is not a bad rate. In addition, Ennis's earnings were up every single year, and the latest quarter showed a 23% gain, which is even higher than the longer-term trend. I like that. At a current price of 37½, Ennis's P/E of 13 is somewhat higher than the 10 to 11 P/E for the market as a whole. But that seems very reasonable given Ennis's steady returns over the years. That's why the stock remains on my potential buy list, although I have not yet recommended it, nor is there any guarantee that I ever will. Indeed, it's been on my potential list for at least a year. Two reasons why I am cool on it as of this writing include the gain of only 8% in sales for the quarter, which I previously noted, and the fact that four insiders have sold stock in the past few months.

In the Lankford charts or the other services you might be using, you can see a brief description of the company's business, which in Ennis's case involves the production of business forms. Use Value Line or Standard & Poor's if you want a somewhat more detailed description of the company's business. Ennis's industry is interesting because companies consistently need its products even during business downturns. Sales might ease off somewhat in a recession, but it's not a highly cyclical business nor is it burdened by heavy fixed costs. Moreover, its growth rate is not spectacularly high, which can actually be a blessing in some cases. Ultrahigh rates of growth attract competition, and competition eventually destroys profit margins and the growth rates. If Ennis and the rest of that industry can "plod" along at 15% a year growth, that's quite good, especially if you can buy the stock at roughly a market P/E. If Ennis's P/E were to drift back a couple of points toward the average for all stocks, it could get very attractive.

Let's move on to the last stock in the *Times* listings of company earnings we've been considering, Federated Group. A perusal through the Lankford *Quote OTC* charts shows that Federated earned $1.16 for the twelve months ending February 1985. Earnings were up 6¢ for the first quarter of the 1986 fiscal year (found by subtracting 19¢ of the year-ago quarter from the current 25¢). Simply add that 6¢ incremental increase to the trailing $1.16 figure, and you'll get $1.22 of earnings for the last twelve months. The day that report came out Federated was 22½, giving it a P/E of 18. That's not exactly cheap for a stock that a few years ago lost 7¢ a share, down from a tiny profit in 1980. While earnings have grown since then, the erratic nature of the net in 1980–81 bothers me.

A second dubious factor here is that the quarterly earnings were up 32%, which is fine, but they had jumped more than sixfold in the previous quarter, so I can't be certain whether growth is slowing or not. Federated might prove to be a good stock, but I'd prefer to pass on it for the moment. So, my work on the earnings reports for June 18, 1985 produced only one stock for my potential buy list, Ennis Business Forms, and that has been on the list for quite some time.

I just want to add another thought or two about earnings trends. I try to look for some stability in the direction. If the earnings are increasing at a steady 15% each and every year, that's great. If earnings are up 30% one year, up 5% the next, up 40% the next, down 2% the next, and up 20% the next, the long-run growth rate might be fine but the lack of stability is a negative. Second, reported earnings are not always what they seem. A variety of accounting methods can "smooth" earnings in a direction the company's management desires. If you use my approach, you don't need to dig further to see whether the reported earnings are overstated or understated. In some cases we will buy bummers, but in the long run you will find a number of excellent stocks based on my criteria. If you have the time and inclination to dig further, go right ahead and do so, but it may wind up being a full-time job.

As I said earlier, I do dig further in our limited partnership, with my partner, Joe DiMenna, doing most of the legwork. We also do a more thorough examination in Avatar Associates, our pension money management firm. In this case each of our portfolio managers, Ned Babbit, Andy Kern, and Francine Goldstein, is responsible for several industries, basically splitting the universe into thirds. For example, Ned might follow the oil group. If a stock screens well after examining earnings trends and P/E ratios, it's his job to check financial statements and talk with analysts who follow that particular industry. But you won't generally be in a position to do that, nor is it necessary as long as you stay well diversified and keep following my methods, especially if you use the fail-safes I will describe in chapter 13, on stops.

Another factor you occasionally might deal with is the amount of debt that a company has. The little Standard & Poor's stock guide will give you the figure of long-term debt as well as the short-term debt measured by current assets minus current liabilities. More details would appear in Value Line or Standard & Poor's other publications. If a company has a tremendously high level of debt, the earnings or earnings growth rate would be worth less because of the potential risk. Companies with high amounts of debt have high interest expense, and interest expense is a fixed cost. If business turns down moderately, the high fixed cost can have a very negative effect on earnings. *So be careful not to overpay for companies with high debt. Indeed, you may want to avoid them entirely.*

PRICE ACTION

We've now screened stocks for earnings and sales growth and for P/E ratios. The next screen is right there in your chartbook, the price action of the stock itself. Recall our Four Percent Model using the Value Line stock price index as described in chapter 5. Even though that study was for the market as a whole, it showed rather clearly that one can achieve excellent results—well above the market's rate of return—by buying strength and selling weakness. The same applies to individual stocks. After all, the market is no more than the sum of all the individual stocks.

I have no hard-and-fast rule on price action for stocks themselves. It's more of an art than a science, although if you have access to a computer and a large data bank, you could employ any number of mechanical rules for screening stocks that have been acting well. When I look at a stock chart I am not specifically looking for the types of chart formations that most technicians follow, such as head-and-shoulder tops and bottoms, rising wedges, or triangle formations. I'm not convinced that stuff works. But I do want to find stocks that are acting better than the market. So, the first place to start is with the market's recent action as a whole.

Suppose the market has been very strong of late. Obviously, then I am going to eliminate any stock that hasn't been keeping pace. Stocks wallowing near their lows, or in obvious downtrends on the charts, are definitely out. Stocks that have been rising but in a very lukewarm way, and that perhaps have not broken out above previous peaks of the last year or so, are probably also not good purchase candidates. After all, if the market is strong, say up 15% or 20% in the past six or eight months, then one has to look askance at any stock that has significantly underperformed that pace. My theory is that if a stock really is so good, it should be acting at least as well as the market. If it hasn't been, that's a caution sign in itself.

In a very strong market, the very best kind of action is a clear uptrend on a chart where you see a series of higher highs and higher lows—sort of a stepladder on the way up. The best buying spots are short-term pullbacks of 5% to 10% from a high, provided that the small downmove does not violate a recent prior low. If the market as a whole is moving sideways for some period, then a worthwhile buy candidate might be one that is just breaking out from a long basing period.

For example, suppose that a stock has been trading between $20 and $25 for a year or so, with the market as a whole generally moving sideways. Now suppose that stock suddenly has managed to break above $25. Clearly, it's suddenly doing better than the market, a positive sign. That's the type of stock I like to buy, especially if it dips back a point or two.

Finally, suppose the market has been bombed out, as it was by mid-1982, with the Dow all the way down to 777 from a peak in 1981 of well over 1000. When prices began to firm in mid-August that year, I began to buy aggressively. Hundreds of stocks had been making new lows, but I was not interested in anything appearing in that list. I wanted stocks that had been outperforming the market in recent months. Back in late September of 1981 the market temporarily bottomed after a 200-point drubbing in the summer. Many stocks made their lows then and rallied in the fall. When the general market slowly sank to lower lows in the spring and early summer of 1982, numerous stocks held well above their September 1981 lows. To me that was an excellent sign of relative strength for those issues, and I bought many of them in the summer of '82.

In some cases the stocks had fallen that summer, but they were falling at a slower rate than the market and had held above a prior low. That indicated the possibility that the worst of the selling was over and that strong buying was beginning to develop in those issues. In fact, many of the defensive-type stocks that were benefiting from the disinflation that had begun at that time were acting very well in late 1981 and early 1982, even as the major averages made new lows. Among such groups were department stores, food stocks, and utilities. Interestingly, in the three years following the major market low in 1982, these groups continued to be leaders, outperforming the broad averages during that stretch. Their early strength before the final mid-1982 bottom proved an excellent harbinger.

Recognizing the relationship between trends and the industries that might benefit from them can lead to above-normal returns. That is what will happen from time to time if you do a lot of reading and thinking. In other words, a major economic trend might develop, such as inflation, disinflation, low interest rates, foreign competition, weak dollar, etc., which may lead to excellent long-term investment opportunities in certain industries. In the late 1970s when inflation was running wild, gold stocks, other precious metals, oil stocks, and forest products responded handsomely. Conversely, utilities, airlines, and automobile firms—oil consumers—were hurt.

If you can latch on to a long-term economic trend, you can profit. Of course, too many people recognize a trend much too late, long after it has been discounted in Wall Street. Later in this chapter, when I go through several examples of stocks I picked in the past, I will demonstrate how one selection—the Dreyfus Corp.—was a play on my feeling that disinflation and the return of the individual investor to the financial markets were long-term trends from which that company would gain.

Whether you are right or wrong about the long-term econom-ic trend, it is important to reject picking any stock that violates your perception of the trend. For example, if you felt that the price of oil would continue to sink, it would be psychologically difficult for you to buy oil stocks, even if the outlook for an individual company looked favorable. In that case, you'd be better off ignoring the group, even if you miss out on a rising stock. That's because if you purchase a stock greatly at odds with your own feelings, you're going to be very uncomfortable with it, and you'll probably sell it on the first tiny reaction, or be tempted to get out with a very small profit if it rises a bit. This would defeat the whole purpose in buying stocks, namely, looking for those that may make a big move and letting your profits ride— but cutting your losses short.

Don't buy stocks if you are going to be satisified with 5% or 10% gains. It's not worth the risk, nor is it worth losing any sleep in buying a stock. So you have to stick with those areas that make you more comfortable. From time to time I have totally rejected various industries because of my perception of long-run economic trends. Fortunately, back in late 1981 and early '82 I began to believe in the disinflation theme very early in its process. For the most part, that kept me away from a lot of natural resource stocks and caused me to drift more and more toward defensive-type stocks.

Even so, in August of 1982 I recommended several gold stocks, because I thought that gold was about to embark on a significant bear market rally, which indeed occurred. It's normally a game I wouldn't play, but I also hedged myself by buying numerous utility stocks at the time. Ironically, over the next couple of months, the gold group was the best performer in the entire stock market, while utilities were among the worst. None-theless, the combination of the two still beat the market. A few months later I sold the golds because I knew that they were a bet against the long-term trend.

INSIDER TRADING

The last major variable I use in picking stocks is the degree of insider trading. Insiders are officers and directors or very large stockholders of corporations. My philosophy is that where there is smoke, there is a much greater chance of fire. If insiders are heavily selling stock, no matter what their alleged reasons, I generally take a dim view. It may not matter if one insider is selling stock because he needs some money to pay for his children's tuition. But if seven or eight of them are doing the same thing, it just doesn't have a good aroma. Conversely, if numerous insiders are buying stock at or about the same time, it's usually an excellent sign.

Several academicians have done studies on insider trading and all have found that stocks insiders buy heavily outperform the market. Years ago I wrote an article in *Barron's* (June 21, 1976) that summarized the results of several of these academic studies. The results are shown in table 36, along with the returns I unearthed in my own study at that time. Those first four studies covered the period from 1958 to 1965. The first column after the date shows the market's overall annualized return during the time frames of those various studies. The next column shows the performance of stocks in which there was heavy insider buying as defined by each of the various researchers. Next you'll see the difference between the insider-buy stocks and the market's return, which in each case was considerable. Finally, in the far right column you'll see that the insider-buy stocks did anywhere from 1.67 times as well as the overall market up to 3.98 times as well.

The brief results of my own studies are on the bottom line of the table, covering a twenty-two-month period from 1974 to 1976. In that span the overall market rose at an annualized rate of 15.3%. But stocks that had insider-buy signals returned just about three times that amount, gaining 45.8% per year. I define an insider-buy signal as a case when three or more insiders buy stock within the latest three-month period but when none sells. Conversely, I would define an insider-sell signal as a case when three or more insiders sell within the latest three months and none buys. I prefer unanimity for a signal.

TABLE 36

PERFORMANCE OF INSIDER BUY SIGNALS BASED ON VARIOUS STUDIES

Annualized Rates of Return

Study	Dates	Market	Insider-Buy Signals	Difference vs. Market	Insider Gain Compared With Market Gain
Rogoff	1958	+29.7%	+49.6%	+19.9%	1.67X
Glass	1961-65	+ 9.5%	+21.2%	+11.7%	2.23X
Devere	1960-65	+ 6.1%	+24.3%	+18.2%	3.98X
Jaffe	1962-65	+ 7.3%	+14.7%	+ 7.4%	2.01X
Zweig	1974-76	+15.3%	+45.8%	+30.5%	2.99X

In my 1974 to 1976 study, 104 stocks gave insider-buy signals and I arbitrarily held each for the following six months. Sixty-two and a half percent of them did better than the market, and the cumulative overall gain for these stocks was 99.5%. During that span the Dow Industrials gained only 24.3% and my Zweig Unweighted Price Index was up 29.8%. Conversely, 275 stocks gave insider-sell signals during that time. Only 37.1% did better than the market. In other words, about five-eighths of the insider-buy-signal stocks beat the market, whereas only about three-eighths of the insider-sell-signal stocks did. Those 275 stocks with insider sells rose a meager 3.6% during the nearly two-year study period, grossly underperforming the market averages. A few academic studies in more recent years have confirmed the results of earlier studies.

It can get even more interesting when one combines insiders' trading with P/E ratios, particularly when heavy insider selling is coupled with very high P/E's. Such signs would surely be indicative of stocks to avoid. In a much earlier *Barron's* article (December 17, 1973) I first wrote about insider trading. I listed a table of twenty-three stocks to avoid. This is reproduced here as table 37.

TABLE 37

INSIDER SALES IN HIGH-P/E GLAMOUR STOCKS

Stock	No. of Insiders Selling During 1973	P/E Ratio (11/30/73)
American Home Products	5	33×
Automatic Data Processing	18	36
Avon Products	42	35
Becton, Dickenson	10	26
Burroughs	11	40
Coca-Cola	11	36
Disney Productions	17	26
First National City Corp.	5	21
Gannett Co.	6	24
Hewlett-Packard	10	44
IBM	10	26
Int'l Flavors & Fragrances	7	55
Kerr-McGee	14	39
McDonald's	13	41
Merck	6	36
Minnesota Mining & Mfg.	13	30
Motorola	16	19
Penney, J.C.	14	21
Perkin-Elmer	10	35
Philip Morris	9	20
Procter & Gamble	8	26
Simplicity Pattern	6	37
Xerox	5	34
Total	266	
Average	11.6	32.2×

Note: In all cases at least 3 insiders sold stock since
July, while in no case did any insider buy stock during the past year.

During the previous year, a total of 266 corporate insiders had sold these various stocks and not one single insider bought any. That worked out to an astounding 11.6 sellers on average per stock. Even more incredible, as fast as the insiders were selling these issues, institutional investors were buying them. They drove the price/earnings ratios on this group up to an average of 32. This is based on prices of late November 1973, which reflected a general market decline for most of that year. In other words, these twenty-three stocks had incredibly high P/E ratios even though they had already been drifting lower in price throughout the preceding months.

All of these stocks were part of what was then known as the "nifty fifty" glamour stocks. This was a group of "growth" stocks that the institutions loved to the nth degree. Indeed, there was a greater fool theory in those days that these stocks were "one-decision stocks." The only decision you ever had to make was to buy them. It was assumed that growth would continue ad infinitum and therefore these stocks could only go higher.

This theory was as dumb as any going back to the one that prevailed in 1929 and was promulgated by Professor Irving Fisher. He advocated buying common stocks because company earnings would always go higher and therefore the stocks would go ever upward. That theory was blamed in part for causing the massive speculation in the late twenties that eventually led to the crash. Some people never learn.

The stocks in the table, and a few dozen others, were driven to incredibly absurd P/E ratios. Imagine International Flavors & Fragrances at 55 times earnings, Burroughs at 40 times earnings, or Coca-Cola at 36 times earnings. Some of these stocks continued to exhibit earnings growth in the years that followed, but many of them couldn't even stay on a growth track. Xerox and International Flavors were only two of the issues that soon became former growth stocks. The point, though, as stated earlier, is that when the P/E ratios get too high, the risk becomes unbearable. There is no room for disappointment.

In the year that followed my article, 1974, the stock market as a whole caved in. It was the worst bear market in decades. That alone chilled the speculative enthusiasm for high-P/E stocks. Then, too, there were many earnings disappointments in this group. Even to this day I still can't imagine how institutional investors were willing to pay 32 times or more for the earnings of these stocks when the insiders were simultaneously bailing out en masse.

One year after I listed the stocks in *Barron's* the Dow had fallen by 27%. However, the twenty-three stocks with multiple insider sales and extraordinary P/E ratios plunged some 41.5% on average, or 14.5 percentage points worse than the Dow Industrials.

In sum, it's just as important—perhaps even more important— to screen out the negatives as it is to screen for the positives. If you could just eliminate, say, the worst 10% of all stocks and choose even randomly from the rest, you would beat the market. A good defense will actually serve to help your offense.

If you want to continue that analogy with football, imagine a team with an excellent defense and just an average offense playing a team that is average in both areas. It's probable that the strong defensive team would score more points than usual, for the simple reason that it would keep turning the ball over to its offense in better field position. In addition, the defense, by preventing the other team from scoring frequently, would make it easier for the offensive squad to run their best plays rather than forcing them into catch-up-type offense. So, good defense will help an offense in football. It's the same in the stock market. Just by avoiding the losers, or at least a good chunk of the biggest disasters, it will help you increase your rate of return vis-à-vis the market.

So, as the studies show, you've got about a five-to-three edge by following the insiders. The question then is, where do you get insider trading data? Corporate insiders are required to file their trades with the appropriate stock exchange and with the SEC. The government then publishes a monthly report on insider transactions, but there are much faster ways to get these same data. Vickers Stock Research (P.O. Box 59, Brookside, NJ 07926) is a service that monitors the insider trading by sending representatives directly to the exchanges to examine the filings as soon as they occur. Each week Vickers publishes a list of all significant insider trades. Over the years Vickers has made its data available to me, and I have in turn published two services utilizing their raw data, The Zweig Security Screen and The Zweig Performance Ratings Report (P.O. Box 5345, New York, NY 10150).

In The Security Screen I show the number of insider transactions on both the buy and sell sides for the most recent single-month, three-month, and six-month periods. The Performance Ratings show that number only for three months. I'm not trying to sell my own service, but I do feel that it is the most appropriate source of insider data for the semiprofessional investor. If you want more detailed information on the insider trading, I would also purchase a subscription to the Vickers Stock Research service. There are other insider services around as well.

By the way, both The Zweig Security Screen and The Zweig Performance Ratings rate approximately three thousand stocks, using computer screens and siphoning through most of the same data to which I've just referred in this chapter. By using the computer we can cull through an enormous amount of data in a mechanical fashion, screening for earnings and sales growth, stability of earnings, price/earnings ratios, the debt structure of the corporation, the relative price action of the stock, the insider trades, and a few other variables that are beyond the scope of this book. Even though I have the computer ratings at my fingertips, and even though they work very well, I still prefer to start my stock-picking procedure by going through the daily earnings reports as I've shown here. It's somewhat more laborious but worth the effort.

I've been doing the computer ratings for just over nine years, following the same methodology throughout that span. My associate, Nick Kaiser, has done all the computer programming. I want to show the results of that procedure, not to motivate you to use a computer, but rather to demonstrate that by applying the same approach (even doing it by hand, which I actually prefer), you can produce superior returns. The computer rates stocks on a scale from 1, the best, to 9, the worst. There is not an equal number of stocks in each group. Rather, only the top 5% of all stocks rated are in the No. 1 group. The next 8% are rated 2s, the following 12% are given 3s, and the next 15% are 4s. The middle 20% of all stocks get a neutral rating of 5; then 15% are rated 6, and 12% are rated 7. The next-to-worst 8% of all stocks get an 8 rating, and the bottom 5% of the universe are rated a lowly 9.

Table 38 shows the results for the 110-month period since I first began to do these ratings in May 1976. Stocks are rated monthly, so this methodology assumes (perhaps unrealistically) that you would switch your portfolio each month so as to stay only in stocks rated 1, 2, etc. Obviously, if you did that in the real world you would encounter transaction costs that would tend to get significant. A more realistic approach would be to buy the stocks rated 1, 2, or 3 and hold them either for an arbitrary six months or until they fall to below rank 5. The results won't be as good as shown here, but they would still outperform the market and would hold down transaction costs.

TABLE 38

RESULTS OF ZWEIG PERFORMANCE RATINGS: MAY 1976 to JULY 1985

Performance-Ratings Group	% of Stocks in Group	% Return in 110 Months
1 (best)	5	+915.2
2	8	+658.7
3	12	+526.8
4	15	+404.9
5 (average)	20	+293.8
6	15	+226.3
7	12	+173.2
8	8	+113.0
9 (worst)	5	+116.3
All Stocks:		+311.0%

Source: The Zweig Performance Ratings Report, P.O. Box 5345, N.Y., NY 10150.

Note that the top-rated group appreciated a cumulative 915.2% in just over nine years. That's about three times the average appreciation of all stocks monitored, which was just over 300%. Conversely, had you held a portfolio only on stocks rated 9 that entire time, you would have made only 116.3%, a dismal return compared to the achievement of all stocks, and an amount that would have had a hard time even keeping up with inflation over that span. Note that the returns of each group are in exactly the order projected. That is, group 1 did the best, group 2 did next to best, and so on right down to group 9, which came in in last place. Remember, these results were achieved by using a method very similar to the one I have outlined here. The only major difference is that this was done strictly with a computer rather than by hand, plus some thinking on the part of the investor.

CHAPTER 12

My Own Stock Selections— Why It's Sometimes Right to Sell "Too Soon"

Real-life examples are probably the best way to familiarize you with precisely how my stock-picking method works. So let's look at the case histories of five representative stocks I've recommended in *The Zweig Forecast* in recent years.

DURR-FILLAUER MEDICAL

Durr-Fillauer is a Montgomery, Alabama–based distributor of medical, surgical, hospital, and laboratory supplies in the southeastern part of the United States. I first recommended the stock in my advisory service on May 19, 1980, at a price of 7½ adjusted for subsequent stock splits. I liked the company's stable business and excellent long-term growth rate, but, most of all, it looked dirt cheap at a P/E of only 8. That spring I was also in the process of turning more and more bullish on the market. By the end of May 1980 I had become fully invested in my advisory newsletter for the first time in several years.

My judgment on the stock proved correct, and in mid-1981 I sold Durr-Fillauer in pieces, netting 115% profit on half the position in July 1981 and 95% on the other half in September 1981, for a net gain of 105% at the average selling price of 15⅜. By contrast, the Dow Industrials had gained less than 8% over that span. This is only a forerunner of the buying example I'll describe in more detail, which took place in mid-1982, the second time I bought Durr-Fillauer.

Obviously, because of my good experience on the first purchase, I had a warm spot in my heart for the stock. I kept my eye closely on it as the price dropped by roughly 40% in the bear market of 1981, after I had gotten out of the position. By the summer of 1982 I was ready to do some buying in general, and since Durr-Fillauer's business-and-profit patterns were the types I prefer, I reexamined the stock. I decided to buy it on July 12, 1982, at a price of 8¼, again adjusted for subsequent stock splits. At that point the most recent quarter reported was its first, or March, quarter of 1982, in which earnings had risen 27% while sales were up 36%. Those were not only solid gains, but they were well above the longer-run growth rate for the previous 5¼ years, which showed sales and earnings per share up an annualized 17% over that span. The earnings had risen every year since 1974.

Even at its somewhat depressed price—the stock was still off close to 20% from its previous high—the P/E was 13. That was quite a bit above the 8 level at which I had purchased the stock a couple of years earlier, but it still seemed reasonable in the 1982 market environment. Moreover, I knew that the June quarterly report would be released within days, and I was expecting a decent gain. In fact, when that report appeared, earnings had jumped 38% for the quarter on a 41% increase in sales. That brought the twelve-month total earnings to 70¢ a share, for a P/E ratio of 12 on my $8.25 purchase price. A further check showed no insider activity in Durr-Fillauer in the previous six months.

So, I had found a stock with solid and stable growth, a reasonable P/E, and no insider negatives. Since I was beginning to like the overall stock market, the only remaining question was the price action of the stock itself. Durr-Fillauer had bottomed at around the 6 area in the 1981 bear market, down from a high of almost 10 (again, these prices are adjusted for the subsequent split in 1982).

In the summer of 1981 the Dow Industrials had dropped about 200 points, temporarily bottoming in late September at 824. After a rally in the fall, the market as a whole drifted down in the first half of 1982, making newer lows. The Dow was flirting with the 800 level in July and would eventually bottom in August at 777. But Durr-Fillauer, at 8¼, was more than 30% above its fall 1981 low. The stock was acting much better than the market as a whole. I decided to recommend it.

A month later the stock market bottomed and Durr-Fillauer began to rise. I held the stock throughout the 1982–1983 bull advance, during which Durr-Fillauer rose to more than $20 a share. I kept raising my trailing stop (a method described in chapter 13). I probably should have tightened the stop more than I did, but since I liked the company so much, and because I had done so well in my original purchase, I tried to give it all the room possible. Finally, in August 1983 the stock fell back to 15 and it was stopped out for an 81.8% long-term capital gain. During that thirteen-month holding period the Dow Industrials had gained 44.7%, not much over one-half the gain experienced by Durr-Fillauer.

At the time Durr-Fillauer was sold the P/E ratio was up to 20, and it had actually been above that figure when the stock was at its highs. It had become overvalued, but I tried to hold on as long as I could because the stock market's overall momentum was still positive. But in the summer of '83 the market as a whole began to waver a bit and higher P/E stocks started to give back some of their gains, which led to the sale of Durr-Fillauer.

CACI, INC.

On the same day in July 1982 that I recommended Durr-Fillauer, I also recommended CACI, Inc. CACI provides analytical and computer software techniques to solve managerial and operational problems, primarily for the government. I had had the stock on my potential-purchase list for several months, having spotted CACI's fourth-quarter 1981 earnings report in which net had increased by 135%. In the latest available quarter before my purchase, first quarter 1981, earnings were 98¢ a share versus 45¢ a year earlier, an 118% increase on a sales gain of 71%. That extremely rapid growth was even faster than in a five-year stretch in which annualized earnings increases were a hefty 64%.

Once again I had found a stock where earnings had grown steadily—in this case even spectacularly—and where the recent quarter found growth accelerating above that of the longer-term trend. Once more, I was expecting another good earnings report within a few days after I had picked the stock, and such proved to be the case. Net for the second quarter of 1982 was $1.67 versus 95¢ the previous year, a jump of 76% with sales rising 53%. That was still above the long-term growth rate and brought the previous twelve-month earnings total to $4.26.

Incredibly, CACI's price at the time I purchased it was only 41⅞ (prior to two 3-for-1 splits in the coming year or so). Thus, the P/E ratio was a very moderate 10 despite the enormous growth in earnings. I could find no meaningful insider activity at that time, so once more the final question was that of price action. Here, if anything, the price action was splendid. From its 1981 low, CACI had roughly tripled by this point even though the P/E was still modest. The stock market was drifting lower and CACI was advancing strongly. The only stumbling block to purchase was having the guts to buy a stock that had roughly tripled in the previous year. Many investors refuse to pay up for such stocks, but I actually prefer doing it as long as the earnings growth is there and the P/E is reasonable. It proved to be a good choice.

By September 30 CACI had surged to 61¼ and I decided to take partial profits by selling half the stock for a 46.3% gain. In that span the Dow Industrials had risen by only 8.6%. In retrospect, selling was a mistake, but at the time I wanted to lighten some positions to use the money elsewhere. I also wanted to sell off just enough so that what was left would not be such a temptation to sell. I was determined to let the profits ride on the rest.

The stock then split 3-for-1, reducing my effective original purchase price to $13.96. The new stock moved up spectacularly, and on December 15, 1982, I sold the remaining holdings at $42 on the new stock, equivalent to $126 on the original purchase price only six months earlier. This netted a profit of 200.9% versus an increase of only 20.3% on the Dow.

Once again, in retrospect, I had sold too soon. But the P/E ratio was already up to 24, and I had a few second thoughts on the market as a whole for the short run (there was a small dip before the market took off again in January). The stock I had sold at 42 reached 78 by mid-1983, although, adjusted for a second 3-for-1 split, the final high was about 26. Earnings then went downhill rapidly, and the postsplit CACI stock plunged all the way to $2 a share in 1984. That was the equivalent of $6 on the stock that I had sold "too soon" at $42. I'd like to make a "mistake" like that anytime.

EMULEX CORP.

The bear market bottomed on Thursday, August 12, 1982, at 777 on the Dow. On Friday, August 13, the Dow was up about 11 points in quiet trading, but the advance did not look impressive. That night the Federal Reserve cut the discount rate for the third time in about five weeks, a bullish move, as we've already seen. However, the market had rallied only for a day or so on the previous two cuts and each time had fallen to lower lows. On Monday, August 16, the Dow was up about 11 points in the morning but then reversed and drifted back to close with only a 4-point gain. The action was not that impressive, and it looked as if for the third time in a row that the market would fail to respond for more than a few hours to a discount-rate cut.

However, most of the signs were in place for a bull market. Monetary conditions were bullish, and the Monetary Model we constructed in an earlier chapter was in a maximum bullish position. Sentiment indicators were in truly excellent shape because pessimism was extreme at that point. The only missing link was tape action.

Suddenly, everything turned around. On Tuesday morning, Henry Kaufman, chief economist of Salomon Brothers, forecast that interest rates would fall. No matter that Kaufman had been wrong for months on end, having expected rates to go higher. Wall Street chose to accept this latest prediction. Interest rates had already collapsed about five full percentage points in a handful of weeks, yet investors still weren't convinced that the trend was downward. Kaufman's change of stance was the catalyst to getting Wall Street in general to change its mind about the direction of rates, and that gave folks the courage to buy stocks.

The market put on one of its greatest all-time shows on Tuesday, August 17, with the Dow zooming some 38 points and up-to-down volume jumping to a record 42 to 1 ratio. That one day's action was enough to convince me that the tape—the missing link—had turned convincingly upward. That evening on my telephone hotline, which is part of my *Zweig Forecast* service,

I moved aggressively to buy stocks, including the golds and utilities I mentioned earlier. There was also a growth stock that I recommended that night, Emulex Corp. It was purchased at the next day's average price of $15 (later adjusted to $7.50 for a 2-for-1 split in early 1983).

Emulex designs and manufactures peripheral products for mini and micro computers. Its second-quarter report, out shortly before I recommended the stock, showed earnings up 50% for the quarter, with sales soaring 95%. The prior quarter had also seen a 50% jump in earnings. Emulex had gone public just a year or so earlier and had a brief financial record going back only two years. However, in that span earnings had grown at a 48% annualized rate. True, the firm did not have a long-run track record, but that's often the story with high-tech stocks.

High-tech stocks are riskier than most because competitive conditions change rapidly and today's growth stock can become tomorrow's bankruptcy case. But when it's all systems go for the stock market—and I've rarely seen better overall market conditions than in August of 1982—it's worth getting more aggressive with stock purchases. The fact that Emulex had only a brief corporate life was merely a minor flaw in an otherwise excellent opportunity.

When I recommended it for *The Zweig Forecast*, Emulex's twelve-month earnings were 96¢ (on the basis of shares outstanding prior to two 2-for-1 splits over the next couple of years—which actually made my effective purchase price $3.75 in terms of graph S). At the then price of $15 per share on the original stock, Emulex carried a P/E of 16, a higher P/E than the general market. But for a company growing at roughly 50% in a very bullish stock market environment, it seemed that there was considerable room for earnings to keep growing and for the P/E to expand further. Once again, I detected no significant insider trading in the stock.

As for price action, Emulex had bottomed in the fall of 1981 at 8½. It rallied a bit at year's end, then fell in the spring of 1982 to the same 8½ figure, holding steady at the previous year's low. By the summer, when the Dow and the other major averages were making new lows, Emulex was rising. It had nearly doubled from its low when I bought it, although the overall market was only a few percentage points above its own lows. Obviously, the relative tape action of Emulex was excellent.

By mid-November, three months later, Emulex had more than doubled. I sold half the position at 33⅝, nabbing a 124.2% profit, during which time the Dow had gained only 23.1%. Once again, my strategy was to sell down to the point where I was comfortable in holding the rest.

If you hold too much of a position, you're apt to worry about it excessively and often wind up selling it too soon. By taking partial profits, I found it a heck of a lot more comfortable to keep holding the stock. Remember that the market then was very volatile and a stock like Emulex was bouncing around quite a bit, and I didn't want to be forced to sell out on a small dip. However,

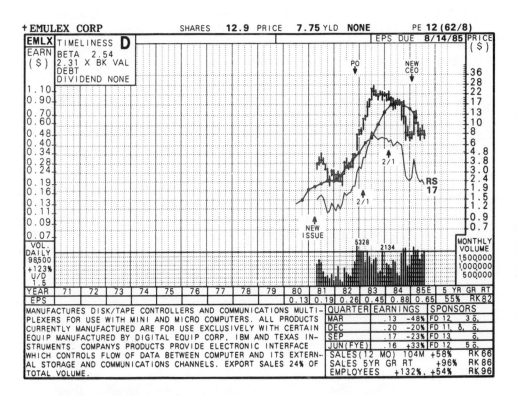

Reprinted Courtesy of Long Term Values, P.O. Box 24933, Los Angeles, Ca. 90024

I needed the gumption to sit with it for the major move, and, by selling a piece of my position, I was able to do that. Then too, Emulex's P/E ratio had already doubled to more than 31, which was not exactly prudent nor for the faint of heart.

Nonetheless, in bull markets, when such a stock gets a head of steam, it can climb to prices that are ridiculously overvalued. I wouldn't risk an entire stake on such a selection, but I had already had a double or more in it. Having then sold half, I had taken out all of the original investment plus some, and was therefore in position to ride a hot stock, even though it was overvalued. I maintained additional protection through the use of trailing stops, which will be described in the next chapter.

Early in 1983 Emulex split 2-for-1, so my adjusted purchase price became 7½. It didn't take long before the split stock was right back to where the presplit stock had been, above $30 a share. On April 4, 1983, I had had enough and sold the split stock at 33¼ (equivalent to 16⅝ on the chart because of still another split later). That sale netted a whopping 343.3% gain in eight months, during which span the Dow Industrials had risen only 35.9%. At the time of the sale, Emulex's P/E was up to an absurd 43. Even in a rip-roaring bull market, that was more than I could tolerate.

Once again, I had sold "too soon." Within three months after I had sold it, Emulex climbed to its all-time high of 27¾, equal to 55½ on the presplit shares I had sold at 33¼. However, by the spring of 1984 Emulex had dipped back to below my sales point. Then, in the second half of 1984, the stock collapsed, dropping to below 7 dollars before a sharp rally in early 1985. Later, in '85, Emulex slipped to another new low at 5¾, down more than 65% from my sales price two years earlier. Thus, as in the case of CACI, I wound up having been right in letting the other guy grab the last few points. Unless he sold soon thereafter, that other guy was left holding the bag.

DREYFUS

I have given you four trades involving three stocks, all of which made a lot of money. But I'm not always right. On July 21,

1983 I recommended the Dreyfus Corp., the big money management firm that runs billions of dollars of mutual funds. For the previous eight consecutive years Dreyfus's earnings had risen. In the latest available quarter, that ending March 31, 1983, Dreyfus had reported a net of 89¢ versus 65¢, a nice gain of 37%. Sales had also been rising in commensurate fashion. Total earnings for the prior twelve months were $6.98. The purchase price for Dreyfus was 68¼, so the P/E ratio was a very reasonable 10, clearly in line with the market's at that time. Yet, Dreyfus had shown superior long-term growth.

However, I made two mistakes in picking Dreyfus at that point—plus I ran into a buzz saw. First, Dreyfus had had three insider sellers in the previous three months. It wasn't a lot, but it was enough to flash a warning sign. My second mistake had nothing to do with Dreyfus. Rather, the market's overall action was starting to get choppy and over the next several months would prove to be no better than flat for most of the blue chips and down for most of the smaller secondary stocks. The third problem was that a few days after I recommended its purchase, Dreyfus reported its second-quarter earnings of only 70¢ versus 75¢ a year ago. I obviously had not expected that drop, and I don't think Wall Street had either. The stock immediately fell several points, and I was stopped out at 61½ for a modest 9.9% loss. In that time the Dow had lost 2.4%.

Despite that bad quarter and three more weaker comparisons that followed, I continued to like Dreyfus. The company's business consists of managing short-term money market funds and longer-term stock and bond funds. I felt that the disinflation, which had begun in 1981 and was well entrenched by 1984, would make financial assets, such as stocks and bonds, the best available long-run investments, far better than real estate, gold, oil, or collectibles, which had been the kings during the late 1970s when inflation ran sky-high. Dreyfus controlled billions of dollars of assets that I felt would appreciate in the long run, plus the kicker that the public would pour in additional assets for Dreyfus to manage as disinflation continued to reign.

In the September quarter of 1984, Dreyfus's earnings got back on track with a net of 85¢ versus 70¢ the prior year, a 21% increase and the first quarterly gain in five attempts. In the fall of 1984 interest rates were starting to come down, and I felt that would increase the profitability of Dreyfus's stock and bond holdings. In addition, changes in pension laws had created individual retirement accounts (IRAs), a vast pool of cash flow in which Dreyfus was gaining a goodly market share. I thought this would help increase long-run results for the firm.

Encouraged by the third-quarter 1984 report on Dreyfus, and much more sanguine about the outlook for the market as a whole, on November 23, 1984, I once again recommended Dreyfus for purchase, at a price of 37⅜. The stock had been split in late 1983 after my first trade, so that its newest recommended price was actually above my previous purchase in 1983, the one that had lost more than 9%. Thus, I had made a mistake once in Dreyfus, and yet here I was coming back in to buy it again at even a slightly higher price. The market, though, little knew nor cared that more than a year earlier I had made a poor trade in stock. All that mattered now were current conditions. Unlike the previous year, market action was considerably better and Dreyfus did not have any meaningful number of insider trades. Moreover, I felt that future quarters would compare very favorably with the more-or-less depressed net results of late 1983 and early 1984.

At my purchase point in November 1984 (by the way, just as the Fed had cut the discount rate), Dreyfus had shown earnings of $3.15 for the prior twelve months. Its P/E ratio was a reasonable 12, especially since earnings were slightly depressed, having declined 7% in 1983, the first such dip in nine years. One small break in the growth rate is clearly forgivable when the company is beginning to show signs of getting back on track—and especially when the outlook for its industry is improving and the P/E remains modest.

Price action for Dreyfus was no problem at that time as the stock was already at its highest price of the year, clearly way outperforming the market as a whole. As I write this in mid-1985, the final result of this second venture into Dreyfus is not yet known. So far, the stock is up to about 68, a new high, or some 82% ahead of its purchase price. I have also raised my protective stop several times, so that by now I am guaranteed a nice profit even if the stock begins to retreat. The two quarterly reports since my purchase have shown increases in net of 22% and 27%

respectively. So, at least to date, I have been right about the growth outlook for this money management company. The P/E is now up to 14, so I do not regard the stock as cheap. But so long as the market behaves, I still feel Dreyfus should outperform it.

MIDLANTIC BANKS

The last example is one of buying a stock that looked extremely cheap. For several years the entire banking group sold at very low P/E ratios, primarily because some of the larger international banks had dubious foreign loans on their books. The middle-sized and smaller regional banks had few such loans and were not vulnerable to them, but they suffered by association anyhow. Also, some of these regional banks had their own problems, particularly in the Southwest, where many banks had loaned heavily to the oil industry, which was coming upon hard times. But in other areas of the country, particularly in the East and Southeast, there were numerous regional banks with excellent earnings trends, small risks of bad loans, and very low P/E ratios. One such example was Midlantic Banks, which I recommended for purchase in *The Zweig Forecast* on August 10, 1984, at 24¼.

On a fully diluted basis (earnings that allow for conversion into stock of all warrants, convertibles, and any outstanding options), Midlantic had reported net for the second quarter of 1984 of 99¢ versus 83¢ a year earlier, a 19% gain. Sales, by the way, are not reported for bank stocks. For the prior four quarters, Midlantic had shown earnings of $3.72, so its P/E was only 6½. Looking backward, I saw Midlantic had shown earnings increases every single year beginning in 1975, when net was 76¢ a share. Thus, in the previous 8½ years, Midlantic's earnings had grown at a very laudable 20% per year. Had Midlantic been a high-tech stock, its P/E ratio would have been three or four times as great, given that long-run 20% growth rate. Because it was a bank, it was generally ignored.

Over the couple of dozen years in which I've been in the stock market, I've seen virtually every industry at one time or another, have its day in the sun. Back in the late fifties and early sixties, the glamour groups included steels, aluminums, chemicals, and public utilities. Can you imagine those stocks today selling at 20 to 30 times earnings? Well, they did back then. I've seen the bowling stocks run wild, mobile homes do the same, and other groups move into the glamour category, such as gambling, gold, restaurants, and aerospace stocks. Each group eventually had its bubble pierced and came back to earth.

In most cases, long before these groups had their big runs, they were regarded as wallflowers. In other words, *today's wallflowers have a chance of becoming tomorrow's glamour stocks, no matter how farfetched it may seem.* My point is that it doesn't matter whether Midlantic is in the banking business or something else. What does matter is that it was able to achieve a 20% annualized growth rate for the better part of the decade, with no down years and with only moderate business risk. When I can buy a stock like that at 6½ times earnings in a fairly decent overall stock market environment, its seems like a very good bet.

At the purchase time Midlantic had had one insider buy stock in the previous three months, with no one selling. That, at the least, was not a negative. As for price action, Midlantic had made a new all-time high, above 24, in early 1984 and then had sold down to 21 and change at midyear. As the market improved that summer, Midlantic moved up to challenge that all-time high when the market as a whole was still below its own former peak. The stock was acting well on both a relative and an absolute basis.

Shortly after I recommended it, Midlantic broke out to another all-time high, above the 26 area. It then consolidated for a couple of months and then ran up above 29 by year's end 1984.

As I am writing this, it's been about a year since Midlantic was recommended, and it's still in the *Zweig Forecast* portfolio. Three quarterly earnings reports have appeared since the purchase price, showing respective earnings increases of 18%, 14%, and 12%. I'm not thrilled about the trend toward somewhat lower growth. However, the economy has been limp and corporate earnings have not done well. Relative to most earnings reports, Midlantic's have not been too bad. The stock has kept moving higher and at this time is up to 39½, showing a profit to date of 63%, while the Dow has risen only 7% in that same time frame. Midlantic's P/E is now up to just about 10, so it's no longer on the bargain counter. However, it's not grossly overvalued either. I've raised the protective stop several times, so even if the price action begins to slide from here, at worst I'll be taken out with a very nice profit. Setting and using stops is an integral part of my market strategy—and you will find complete details on this risk-limiting method in the following chapter.

CHAPTER 13

Stop! How to Manage Your Investments to Minimize Risks and Maximize Profits

s I said before, I'm proud of my record in the stock market. Since the *Hulbert Financial Digest* began to rate most of the investment advisory services in mid-1980, I have not had a down year—and only three other stock advisories out of more than seventy now rated can make the same claim. But I also make my share of mistakes, and it's certain that I'll make more mistakes in the future.

Suppose I make a wrong call on the market as a whole. Or, at the least, let's say out of the dozens of stocks I recommend, some of them head south. What then? The answer is simple: *I use stop points on every single recommendation I make.*

WHAT IS A STOP?

A stop order can be placed directly with a specialist of the New York Stock Exchange through your broker. It tells the specialist to sell your stock "at the market" the moment it hits your stop point, or "trigger price." On over-the-counter stocks, where there is no specialist, you cannot use a stop as such. The same is true on the AMEX, where the stop rules are a bit different and, in my opinion, normally not workable. So, for OTC and AMEX stocks, I suggest using a "mental stop." This means that you or your broker will have to follow the stock in question and, when it hits your mental stop, the broker will have to sell it right away.

Getting back to the NYSE, the stop is automatically triggered when the stock falls to your stop point. You don't have a chance to second-guess yourself, cancel the stop, and then ride the price down because you have gotten stubborn—an often-fatal error. There are some people who don't want the specialist to see their stop order on the assumption that he will let the price slide just enough to trip their stop. That has *not* been my experience. I don't blame the specialist when my stop is hit, only to see the stock rebound. If you have the discipline to follow through with a mental stop, then go ahead and use it. But in most cases, at least for issues on the NYSE, you would be better off giving your stop to the broker. But whatever you do, don't back out of your original plan when prices fall. If so, the whole idea of the stop is ruined.

You'll recall my earlier reference to Jesse Livermore, sometimes regarded as the greatest speculator ever. His words of more than sixty years ago say it all: *"A loss never bothers me after I take it. I forget it overnight. But being wrong—not taking the loss—that is what does damage to the pocketbook and to the soul. Of all the speculative blunders there are few greater than trying to average a losing game. Always sell what shows you a loss and keep what shows you a profit."*

The purpose of a stop is to stay consistent with Jesse Livermore's rules—to let your profits run but to cut your losses short. If you buy a stock at 20 you won't be too badly hurt if you stop yourself out at 17 for a 15% loss. You'll still have the bulk of your capital left. A 20% drop is about as much as I would be willing to take, because that needs a rebound of 25% to hit the break-even point. That is, if a stock drops from 20 to 16, it's down 20%. On a return trip from 16 back to 20, it works out to a 25% increase. That's not necessarily so difficult to achieve.

However, if a stock is slammed for a 50% loss, say from 20 down to 10, you'll need a double to break even. Or, if you allow the situation to get totally out of hand, and you ride a stock down 90% from 20 to 2, you'll need a tenfold increase, or a gain of 900%, before you can get your money back. Such gains are hard to come by. So, it is sheer folly to let losses run wild. Remember: *Your first loss is your best loss!*

Generally I set my stops 10% to 20% below my purchase price. The exact level depends on my own analysis of the stock's trading pattern and the "feel" I've gained from two dozen years of experience in the market. Usually, I will give more room to more volatile stocks, such as high-tech issues, and less room to more conservative stocks, such as utilities. A 10% margin is generally too little for an extremely volatile stock. It's no big deal for a $30 high-tech stock to drop quickly to $27 on a normal correction and then turn and go back up again. A stodgier utility stock, though, doesn't usually do that unless it's about to reverse its major course.

I often try to set a stop point just below a previous low that a stock has made recently. Or perhaps I'll draw a trendline on a chart and set my stop just below the upward-sloping trendline, on

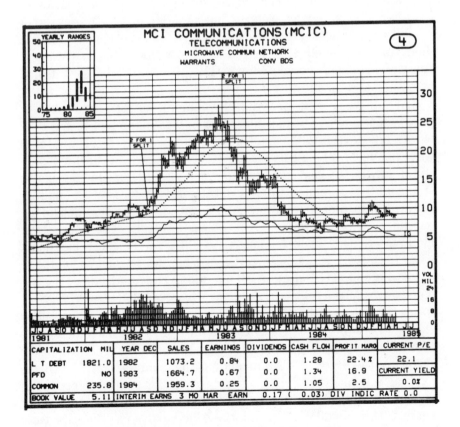

the assumption that if that uptrend were to break, it might lead to a downward reversal in the price. Admittedly, setting stops is an art and not a science. Sometimes I wind up getting stopped right at the bottom eighth on a correction and wishing mightily that I had given myself a bit more room. But other times I'm stopped out as a stock is breaking down from a trading range and, after I take my reasonable loss, I watch as a bystander while the stock plummets.

Graph T (p. 239), on MCI, shows how unlucky one can get at times using stops. I had recommended MCI in late July 1982, just three weeks before the brand-new bull market boomed. My recommended price was 42⅞ and I set a fairly tight stop at 39⅞. I should have given myself a bit more room. As you can see on the graph, MCI backed off for a few weeks, hitting $9, which was made after a couple of 2-for-1 splits. That price was equal to $36 back in 1982. In other words, I was stopped out of MCI in two weeks for a 3-point loss, and the stock backed down about another 4 points. It then turned around and soared to more than $28 on the split stock, which was equal to over 112 on the shares that I had recommended at 42⅞.

What went wrong? Well, my timing on the market was pretty good, since my recommendation was made just a couple of weeks before the August 1982 bottom. And my stock selection was excellent; MCI nearly tripled over the next several months. But I ran into a bad combination of a short-term decline and a stop that was a bit too tight. Consequently, I was taken out just before its spectacular surge. Had I set the stop 17% below my purchase price, I would have enjoyed a very profitable run. However, at that time I felt that would give the stock too much room because I was not so certain about the market's direction.

I could easily find more MCIs among the hundreds of recommendations I have made in the past. However, I can find far more cases where my stops greatly protected my subscribers. For example, when the bull market began to explode in mid-August 1982, I recommended the gold stock ASA at 32¾ (see graph U). Two months later I recommended the sale of ASA at 51½, nabbing a healthy 57.3% profit. In July 1983, near the top of the market, I decided to recommend ASA once again (unwisely going against the disinflation trend described earlier). By this time the stock was 70⅝, and I placed a stop at 64¾. In September

1983, less than two months after I recommended it, ASA hit its stop and I was taken out for an 8.3% loss. By November ASA had nose-dived to 50. Later, after a rally, it worked its way irregularly downward, reaching the 44–45 area several times from 1984 to 1985. Finally, in mid-1985, ASA plunged to 35. Clearly the sale at 64¾ prevented much greater damage.

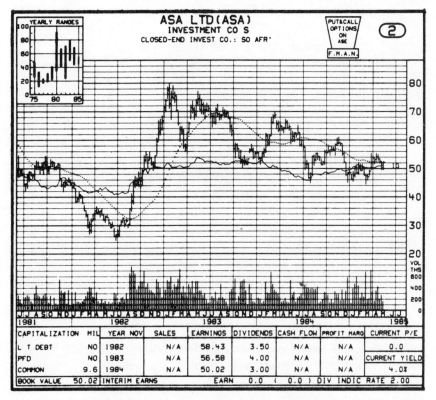

ASA LTD (ASA)
INVESTMENT CO S
CLOSED-END INVEST CO.: SO AFR'

CAPITALIZATION	MIL	YEAR NOV	SALES	EARNINGS	DIVIDENDS	CASH FLOW	PROFIT MARG	CURRENT P/E
L T DEBT	NO	1982	N/A	58.43	3.50	N/A	N/A	0.0
PFD	NO	1983	N/A	56.58	4.00	N/A	N/A	CURRENT YIELD
COMMON	9.6	1984	N/A	50.02	3.00	N/A	N/A	4.0%
BOOK VALUE	50.02	INTERIM EARNS		EARN	0.0	(0.0)	DIV INDIC	RATE 2.00

Chart Courtesy of Trendline, a division of Standard & Poor's Corporation

In September 1983 I recommended an electronics firm, Sanders Associates, at 55⅞ (see graph V, p. 242). Sanders quickly moved up to over 60, and I raised my original stop a couple of points to 53½ (more about trailing stops later). Sanders quickly reversed and fell through my stop point, generating a small 4.3% loss. By March 1984 Sanders had fallen to $35, some 35% below my stop point. Even on a good rally in 1984, Sanders failed to reach

my stop level. From there it was downhill again to $31 in early 1985. Clearly the stop proved useful in this case.

In November 1983 I recommended the purchase of an OTC company called St. Jude Medical at 17⅝ (see graph W). I placed a stop at 14⅞. St. Jude managed a weak rally to a bit over 19 and then fell apart, triggering my stop in February 1984 for a 15.6% loss. By early 1985 the stock was below 7½, down 50% from my stop point. Had I held it that long, I would have needed a double to break even.

Remember, if a stock drops right away—which is about the worst thing that can happen after you purchase it—I'm stopped out with a moderate loss, but I've got most of my money left. This gives me the opportunity to find a better stock. That's right.

A small loss, when realized, becomes an opportunity for profit elsewhere. It gives you the chance to turn a liability into an asset, instead of just sitting there praying that your old stock will come back.

So, when I was stopped out of ASA, Sanders, and St. Jude, I took my moderate losses and had the capital left to redeploy into much more promising situations, and happily so, especially since those three stocks were pummeled after I was stopped. Even in the case of MCI, which soared spectacularly shortly after I was taken out, I at least had most of my money left to use elsewhere. I had bought the MCI on July 21, 1982. I did not buy another stock until August 18, the day after the market began to shoot upward. I bought thirteen stocks on August 18, about as many as

Chart Courtesy of Trendline, a division of Standard & Poor's Corporation

I've ever purchased in one day. Five days later, as the market continued to roll, I recommended the purchase of another six stocks, and three days later I added three more positions. Some of the money used to buy those stocks came from the proceeds of the MCI sale, plus a few other issues in which I had been stopped in July.

One of my purchases on August 18 was an OTC stock in the computer area called Emulex, mentioned in the last chapter (graph S). I paid 15 for it and sold the last of it in April 1983 at the equivalent of 66½ (it had split 2-for-1, so it was 33¼ on the new stock) for a huge 343.3% profit. I don't know exactly what I might have done on August 18 had I not been stopped out of MCI. Certainly, at least one stock I bought that day would not have been purchased. Because Emulex, like MCI, was a volatile, high-tech, OTC stock, it was in some sense a good substitute for MCI. Most of the stocks I recommended that day, including the golds and utilities, were not at all good substitutes. Indeed, Emulex was the only one having those characteristics.

It's a fair probability that I never would have purchased Emulex had I not been stopped out of MCI, and I actually did better in the latter than I would have done at the former, even if I had somehow managed to sell MCI at its exact high in 1983, a most improbable event. Thus, *I never look back when I'm stopped, even if that issue turns around on a dime and soars mightily. Rather, I focus my attention on what to do with the proceeds.* Granted, there aren't many Emulexes to be found, but there's no point in moaning about the fish that got away. One is best off simply trying to hook the next fish.

LOCKING IN PROFITS

As we've seen, the first use of a stop is to protect against losses. If the stock goes down shortly after you buy it, the stop forces you to take a moderate loss while keeping the bulk of your capital intact. The second use of the stop is to lock in profits after the stock has begun to rise, obviously a more pleasant task. The idea is to let your profits ride as the stock keeps rallying. As it continues to climb, you keep raising what is called the "trailing stop." Finally, at some point the market will turn down, and you'll be taken out with your trailing stop, often showing big profits.

Let's take a theoretical example. You purchase XYZ at $20 a share, setting a protective stop at $17, 15% below the purchase price. Happily, your stock begins to rise. There is no precise point at which to raise the trailing stop; it's an art. If I'm still very positive on the market as a whole, I'll be a bit slower in raising the trailing stop. If general market conditions begin to deteriorate, I am quicker to lift the trailing stop. Occasionally, the stock might rally only a fraction and I'll still raise the trailing stop because of concern over market conditions. Once in a while I may even become cautious because of something negative about that particular stock. It may not be quite enough to cause me to sell it outright, but for added protection I will tighten the initial stop.

Another factor to consider is the trading behavior of the stock itself. As noted in chapter 11, I favor buying stocks that are generally strong to begin with. Suppose the XYZ was in an uptrend when we purchased it at $20. Suppose that earlier the stock had made a couple of minor downticks from $21 to $20, our purchase point, but had risen from $15 prior to that. Let's also assume that the stock went no lower than about 19½ on the small reaction after we originally bought it. Now let's say that XYZ climbs to about $24 a share, giving us a 20% paper profit. This is about the time we should think of raising the stop. One logical spot to put our trailing stop would be around the 19½ area, the low of the previous minor reaction. If all is well with the stock, it ought not break below that point. So a logical stop might be 19⅜, a fraction below the previous minor low.

Another possible way to determine where to place the trailing stop is to construct an upward trendline connecting the last several low points of the stock. Let's assume that the upward-sloping trendline currently is at about $20 a share. So an alternative logical point for placing the stop is a fraction below that upward-sloping trend, at about 19⅞ or 19¾.

Sometimes there is no logical place to put the stop, especially in the case of a breakaway stock. Suppose XYZ suddenly zooms to $30, having never gone higher than the low 20s in its history. At the new price, there's a very limited trading pattern to analyze. There are no minor bottoms below which to place the trailing stop, and the upward-sloping trendline is so steep as to be useless for this task. This is where it becomes totally an art.

I'll generally attempt at least to raise the stop above my purchase price in order to make sure I don't lose any money. However, at $30 XYZ would have a 50% profit, and that's far too much of a gain to lose all of it back.

I would then try to determine how much of a percentage loss would be a "reasonable" reaction without doing any major technical damage to the stock. Suppose I estimated that a 25% reaction, while harsh, might be within reason for a volatile stock. That implies a 7½-point drop to the 22½ zone. So I might set my stop at, say, 22¼. That would lock in a gain of at least 12½% on my purchase price and give me more than enough room to handle a relatively normal reaction. Of course, I wouldn't ordinarily allow as much room as a 25% drop unless I were still very bullish on both the stock and the market as a whole.

Let's assume that we raise the trailing stop to 22¼. Now the stock begins to back off the 30 level down to 27. From here it rallies, breaking out to a new high and reaching 32. At this point the drop from 32 to our trailing stop at 22¼ is far too much, so it's time to raise the stop again. At least here we have a logical point to which to raise our trailing stop, namely the 27 zone, which marked the low of the last minor decline. Giving the stock a little bit of extra room, we might raise our stop to, say, 26½. This is about 17% under the current 32 price and 32½% above our purchase price, locking in a very nice profit.

Now suppose XYZ begins to falter and eventually breaks down and triggers our stop. We're out, but we've taken a 32½% profit and we haven't given up an extreme amount from the peak. We've protected ourselves by, first, putting in a protective stop at 17, 15% below the purchase price. Next, we raised our protective stop to just under the purchase price at 19¾ when XYZ began to move upward. Third, as the stock continued to climb, we raised our protective stop to 22¼, locking in better than a 12% profit. Fourth, as the stock advanced further, we raised our protective stop one more time, to 26½, locking in our final profit of 32½%. It would have been nice if our theoretical stock had kept on climbing, and if it had, we would have kept raising the protective stop. But all good things come to an end, and the final result, a 32½% profit, is certainly nothing to be upset about.

I suggest raising stops to points that will make you most comfortable, and you are the only one who can choose those levels for yourself. If your protective stop is 25% below current prices, you may find that that's far too low for you to feel relaxed about. Certainly, it's not pleasant to see a stock drop a whopping 25% before you sell. On the other hand, if you raise your protective stop to, say, 5% or 6% below the current price, it would be very easy to have it tripped on just a minor reaction.

The main idea is to make the best guess you can about what an ordinary reaction in the price would be, as opposed to a drop commensurate with bad news or lower expectations for the company—or perhaps more negative general stock market conditions. You're trying to separate the random and normal short-term sell-offs from the nonrandom and abnormal sell-offs inspired by more negative conditions. No one can do this correctly all the time, but with reasonable judgment you can stay ahead of the game by judiciously setting both the protective and the trailing stops.

Here are a couple of actual examples where I used trailing stops. The first is U.S. Air, a stock I recommended in *The Zweig Forecast* on August 24, 1982. The market was in the early days of its strong bull run and U.S. Air had just broken above the previous minor high of around 17¾. My purchase price was 18½. At that time I put in a protective stop at 15¾. As you can see from graph X (p. 248), the last minor low was about 14¼, which might have been a more natural protective stop point. However, 14¼ would have represented a loss of 23%, which I felt was too large. I decided to use the 15¾ price as a compromise. It was, however, about half a point below the trading high set in the spring of 1982, which I thought would offer reasonable support.

U.S. Air surged to 21 and then retreated to about 17¾. In that initial jump I raised the protective stop one point to 16¾, which was about one point below the previous trading high at 17¾. That 17¾ region proved to be the support point in early October, after which U.S. Air and the whole market began to surge once again.

As the stock rose I lifted the stop to 17¾, and then, as the stock shot up to 25 in October, I raised the trailing stop to 19¾. That locked in a gain of about 7%, or 1¼ points above my purchase price. I felt that at 19¾ it gave me more than five points, or around 20%, of downside on a normal reaction. Also, it was 1¼ points below the last rally high, which seemed reason-

Chart Courtesy of Trendline, a division of Standard & Poor's Corporation

able. In fact, I might even have set the stop slightly higher, at, say, 20½, which I did rather quickly when the stock rallied about another point.

As U.S. Air began to climb even further, reaching the 28 area, I advanced the trailing stop to 22¼ and then in November to 23¼. No sooner had I done that than U.S. Air broke above 30, prompting me to raise the stop once more, to 25¼. It was rising so quickly that it was difficult to find the most reasonable points to place the trailing stops. But I didn't want to lose more than 20%–25% or so back from the top at that time. I kept the stop at 25¼ for a couple of months, during which the stock reached 36.

I could have raised the stop again, but I decided not to do so because I felt that a normal reaction could take me out. Normal, in that case, would have been an enormous reaction because the stock had more than doubled in just a few months. Sure enough, in January U.S. Air was hit all the way down to 26, a 10-point decline from the top. Because my stop was at 25¼ I was fortunate not to have been taken out. Quickly, U.S. Air turned around and raced toward the 36 level again. At that point I felt it should not drop back below the 26 area again, since it had already undertaken its major correction and the stock market as a whole was off and running toward new highs.

So in January I raised the stop to 26¼, with an increase in February to 27¾. The next reaction carried down to 29½, again failing to take me out. I didn't touch the stop again until May 1983, by which time U.S. Air had finally managed to break above the 36 zone. As it ran to almost 40, I raised my stop to 29⅝ in May, and again, to 30¾, in June.

In all I had raised the stop eleven times after first having set it at 15¾. With 20/20 hindsight, perhaps I should have raised the stop somewhat more. It's easy to say after the fact, but somewhere around the 34 level the upward trend was broken, and just below 33 the stock dropped under its last minor trough. With the comfort of hindsight, I would estimate I should have raised the stop again, perhaps to 32¾, but I opted to leave my stop at 30¾, namely because the stock was extraordinarily volatile. Finally, on August 16, 1983 I was stopped at 30¾, nailing down a gain of 66.2% in just under one year.

The main regret is that I was only a week or so away from establishing a long-term capital gain (since that time the holding period for long-term capital gains has been reduced to six months and one day). Actually, that is why I left my stop at 30¾ rather than 32¾, figuring that I was so close to the long-term gain that I was willing to sacrifice a couple of extra points to have room to make it. Unfortunately, I was stopped shortly before I achieved that objective.

The stock immediately dropped toward the 26 area, and it managed to have a rally in the fourth quarter of 1983 that finally carried U.S. Air back to 35 in early 1984. But after that it was downhill to $22 a share in mid-1984. That was nearly 29% below where I had been taken out with the trailing stop, enough of a decline to make me feel rather good about having sold the stock about a year earlier.

Let's try one more example. In August 1984, a sharp market rally began, prompting me to recommend, among others, an OTC issue called First Data Resources (ticker symbol FDRI), a company involved in the data-processing field. The purchase price was 15, and the initial protective stop was set at 13¼. You can see on graph Y that First Data Resources fit my criteria of a stock acting well, because at that point it was breaking to a new high. The earnings were also excellent. At 13¼ my protective stop was only 11.7% below the purchase price, somewhat on the tight side. However, I wasn't a roaring bull on the market then, and I didn't want to take much of a loss in case prices turned down. The 13¼ stop was a hair below the previous minor reaction low in June.

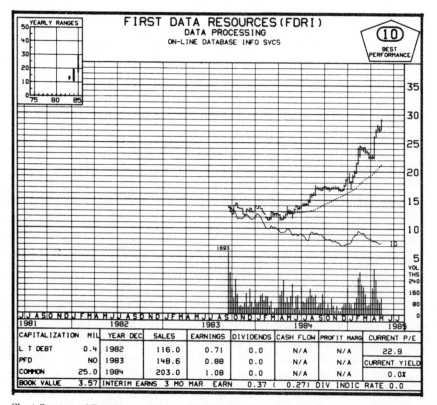

Chart Courtesy of Trendline, a division of Standard & Poor's Corporation

First Data Resources immediately rallied to the 16 area, and I followed suit by raising the protective stop to 14. It had traded between 14 and 14½ for a few weeks during July without going below 14, so I figured that if the stock and the market remained in a positive trend, there would be no valid excuse to break below 14. In September, First Data Resources climbed to 17½, and I elected to raise my stop to 15½. Once again, this was a rather tight stop. However, it enabled me to lock in a half-point profit, or about 3%. The market as a whole had stopped going up, and I was, at best, neutral on the trend at that time; hence, the continuance of the tight stop. (Later that fall I would turn bullish.) The 15½ point was also used because it was just below the bottom of a tiny trading range in which the stock had traveled in August, after the original breakout.

I could have gone to sleep for a few months after that as far as FDRI was concerned. Finally, in the last couple of weeks of 1984, FDRI began to break out, making a new high at 18 and continuing to climb to about 19¾ in early January. I quickly raised my stop to 16¾, roughly the bottom of the trading range since September. Once again, I deemed that there would be no sound reason for the stock's dropping below that point if it were truly in a major uptrend. I really cut it close that time, but luck was on my side. FDRI dropped to exactly 17. I was a scant quarter point away from having been stopped. But the stock market as a whole turned around mightily in the second week of January and took off like a shot, with FDRI following suit.

By February, FDRI was above 24 and I had raised my trailing stop to 18 and then to 19. Nineteen was still a good fraction below the minor trading peak in January, and I felt that FDRI would not break below that point unless something serious was brewing. The stock retreated to just under 22½ in late March and early April, still comfortably above my trailing stop at 19. Even if I had been taken out, I would have shown a 4-point profit, or some 26.7%.

In mid-April FDRI once again began to rally, breaking through a new high above 25. That prompted me to raise my trailing stop once again, to 21¾. This was about half a point below the reaction low set in March and April. No sooner had I raised my stop than FDRI shot ahead to over 27. So, once again I faced the pleasant task of raising the protective stop, this time to

22¾. I did this because I didn't feel like giving up as much as 20% should the stock decline from the 27 area, which would have been the case with the previous stop at 21¾. Also, a rough upward trendline drawn between the last important lows, at 17 and at 22½, showed the trendline cutting through at somewhat above my 22¾ stop. Recall, it's often a reasonable idea to set your stop slightly below an upward-sloping trendline.

As this is being written (there's quite a lead time between preparing a manuscript and the time a book hits the bookstores), FDRI is trading right at its high of 29½. I still have my stop in at 22¾, which is about 23% below the peak. At the moment I'm willing to give it that much room because market conditions look quite favorable. However, if it moves up just a little bit more, I will probably raise the stop to somewhere near the 24 area, just a bit below the previous minor peak in February and more in tune with the upward-sloping trendline. A stop at 24 would be about 19% under the 29½ price. In fact, it sounds like such a good idea as I'm writing this, that I probably will undertake doing that within the next few days.

At this point FDRI is just a half a point away from producing a double. I have no idea how much higher this stock can go. Its P/E ratio is already about 25, which is on the high side. However, the earnings trend is excellent and so is the tape action. Mix in the market here, and I would prefer staying with this stock. Also, as I write this, I'm beginning to favor the secondary growth stocks once again, a category to which First Data Resources obviously belongs.

Assuming I do raise my stop to around 24, I will have locked in a gain of 60% (this time, under the new tax rules, a long-term capital gain since it has been held for more than six months), and I will still have a chance for additional profits if the stock keeps climbing. I have raised the stop eight times since setting the initial one, and to date the action has served me well. If the stock continues to boom, I might sell it outright if I feel the time is ripe. However, I have a general distaste for selling stocks that are exceptionally strong, because more often than not they continue to stay strong.

In that case I will just raise the protective stop and probably wind up getting stopped out of it on a reaction at some point. If that sale winds up at the exact bottom eighth of a minor reaction, and the stock turns and soars mightily afterward, I'll just shrug it off and go on to the next issue with the capital raised from that sale. There is no looking back. Remember, U.S. Air dropped considerably after I was taken out with a trailing stop, nailing a nice profit in the process.

I can also recall numerous stocks in the past on which either protective stops or trailing stops prevented disaster later on. It hurts when you're stopped right near the bottom of a minor reaction, but you have to make a finite decision at some point. Occasionally, I miss getting taken out by a fraction, as I did in FDRI when it retreated to 17 on a minor dip and my stop point was 16¾. So I had an element of luck then, and perhaps the next time I won't be as lucky. *However, I'll always continue to use stops. In the long run they enable me to cut my losses to reasonable size and to let my profits run. I can't think of anything more important in managing money.**

---

*Between the time this was written and my final proofing of the manuscript, First Data Resources was taken over by American Express for $38.25 a share in cash. I advised my *Zweig Forecast* subscribers to tender their stock, establishing a long-term capital gain of 155%. The fortuitous takeover made my last stop point academic.

C H A P T E R   1 4

Selling Short—
It's Not Un-American

No discussion about making money in the stock market would be complete without some attention to short selling, a subject that many traders do not truly understand. The idea in short selling is simple—you're betting that a certain stock will go down. So you sell it now and hope you can buy it back later at a lower price. When you think about it, *this is similar to any transaction where you try to buy at a lower price than you sell. The only difference in this case is just that you're selling first.*

Technically, when you sell short you borrow the securities from a brokerage house and sell them in the market. You owe the broker these securities. For collateral, you deposit a certain amount of required cash with that broker. Since he knows that there's enough money to repurchase the securities if necessary, there is no time limit. Don't be concerned about that old saying, "He who sells what isn't his'n must buy it back or go to prison." But, sooner or later, all shorts are covered or bought back.

There are at least two good reasons for selling short. If you think it's a bear market or that a particular stock is on the skids, you can garner good profits by selling short. You may also want to sell short to hedge your portfolio. Let's say you have a $100,000 portfolio. You think the market will weaken over the next six months but you don't want to disturb some long-term holdings, perhaps for tax reasons. What you can do is sell short other stocks as a hedge. For example, you own some General Motors on which you're hoping for a long-term gain. In the short run, you might want to sell short Ford to protect yourself. So for either speculating or hedging, short selling can be very useful.

I personally like to sell short and frequently feel more comfortable on the short side of the market than on the long. But short selling has a bad rap. The average person has a tremendous hang-up about selling short. I don't know why but it exists. In no particular order, here are some of the perceived negatives about short selling, none of which is true.

The first misconception is that short selling is un-American. Somehow it just doesn't seem like apple pie and the flag to sell short. People perceive it as a bet against the country and that's just wrong. If you sell short General Motors or AT&T, you're not betting against the United States. All you're saying is that at times these stocks may be overvalued. If the stock is worth $50 and it's selling for $70 or $80, there's a good chance it may recede to $50 or even $40, especially if it's a bear market. There's nothing unethical about that appraisal. It's just reality—the stock may go down.

Sometimes you may sell a stock short when you feel that the company will go bankrupt. That's not un-American either. There are thousands and thousands of bankruptcies each year in the U.S. Your selling short is not going to cause any company to go under. All you're doing is wagering in the stock market that a firm is in trouble. Even if it doesn't go bust, it may have poor earnings and the stock may decline. *If you profit from your judgment, it's not different in principle from profiting on the long side when you anticipate that a company's earnings will increase.*

Also, selling short is a very common business practice outside the stock market. They just don't call it selling short. For example, you go to a car dealer to buy a Chevrolet and you want it with fancy red paint, a stereo, and an automatic seatwarmer. You order all these extras and the dealer says, "I don't have such a car in stock, so I'll have to order it for you." You say, "Okay, that's fine. Order it." He says, "I'll have the car in a month. Pay me a deposit now. We'll order the car and deliver it to you." You agree. What's happened is that the dealer has sold short a car. He has actually sold you something before he's bought it from the factory.

The second rap on selling short is the belief that your profits are limited and your losses unlimited—and that is absolute nonsense. For example, there is a misconception that if you were to sell short a $50 stock, the most you could earn is $50, or 100% on your investment, if the company were to go bankrupt. Conversely, people believe that if you guess wrong there is no theoretical limit to how much you can lose. The stock could go to 1000, in which case you're out twentyfold on your money. Such thinking is faulty to say the least.

In the first place, when you sell short you put up collateral with a broker, which can be in the form of Treasury bills if you want to continue earning interest on the money. The minimum collateral is 50% of the transaction. So, if you were to sell short 100 shares of a $50 stock, that's $5,000, and you'd have to put up at least $2,500 in collateral.

To simplify it, let's say you put up the whole amount. You place $5,000 in T-bills with a broker. If that stock were to go up, he would eventually call you for more money. By the time the stock rose to $80, you would have a $3,000 loss. Your equity would be down to $2,000. Before that point, the broker would have requested more collateral. If you didn't put it up, he would cover the sale by buying the stock and you would be out.

The only way you can lose an infinite amount is to keep advancing more and more money, which is like pyramiding your loss. *Remember the golden rule, "The trend is your friend. Don't fight the tape."* If you have a loss like that, get out. Nobody's holding a gun to your head for more money. Only a fool would keep putting up money on a losing short sale like that.

On the brighter side, your profit potential in a short sale is not limited to 100% profit. It is virtually unlimited. For example, you short 100 shares at $50 and the stock falls to $25. That's a $2,500 profit for you. If you started with $5,000 in equity, your total equity in the account is now $7,500. At this point the stock is trading at $25, which is $2,500 per 100 shares. To maintain 100% equity behind your position, you only need $2,500 in the account.

You then pyramid (without using margin as such), selling short an additional 200 shares. You now have 300 shares short, which would require the $7,500 backing. If that stock were to go to zero, you'd make an additional $7,500 in profit. So your total profit would be $10,000 on a $5,000 investment, which is 200 percent.

But it doesn't have to stop there. Suppose the stock then drops from $25 to $10. Now you have 300 shares of a $10 stock. The total capital you need in the account without margin is $3,000. Remember, you have $7,500 in capital. On the drop from $25 to $10 you've made 15 points, or $1,500 per hundred shares, which is $4,500 in profit added to your $7,500 of equity. That gives you $12,000 of equity when the stock is at 10. You're only short 300 shares. You could then short another 900 shares at $10 without putting up any more money or without using margin.

Let's say you did that. Now, at $10 you're short 1200 shares. What you're doing is following the tape. You're shorting more as the stock drops. Now suppose the company goes bankrupt. The stock falls from $10 to zero. You've made $12,000 on the drop, but you had an additional $12,000 in the account when the stock was $10. So your total ending equity is $24,000 when the stock is at zero. Since you started at $5,000, you have made almost a five-fold profit. If you want to, you can pyramid a lot more on the way down than in the example. You could short more at $5 or at any other price. So your profit on the downside is virtually unlimited.

Remember, if the stock goes down and you don't short any more, you have excess equity in the account. If a $50 stock falls to $25, you've got $7,500 of equity in the account. Since you need only $2,500, you could take out the extra $5,000 and earn interest on it or do something else with it.

On the other hand, if you are on the long side and the stock goes from $50 to $100, you can't pull any money out unless you go on margin. Therefore, on the upside you are always pyramiding, because you have to let your money ride all the time. On the short side, to be fully invested you actually have to keep shorting more and more as the stock goes down. People don't think of that for some reason.

Many investors believe it's risky to short more on the way down. It really isn't if you know what you're doing. If the company is going to go broke, it doesn't really matter where you short. You'd make just as much money shorting at $5 as you could at $25. Stocks that are already down from $100 to $10 are still pretty good shorts if the stock is going lower. If the stock eventually dips to $2, you can make 80% by shorting at 10, even without pyramiding. If you short it at $100, you'd make 98%. Returns of 80% and 98% are not all that different.

That's one reason I find shorting very reasonable. If you're willing to let your money ride, you can make far more than 100% without even using margin. Your loss is not unlimited. The only way it becomes unlimited is if you're crazy enough to throw more money away in a losing cause. Yes, short selling has a bad rap.

There is a third negative on short selling that *is* real. After the crash in 1929, the government had to blame somebody. The cause did not rest with the short sellers, but they were a vulnerable target. Attributing the market collapse to the fact that some people sold short, the government decided to make short selling more difficult. That's why they imposed an uptick requirement. That means that if you're going to sell short, you have to sell at a price higher than the previous price for listed stocks. That makes it a little harder to get off the short sale, but it doesn't preclude it.

Additionally, the tax people discriminate against short selling. Even if you hold the short position for more than six months you can never get a long-term capital gain on it. No matter how long you hold the short sale, it will always be considered a short-term gain or loss. However, the alternative might be worse, such as bear market losses or a bear market without your participating on the downside.

Another plus about short selling is that not many people do it. So you have the field relatively to yourself as opposed to participating on the long side.

I also find that negative research on a company is usually superior to positive research. An extensive study covering several years of market activity disclosed that following buy recommendations of brokerage houses was really no better than choosing at random. In other words, on buy recommendations you could do just as well by throwing darts at the stock market page. Sell recommendations are a different story. About three-quarters of them underperformed the market. That is, they went down more than the market. Partly because sell recommendations are so rare, they tend to be better.

Based on personal experience, it's easier to ferret out negative information. If a company has taken advantage of permissible accounting rules and has overstated earnings, that will catch up with it eventually. Or if a company has a fundamental problem, such as inventory accumulation in the face of declining orders, that will surface sooner or later. Since it's already in the works, the bad news will get out and the stock will probably decline. If you're betting on the long side, frequently you're depending on a prediction that may not work out.

For example, XYZ has a terrific product and forecasters estimate that sales and earnings should grow 20% a year for the next five years. All too often, unexpected competition appears or the economy turns down, and the earnings don't climb as antici- pated. It's harder for a story on the long side to work out as well as one on the short side. Once the bad news is in the can, it's there and you can't get rid of it. Eventually the stock should get hit. That's why I think playing the short side is easier than the long side. Of course, short selling in the wrong market can kill you. You don't want to sell short in a bull market unless you are hedging something.

I happen to feel comfortable with short selling, a practice I think is terribly misunderstood, and have written this chapter to clear up some of the misconceptions about this investment strate- gy. *However, at this point I am not recommending that the average investor engage in short selling. I consider it a supplemen- tal strategy for the really sophisticated investor.* Perhaps if I write a second book and decide to get a little more complicated, I'll go into short selling in greater depth.

CHAPTER 15

Questions and Answers on Investing

Why *should people with money in certificates of deposit, Treasury bills, or money market funds consider investing in stocks at this time?*

From 1966 to 1982, we were in a long-term bear market. The Dow Jones Industrial Average dropped from roughly 1000 to under 800 in about sixteen years while the inflation rate just about tripled. Inflation-adjusted, the Dow slid from about 1000 to, let's say, 250! As "real," or inflation-adjusted, prices eroded, the public got turned off and was a seller of stocks—rightfully so, I might add. With other vehicles available at higher yields, a whole generation of investors has not put much of its money into the stock market.

Now, however, conditions have changed from the inflationary era of the sixties and seventies to the relatively stabilized environment of the eighties. People with money in CDs, Treasury instruments, and money market funds will discover that their rollover rate is not nearly as appealing as it had been. As stocks become more attractive, investors will return to the market in increasing numbers. Real estate, collectibles, and gold took turns as kingpins in recent years, but I don't expect these areas to do as well as stocks or bonds in the eighties and possibly even the nineties.

Do well-informed individual investors have any advantages over large institutional investors?

Yes. I think that an individual investor, well informed, can beat the pants off institutions because he has tremendous flexibility. If you are running, say, $50,000, your money isn't going to affect the market. An institution with several billion dollars is like a battleship. It's very hard to maneuver. You can't trade. You're limited in what you can do. You can't buy meaningful positions in small stocks when you're that large because you'll wind up owning the whole company. The little guy might find an over-the-counter stock that trades five thousand shares a day and is a $10 stock. He can buy a couple of thousand shares or even a couple of hundred shares, which could be meaningful. Simply by being more maneuverable, the little guy has a tremendous advantage over institutions.

Are common stocks still a good inflation hedge?

I'm not sure that common stocks were ever a good inflation hedge. Studies have shown that stocks do best during periods of relative price stability. The worst performance for stock prices accompanied extreme deflation during the bear markets of 1920 and the early and late 1930s. The next-worst periods for stocks came during periods when inflation rates reached 8% or 9% or higher.

Investors should consider "real" returns in the stock market rather than nominal returns. If inflation rises 10% during a year and the stock market stays even, you actually lose the equivalent of 10% of your purchasing power. In other words, your dollar would only buy 91 cents' worth of goods at the end of the year (100 is 10% greater than 91).

Of course, some stocks tend to do well during periods of inflation. These include holdings in extractive industries, such as gold, silver, copper, and oil, as well as timber. The prices of these commodities generally rise faster than their costs, increasing profits and making the stocks more attractive.

Most other industries suffer during times of inflation. Utilities, for example, have dramatically increased fuel costs and don't have the latitude to raise prices proportionately. Airlines also have a problem with fuel prices. Companies heavily dependent on raw materials and labor find their profits squeezed. The total result is that the market usually does poorly during a heavily inflationary period.

One reason most people have misconceptions about the performance of stocks during inflationary periods is that they compare stock values today with those of, say, fifty years ago and find they have surpassed the inflation rate. That's faulty logic because, during the subperiods within that fifty-year span, the markets did extremely well during times of price stability and very badly during high inflation. Generally speaking, it's a myth that stocks provide a good inflation hedge.

How much money do I need to start investing in the stock market?

You don't need a lot of money, but if you have a small amount—$500 or $1000 or even up to $5000—I suggest that you buy no-load mutual funds rather than stocks. These are the funds that charge no fee for buying or selling the fund. If you try to trade stocks with less than $5000, the broker's commissions would be relatively high because you'd be buying in small quantities, and your diversification would be limited because you couldn't buy very many stocks. So you're better off with no-load mutual funds.

Which news and information sources do I need if I want to play the market in a fairly serious way?

First, you need one good daily source of general information. Three valuable sources are the financial section of *The New York Times* (from which I get a lot of the data I track), *The Wall Street Journal*, and the new *Investor's Daily*. Since most local papers around the country don't have really adequate financial sections, one of the three above is a must.

For overall data, my most indispensable publication is *Barron's*. You can subscribe, but I buy it at the newsstand on Saturday morning. *Barron's* is a great source of information of every description, and there really isn't any newspaper or magazine that is a substitute.

When it comes to specific investment advice, there is a great deal of competition and I would not rely entirely on any one source. From time to time, you may want to consult reference services like Standard & Poor's, Moody's, or Value Line. Then there are the stock market newsletters, including my own *Zweig Forecast*. You might even want to read some of the research from brokerage firms—at your own peril. Material from brokers varies from interesting to undistinguished. If you want, you can read an incredible amount of material. I try to limit what I read, otherwise it gets out of hand. However, I do spend a lot of time with statistics and other data from government publications and elsewhere that the general investor would not require.

How should I go about building a modest portfolio for, say, $20,000?

First, you should diversify. When I say diversify, I not only mean with several stocks, but with stocks in different industries. That old adage about not putting all your eggs into one basket really applies to the stock market. It's too risky. The worst thing in the world is to win the battle and lose the war, the battle being the direction of the market.

Let's suppose that you turn bullish and the market does indeed go up—but you have put all your money into one stock and it drops. You don't want that to happen, so you try to diversify. However, you don't want to buy too many stocks, either. The average investor should try to get in the zone of five to eight stocks. With five stocks, you're talking about $4000 apiece, which may be enough depending on the price of the stock. To get a much better break on commissions, try to buy two hundred shares of a stock rather than a hundred, where possible. If you're dealing in $15 or $20 stocks you can do it. If you buy a $50 or $60 stock, you'll have to restrict yourself to a hundred shares or so.

Would your indicators work if I invested only in mutual funds?

Sure. You could use the Super Model developed in chapter 6, and invest in no-load mutual funds on a buy signal and move to money market funds on a sell signal. Or, you could modify it. You could get fully invested when the model is very good, say 8 points or higher, and you might move to a 50% position when the model is neutral and then get completely into money market funds when the model is, say, 2 points or less. You can also trade the no-load funds with the model presented in chapter 5, the Four Percent Model, which follows the tape, or with the Monetary Model discussed in chapter 4.

Incidentally, there are mutual fund families with industry funds that offer a small one-time load when you first come in, after which you can move in and out without further charges. If you wanted to buy oil stocks or computer stocks or utility stocks or gold stocks, you could move from one of their funds to another. And if you had only $5000 to invest, you might diversify a portfolio by perhaps putting $1000 into each of five different industry groups.

What do you consider a reasonable rate of return on a stock market investment?

Studies of stock market activity over the last sixty years or so have found that one would have earned in the vicinity of 8% to 9% a year, assuming reinvestment of dividends. Roughly half of the returns would have come from dividends and the rest from capital appreciation. That's before inflation. If you factor in inflation of perhaps 3% over that period, it gives you a real return of 5% to 6%. Of course, that includes periods of several years when returns were negative.

At this writing, with relatively low inflation, I don't think that 8% to 9% is an appropriate return. Probably something more on the order of 12% to 13% might be reasonable for a few years—at least until inflation heats up. My goals include beating the market by 3 or 4 percentage points a year and achieving a positive rate of return after inflation. I'd like to beat inflation by a minimum of 5 points.

If you're playing the market, you have to realize that you are somewhat at the mercy of what the market as a whole will do. You're not going to earn 20% to 30% a year if the market is doing nothing or going down.

I prefer to stick with blue chips. Is this a wise investment strategy?

The problem is that a blue chip company is mature and might not have a lot of growth left in it. It might sell at a premium because of the safety, lowering the long-run rate of return. Also, stocks that are regarded as blue chips today may not have that status in a few years. Not so long ago, U.S. Steel was one of the strongest of blue chips, but over the last decade or so it's been viewed as more of a dog, which, ironically, might make it a better investment since it is out of favor and possibly undervalued.

On rare occasions even blue chip companies cash in their chips, with disastrous consequences. I remember the story of what happened to a New England family in the nineteenth century. When the head of a very wealthy household died, he left an irrevocable trust, putting all his assets into the bluest of blue chips of that day—the New Haven Railroad. It was as blue a chip then as perhaps IBM is today. Over the years, the railroad's fortunes sagged and sagged, and the heirs desperately tried to break the trust but couldn't. Eventually the railroad went bankrupt and they lost all their money.

Generally speaking, blue chips do offer, despite the above example, more safety than the average stock. They also offer less return. Normally, the higher the risk, the greater the expected return.

Should I ever buy a stock because it pays a good dividend?

I wouldn't buy a stock just because it pays a good dividend. But if other aspects are favorable and the stock has a high yield, that's a bonus. What you have to be careful about are stocks with exceptionally high dividends. These yields may be excessive for very good reasons, possibly because the company has undisclosed problems. You are probably better off going into the next rung, buying the blue chip stocks with high but not ultrahigh dividends.

If, over the past twenty, thirty, or forty years, you had bought eight or ten stocks from the Dow Jones Average with the highest dividends and adjusted your portfolio each year to stay with the highest dividend payers, you would have done better than the Dow in terms of total return over that period. In other words, appreciation plus dividend return would have been higher for the high-yielding stocks than for the lower-yielding ones. And yet the low-yielding stocks, which pay low dividends or even no dividends, and usually have high price/earnings ratios, are those associated with growth.

In the long run, the plodding types of companies with high dividend yields and low P/E ratios have tended to outperform the growth stocks. So there's nothing wrong with buying high dividends. In fact, other things equal, it would be the preferred thing to do. I just want to warn you that perhaps 1% or so of the stocks with the highest of all dividends may be somewhat risky.

What about new issues? Should I try to find them?

There are good new issues and bad ones. They tend to run in

cycles. When the stock market is speculative, many hot new issues come out. A hot new issue is one that opens at a big premium over the offering price. Suppose the offering price is 20. If you are fortunate enough to buy at that, the stock may open at 25 or even 30. It causes a lot of excitement and a stampede into new issues. Unfortunately, companies of lower quality also rush in to sell their stock. If you get a tremendously speculative period, such as 1961 or 1968 or 1983, a lot of garbage is underwritten and eventually somebody gets left holding the bag.

If you're buying new issues, buy the better ones. Studies have shown that new issues tend to outperform the market for the three to six months after they appear. But you don't want to overstay the game. If you had bought new issues at the end of 1968, you would have had a disaster on your hands the following year. The same is true of 1983. If you had bought late in the 1983 new-issues craze, you would have been hurt badly in 1984. So, it's like everything else. New issues are okay if you know what you're doing and don't get left behind when the party's over.

I would avoid new issues at excessively high price/earnings ratios. I would avoid low quality. I would avoid new issues from the schlock houses of Wall Street. I would stay away from start-up companies and concept companies (companies that don't even have a business going), and I would pass on new issues in which the original owners are big sellers. It's fine if the company itself is trying to raise money, but it's not so good in the case of a bailout, where the company's owners sell huge amounts of stock. If they're selling modest amounts, it may be okay, but the more they sell, the warier you should be.

How do you feel about dollar-cost averaging when buying stocks?

I'm not too thrilled about dollar-cost averaging because it means that you buy more if a stock declines. I don't like buying weakness. If you buy a stock at $50 and it drops to $40, maybe there's something wrong. If it's such a great stock, why did it drop in the first place? I'd rather buy strength and sell weakness. If you are investing income regularly in the market, perhaps in an IRA, where you put in $2000 each January, that might be okay. You're sort of dollar-cost averaging. If the market is lower, you'll wind up buying more than if the market is higher. But if market conditions are lousy in a particular January (when it's time to make the next IRA contribution), I wouldn't invest my $2000 right then. I'd put it in a money market fund and wait for conditions to improve.

Do stock splits really help you at all?

No. Stock splits are much ado about nothing. They only help the brokers because they create more shares and generate higher commissions. The effect of a stock split is not different from cutting a pie into more pieces. If you cut a twelve-inch pie in half, you still have a twelve-inch pie. No matter how many slices you cut, it's the identical amount of pie. It's the same with a stock split. It has absolutely no value, and yet many naïve people believe they are getting something for nothing. On the positive side, a split might provide more liquidity for the stock, making trading a little easier. But it doesn't add any value to the company.

Is there a way to spot special situations like takeovers?

A lot of money has been made in searching out takeover situations, and there's nothing wrong with that technique. It's just not my approach. As I see it, takeovers are the domain of professionals who specialize in this most difficult and time-consuming area.

Basically, to uncover takeover candidates, you look for companies with assets substantially in excess of their stocks' market value. With public information, however, it's hard to determine actual value of assets. For example, a company might have land in downtown Dallas purchased fifty years ago for $1 million and worth $100 million today. It's not on the books for that. So you'd have to find some way of determining what the assets are worth.

If you're interested in combing through annual reports and all sorts of statistical information, you might dig up potential takeover targets. But that doesn't mean they will be taken over and, if they are, it could take several years. If you favor that approach and can handle it emotionally, then by all means go ahead. It's not right for me but is right for some people.

Are there any advantages to buying low-priced rather than more expensive stocks?

The public is often tempted by low-priced stocks, say those

under $10 a share. People figure that if they buy a $5 stock, they only have to put up $500 for a round lot and that it would be easier for a $5 stock to go to $10 or $20 than for a $50 stock to reach $100 or $200. Actually, that happens to be true in bull markets. However, in a bear market it's just the reverse. At the bull market top there are a lot of stocks selling for $15 and $20 that have come up from $5. These stocks are going to make a round trip and plummet again. So you've got a lot more risk with low-priced stocks, and you've got a lot less quality.

Stocks sell for a few dollars a share for a very good reason—they tend to be junk. An exception might be in a year like 1974, after the market had been annihilated for a few years and stocks that had formerly been $30 or $40 were selling at $5. In the long run, I think you'll make more money by eliminating the junk stocks and concentrating on stocks of reasonable quality that have real earnings or real assets behind them.

While I'm on the subject, there's a kind of stock even worse than the typical $5 stock. That's the so-called penny stock, which trades for under a dollar a share. Generally, you'll find them at some regional markets, such as Salt Lake City or Denver or the Spokane Mining Exchange. Most are mining stocks—very few with earnings or even working mines. In Salt Lake City and Denver they underwrite a lot of high-technology stocks that sell for pennies but frequently don't even have a product. You've got to be very careful, but in periods of speculative frenzy, a 10¢ stock might go to $5. People think they can make a killing in these markets but most wind up getting burned. I would, as a general rule, stay away from penny stocks, particularly if you're dealing with your IRA or Keogh plan.

Should I consider buying stock on the American Stock Exchange or Over-the-Counter?

I have no problem with the AMEX or OTC except when it comes to placing orders. Because these markets are generally thinner and dealers have less capital, you usually get better trades on the New York Stock Exchange if you are buying or selling in quantity. As for the stocks themselves, those of the AMEX and OTC tend to be more speculative and represent smaller companies than those listed on the NYSE.

The real question is whether you want to buy secondary-type

stocks or the blue chip variety. I would tend to go heavily into the secondary stocks only when conditions are very, very bullish for the market as a whole. This would be a time when our Super Model turns extremely positive and the Fed is loosening credit, especially if we're in or just coming out of a recession. Then you could probably buy the secondaries with the greatest safety. In a more neutral period, when the models are mixed, I would tend to favor the more conservative companies. And, of course, when the models are unfavorable, you wouldn't want to be in stocks at all.

What about buying stocks in foreign countries? Does it ever pay?

It can pay. It's a completely different ball game and, again, goes beyond the scope of this book. The truth is, it generally goes beyond my own experience. I have put very little time into trying to ferret out foreign investments for the simple reason that I have my hands full coping with the U.S. market. However, I have had some success with foreign gold stocks, particularly the South African ones, although I haven't touched them in a while. During the bull market in gold, in the mid and late 1970s, there were very few U.S. stocks to buy. ASA, Homestake, Campbell Red Lake, and Dome Mines are the only big ones in this country or in Canada. As a matter of fact, while ASA is listed on the New York Stock Exchange, it's really a fund of South African golds. So, for that industry, you were almost forced to go to Canada or South Africa.

Outside of that, I've bought very few foreign stocks. I just don't have all the data I'd like to have. If you can get enough information and feel you know what you're doing, it's fine. In buying a foreign stock, you are getting a little bit of diversification and cutting your risk somewhat. That's because if our market goes down, the odds are less than 100% that the foreign markets would move similarly. But it's not the best diversification in the world.

Most of the references in the book are to stocks. What about bonds? Should I buy them? How do you select them?

There is nothing wrong with bonds. My specialty happens to be stocks. I don't get into bonds for various reasons. When the bond market is strong it generally reflects conditions that are also bullish for stocks. During those periods stocks tend to do even better than bonds. Although stocks probably decline more than bonds during the bad periods, they outperform bonds over the long run. At least, that's been the record over the past five or six decades. Stocks, however, are more volatile and riskier than bonds. So if you don't want the risk of stocks, that's okay; but telling you when to buy bonds is beyond the scope of this book.

Even if I were a long-term investor with an individual IRA or Keogh account and didn't plan to retire for ten, twenty, or thirty years, I would pick stocks rather than bonds. Many brokers are pushing the so-called Zero Coupon Bonds, which mature in twenty or thirty years with an interest rate that works out to 10% to 12%. While this seems tempting for an IRA, I feel that if you have that kind of time working for you, you're better off with stocks even though there may be a period of a year or two when you don't do that well. I think that stocks would provide more money in your retirement account at the end of the period.

What about annual reports? Should I get one before I buy into a company?

I don't use annual reports very much. If you really want to buy companies based on value, you should consult annual reports and also the even more comprehensive 10-K reports filed with the Securities and Exchange Commission. Of course, you'd want to back that up with statistical information from Standard & Poor's, Moody's, or Value Line, where you can get a lot of balance sheet information and financial history and tear it apart. If you're really into it, you can read the footnotes. You can spend an inordinate amount of time analyzing just one stock. By now you know I have a different approach to the market. But there is no one right way to do it. Reading annual reports and related material can be helpful in specific investment decisions.

Can the stock market foretell business conditions?

Actually, yes. The stock market is one of the twelve leading indicators published by the government—and the one with the best track record for calling the economy. That's ironic because you hear an awful lot of stock market forecasts based on what the economy will do. The market is a discounting mechanism. It discounts what the economy will do, not the other way around. The market tends to peak well before the economy does and also bottoms first. In general, the market will bottom six months before the economy does. The best time to buy stocks is during a recession. Once the economic downturn has become widely recognized, it's no great help in the stock market to know what the economy will do. On the other hand, if you want to forecast the economy, look to the stock market.

How representative is the Dow Jones Industrial Average of what's happening to the overall market?
   The Dow isn't that representative because it comprises only thirty blue chip stocks. There are intervals such as in 1972, when the Dow went up roughly 10% while the average stock fell by a like amount. In other periods, such as in 1977, the average stock rose slightly but the Dow dropped about 15%. So there are times when selected blue chip returns vary greatly from those of secondary or smaller companies' stocks.
   Arbitrary decisions can also substantially affect the Dow performance. For example, IBM was taken out of the Dow back in the 1930s, and not replaced until the late 1970s. The company enjoyed fabulous growth during the forties, fifties, and sixties. Had IBM not been removed, the Dow would have stood at perhaps 1700 or 1800 sometime in the seventies, when the actual figure was 1000. Meanwhile AT&T, primarily a utility rather than an industrial company, stayed in the Dow during that entire time.
   While the Dow is not totally representative, the chances are that if it does very well or very poorly over a period of time, the rest of the market will move in line.

Brokers' advertisements promise 11½% return guaranteed by the U.S. government for Ginnie Maes. Do the ads leave anything out?
   Yes they do. Ginnie Maes represent pools of government-backed mortgage securities that may be quite volatile. The maturities in them might run ten, fifteen, or even twenty years. The longer the maturities, the more sensitive these portfolios are to changes in interest rates. For example, on average, for every one percentage point change in interest rates, a portfolio might change by 6%. In other words, if rates went from 11½% up to 12½% the portfolio might drop 6% in price. That's what they leave out.

How should I go about picking a broker?

First I would decide what I want from a broker. If you're a total do-it-yourselfer—that is, if you have your own stock ideas, your own opinions as to where the market is going, and you just want to place orders—go to a discount broker and save two-thirds or more of your commission cost. Discount brokers won't give you much service other than placing your orders and providing the regular transactions information. They won't call you. You have to call them. That's okay if that's all you need. Why pay for more?

On the other hand, if you want full service, you might want to go to a full-service broker. What would full service entail? For one thing, it might entitle you to some handholding. There are people who need that. Sometimes I think it would be cheaper to employ a discount broker and use the savings to pay a psychiatrist for the handholding. But if you want a broker to call you three times a day and tell you not to worry about the fact that your stock is down because it's a good company, that's your privilege. But you're paying for it in excess of the normal transaction charges.

Brokers at big firms might offer other services. For example, they have products such as tax shelters, municipal bonds, options, and so forth that a discount broker might not have. But you're also going to have to pay for each of these items. If you're a good customer of a big retail firm, it's possible they might let you in on the ground floor of some hot new issues. But there's no guarantee that an issue is going to be hot. They don't always go up. Even if they sometimes do, I don't know if it's worth opening an account and paying a lot of high commissions in order to be entitled to take a flier.

I have a broker I trust. Why do I need this book?

This book may be a good supplement to a broker you trust. First of all, you shouldn't have a broker you don't trust. That's ridiculous. A broker can be trustworthy but still not know which way the stock market is going, or he may not have good sources of investment ideas. Frankly, I think that you are probably better off using a broker to place your orders, to introduce you to other products that might be suitable for you, such as tax shelters, bonds, municipals, and whatever, but not to rely on for investment advice, especially when it comes to the stock market.

What about trading on margin? Do you recommend it for the average investor?

First, I'd like to explain precisely what margin is. Margin is the difference between the equity in the brokerage account and the market value of the stocks. The difference is what you borrow "on margin." Brokers are only too happy to provide it. For example, if you have $25,000 in equity, you could put it into a margin account and, under current regulations, borrow 2-for-1. That is, you could have $50,000 worth of buying power. You would have to pay interest on whatever sum you borrowed above your $25,000 equity. The interest rate is always higher than the prime rate.

Brokers can borrow money using your stock as collateral. They borrow at what's called the broker loan rate, which is a little less than the prime rate. It's a great loan for the banks because of the collateral involved. Brokers typically will add on several percentage points. If you are just a so-so customer, they may add 2 to 3 percentage points. If you're a great customer, you may get a smaller spread. In any event, you're paying a pretty high interest rate, which is charged to your account. Brokers do very well on margin business. In fact, many retail brokerage houses make more on interest than they do on commissions. That's why brokers love margin accounts, but they may not be right for you.

If you have $25,000, you probably shouldn't buy more than $25,000 worth of stock, if that. The average guy comes in, uses margin, and suddenly has $50,000 buying power. He's all set to hit the home run but he has no staying power. If the market dips for a few days, he worries he's going to go broke and gets out. While he's in, the interest keeps adding up. The interest isn't exactly chopped liver. At current rates, you're talking about double-digit figures. You're paying, say 1% a month to carry the stock, which really cuts into your profits. You are extended and leveraged and tempted to take small profits, rather than letting profits run.

Also, if you use margin, you tend to buy too much of a stock. Let me give you an example. Back in 1966, when I was trading for myself, I did a lot of research and decided I really liked Sperry Rand. I thought the stock was relatively cheap and would do very well. Believing that the more I bought, the more money I'd make, I went totally on margin. I had $20,000 in equity, borrowed another $20,000 and bought two thousand shares at $20 a share. I was right on the stock but, with almost all my money in this one stock, had almost no staying power. Within a short time, I got out of the stock, breaking even. Afterward, Sperry did pretty much what I thought it would do. The stock went up to about $70 a share in the next couple of years. Had I stayed with it, I would have made 50 points and earned $100,000 on my equity of only $20,000. But that's only a fantasy.

First of all, I would never have sold at the exact top. Secondly, I obviously overowned the stock. I owned so much of it that I couldn't stand the pressure. I would have been better off buying at most five hundred shares. With more staying power, I would have captured some of that 50-point gain. I always think back to Sperry Rand when I think about margin. I just don't feel good about using it.

C H A P T E R   1 6

Concluding Words to the Intelligent Investor

"People don't seem to grasp easily the fundamentals of stock trading. I have often said that to buy into a rising market is the most comfortable way of buying stocks.... Remember that stocks are never too high for you to begin buying or too low to begin selling. But after the initial transaction, don't make the second unless the first shows you a profit."*

The above words of wisdom, with which I agree completely, came from Jesse Livermore, one of my heroes in stock market lore, whom I have mentioned earlier. He was a big speculator during the first third of this century and was immortalized, so to speak, in a book called *Reminiscences of a Stock Operator* by Edwin Lefevre, first published in 1923 and reprinted some forty years later. I strongly suggest you read it.

It's remarkable how pertinent Livermore's views are to today's market. Here's what he says about the importance of momentum and following the tape:

"They say you never grow poor taking profits. No you don't. But neither do you grow rich taking a four-point spread in a bull market."

In other words, as I've emphasized throughout this book, the idea is to let your profits run and to cut your losses. Too many people are apt to redeem their profits too quickly. In a huge bull market they wind up with piddling profits, only to watch their former holdings soar. That usually prompts them into making mistakes later when, believing the market owes them some money, they buy at the wrong time at much higher levels.

To avoid these mistakes, use my timing models—Monetary, Four Percent, and the Super Model. They do a good job in identifying bullish and bearish trends in general. Obviously, you should do the bulk of your buying when the timing models, especially our Super Model, turn bullish.

Buying on declines can lead to big trouble. Of course, there are declines and there are declines. If the market is extremely strong and backs off for a half hour and your stock dips three-eighths of a point, there's nothing wrong with entering then. But when the market acts poorly for days on end and the stock is down four or five points, buying could lead to trouble.

No matter what the market conditions, you must houseclean your stocks periodically, even in an overall bullish environment. For example, if a company you are holding reports mediocre earnings, or if too many insiders begin to sell the stock, or if the stock climbs to loftier and loftier P/E's, you will want to replace that stock and find others to round out your portfolio. Aside from the normal amount of portfolio watching, the big increases in your stock exposure—say, going from zero invested to 100% invested—will come when the models described earlier turn from bearish to bullish.

What about the times when the market indicators are relatively neutral or mildly bullish? Such conditions may call for being less than fully invested. But even more important, they would imply that risk, while not exceptionally high—as it would be if our models were outright bearish—is high enough to warrant caution on owning aggressive-type stocks. Under such circumstances, I prefer more conservative stocks. Conversely, I gravitate toward the more aggressive stocks when our timing models are moving from a bearish to a bullish mode, as they did in, say, mid-1982 or in the fall of 1984.

The conservative stocks are those such as the Midlantic Banks example, where there is a high degree of earnings stability but where P/E ratios are quite low. The more aggressive stocks are those generally regarded as growth stocks, where earnings are up sharply in the more recent past but where P/E ratios are also high. A good example is that of Emulex back in 1982. I like the aggressive growth stocks when all systems are go for the market as a whole. In the rip-roaring stages of bull markets, these stocks tend to do better than the overall market.

But when the market indicators are less than outright bullish, I prefer retreating to more defensive and conservative-type stocks with lower P/E's and greater earnings stability, even if it means a slower rate of growth.

I'm willing to get very aggressive when overall market conditions are right. But when the indicators are mixed or only moderately bullish, I'd just as soon ease out of stocks somewhat and hold some cash equivalents. When the indicators are very negative, I would rather be mostly out of stocks and sit with cash. I've learned to avoid looking for that elusive needle in a haystack. If I do have a handful of stocks at such times, say 10% to 20% of my money, I still prefer to be in the conservative-type stocks.

The average guy buys his stocks when the market is on a decline and sells in the initial phases of a rally. That's what happened in 1973–74 when the Dow dropped almost 500 points. Data from Bob Farrell at Merrill Lynch show that cash buying by the public began in February 1973, nearly two years before the market bottomed. It's true that by December 1974, when the market hit its lows, the public was buying heavily and it looked as though the crowd had been right. But this was the culmination of buying that had persisted for almost two years, and many people were badly hurt in the process.

Finally, *when you buy stocks, you must diversify.* How much diversification is proper? That depends on the size of your portfolio. The drawback with diversification, if you have a small portfolio, is that your transaction costs will increase. So, here are some rough guidelines. If you have less than $5,000, I would hesitate to buy stocks outright. Instead, I'd just as soon put that money into a no-load mutual fund, where you can get diversification.

If you have between $5,000 and $20,000, I would try to buy 4 or 5 stocks. As you move toward about a $50,000 portfolio, I would try to purchase 8 or 9 stocks. At the $100,000 level, you can step up to about a dozen different positions. For the $250,000 range, a portfolio of roughly 20 stocks is adequate. In *The Zweig Forecast* I will have anywhere from about 25 to 33 stocks. With 25 stocks in a fully invested portfolio, each one represents 4% of the portfolio. If I expand the portfolio to 33 stocks, each represents about a 3% position. That's enough diversification.

Academic studies have shown that if you diversify among

different industries, you'll get roughly seven-eighths of the total benefits of diversification once you reach about eight stocks. It is important not to put all your nest eggs into one basket. If you buy only one, two, or three stocks, you might win the battle by buying when the market as a whole goes up. But you may lose the war because your particular stocks may underperform, or possibly even decline, while the market is advancing. If you diversify, you're probably pretty sure of doing reasonably well as long as the market behaves. Moreover, if one or two stocks bomb out on you, it won't do any major damage if you're diversified. But if you have only one stock and it lays an egg, you're in trouble.

One last word about my stock-picking approach. Recall, I start by going through every earnings report in the daily newspapers. Some of you may find this is more of a chore than you are willing to take on. Of course, you cannot expect to get something for nothing. You have to do at least a little work to achieve above-normal investment returns. However, if you want to cut down on the magnitude of the task and are willing to pass up some pretty good opportunities, you can filter out the earnings reports according to your personal preference.

For example, you might look only at the reports on the New York Stock Exchange if you want to gravitate toward the somewhat more conservative stocks. Or, if you're more aggressive and wish to operate in an area where there is somewhat less competition, you might concentrate only on over-the-counter stocks. Another possible screen is to pick stocks whose quarterly sales are above, say, $100 million. That way you'll be sticking with larger companies that might be more to your taste. Conversely, if you're more aggressive, you might want to stay with companies that are far smaller, with perhaps as little as $10 million in quarterly sales.

Obviously, there are a number of ways to chop up the universe to reduce the number of stocks you may want to follow. I myself like to cover the entire gamut because I have found stocks to my liking both on the very small end, such as CACI or Emulex, which I mentioned earlier, right up to the bluest of the blue chips, such as IBM and American Telephone, which I've recommended at various times in the past couple of years.

Regardless of the stocks you buy, there's no point in going to bed at night with a position that's going against you or with a position that's too large. If you can't sleep, you're doing something wrong. Remember, if you take a small loss, you can always make it back. If you wind up with a big loss, forget it. It's a matter of simple arithmetic. Should you lose 10% on a stock, you need to make 11% to break even. If you lose 20%, you need to make 25% profit to recoup. But if you were to lose 90%, say by riding a stock down from 100 to 10, you'd need a tenfold increase to break even, and that's almost impossible.

On the more favorable side, I want to stress that *if you have a nice profit riding in a bull market, hang in there.* You may even want to buy more—it's easy to average up. What you don't want is to sell too soon. Imagine if, in the great bull market that started in August 1982, you had sold out in September or October. You might have made 15% to 20% on some of your positions, but you would have given up the chance to double your money by holding on for three, six, or twelve months.

Summing up, I want to leave you with a few clear and simple rules: *Buy strength, sell weakness, and stay in gear with the tape.* As with any rules, I suppose there is a time to break them, but I urge you to resist the temptation. Even as astute a trader as Jesse Livermore found that when he didn't practice what he preached, he got clobbered, going broke three or four times after making millions. I can't guarantee that you'll make millions in the market, but, if you heed the advice in this book, I think you'll consistently come out ahead, have some fun, and enjoy relatively untroubled sleep at night.